PHARAOH'S COUNSELLORS

Program in Judaic Studies
Brown University
BROWN JUDAIC STUDIES

Edited by

Jacob Neusner,
Wendell S. Dietrich, Ernest S. Frerichs,
Alan Zuckerman

Editorial Board

Number 47

PHARAOH'S COUNSELLORS
Job, Jethro, and Balaam in Rabbinic and Patristic Tradition

by
Judith R. Baskin

PHARAOH'S COUNSELLORS
Job, Jethro, and Balaam
in Rabbinic and Patristic Tradition

by
Judith R. Baskin

Scholars Press
Chico, California

PHARAOH'S COUNSELLORS:
JOB, JETHRO, AND BALAAM
IN RABBINIC AND PATRISTIC TRADITION

by
Judith Baskin

© 1983
Brown University

Library of Congress Cataloging in Publication Data
Baskin, Judith Reesa, 1950–
  Pharaoh's counsellors.

  (Brown Judaic studies ; no. 47)
  Bibliography: p.
  Includes index.
  1. Job (biblical figure) 2. Jethro (Biblical figure)
3. Balaam (Biblical figure) 4. Rabbinical literature—
History and criticism. 5. Fathers of the church. I. Title.
II. Series.
BS571.B39 1983   221.6'09'015   83–11535
ISBN 0-89130-637-4

Printed in the United States of America

For my

Mother and Father

TABLE OF CONTENTS

A NOTE ON TEXTS AND TRANSLATIONS

Editions of rabbinic and patristic texts used in this study are indicated in the bibliography, and where pertinent, in the notes and indices. Translations of some of these texts have also been consulted and are often reflected in passages quoted in the body of the text; these translations are also listed in the bibliography.

Quotations from the Hebrew Bible are taken from the Jewish Publication Society *Holy Scriptures* (Philadelphia, 1917). Quotations from the New Testament are from the Revised Standard Version.

INTRODUCTION

In the process of interpreting sacred scripture, biblical exegetes reveal the concerns and attitudes of their own circumstances. Even as the biblical authors themselves had shaped events and personalities to fit a dominant theological pattern, so rabbinic and patristic commentators, with greater or lesser awareness, refashioned episodes and characters to answer the spiritual and practical needs of their own eras. Using a variety of exegetical methods, the Rabbis found proofs and buttresses for a legal system far more complex than any prescribed in biblical times. Through a reunderstanding of ancient adversity, their homilies and consolation texts were able to ease Israel's present misfortunes and offer hope for the future. Christians similarly found in their versions of the Hebrew Bible not only moral encouragement, but also foreshadowings and premonitions of a fulfillment to come, albeit of a rather different nature. In the Christian schema, the history of Israel now pointed to the life of Jesus, and beyond, to the soul of the individual Christian. These exegetical traditions of rabbinic Judaism and patristic Christianity, although tending to radically different conclusions, share in common a basis in Scripture and the influence of contemporary concerns. They share as well a lasting longevity, for the law and creed they established formed the foundation of each religion for the ensuing thousand years.

A further factor which shaped Jewish and Christian religious and exegetical traditions was knowledge of each other. From the advent of Christianity, there were intellectual contacts, often on scriptural subjects, between Jews and Christians. These meetings of minds, occasionally pleasant, more often polemical, also played a part in deciding attitudes, beliefs and interpretive patterns. A comparative approach to Jewish and Christian exegesis of similar biblical passages or figures can therefore yield a double harvest: both contemporary attitudes in Jewish and Christian scriptural commentary, as well as Jewish-Christian contacts and their effects, can be illustrated. This study undertakes to fulfill both these aims by gathering and analyzing exegeses of three biblical gentiles, Job, Jethro and Balaam, and by comparing rabbinic and patristic responses to them.

These biblical gentiles are linked together in a rabbinic midrash which names them as the three wise men who advised Pharaoh

1

how he should treat the enslaved Israelites in Egypt.[1] Ultimately
they came to epitomize for the Rabbis three aspects of the gentile
world. Job was the righteous gentile who acknowledged God, and
lived a life acceptable to Him outside the boundaries of Israel.
Jethro became an example of the gentile who went a step further,
forsaking his former life to become a proselyte to Judaism.
Balaam, by contrast, was perceived as representative of the third
and largest gathering of the nations of the world. Wicked and
blasphemous, his aim was the constant oppression and eventual
destruction of the people of Israel. Each of these figures, in
effect, represented one solution to the existence of non-Jews in a
world created and ruled by the one God. Reflections of both rabbinic and patristic attitudes towards the gentile nations in the
exegesis of these figures is a major theme of this work.

In the process of contrasting Jewish and Christian
exegeses of the same figures and texts, rabbinic and patristic
approaches to Scripture are also compared. Jews and Christians in
late antiquity shared not only a common text of inspiration, but
also common physical and cultural environments. It is not surprising that each body of exegesis should reflect some knowledge
of the traditions of the other. Much scholarship on Jewish-
Christian contact has concentrated on apparent patristic knowledge
of Jewish sources.[2] Origen and Jerome, for example, are known to
have consulted contemporary Rabbis, and to have occasionally
incorporated what they learned into their elucidation of specific
scriptural passages; such Fathers as Ambrose and Cyril of Alexandria made frequent use of Philo's commentaries. Parallels of this
kind are readily discovered in an examination of patristic writings on Job, Jethro and Balaam, and are pointed out in the body of
this book. Similarly, it is apparent that rabbinic commentators
were often aware of and affected by Christian exegetical trends.
Examples of such influences, however, have been pointed out and
discussed rather less frequently than cases of rabbinic elements
in patristic literature.[3] The instances cited in this study of
rabbinic responses to Christian teachings on Job and Balaam,
therefore, are of importance to the comparative study of Judaism
and Christianity in late antiquity, for they testify to the ways
in which one tradition's exegetical models could become altered in
reaction to the teachings of the other. In the end, however, such
a comparative study also makes clear that despite shared or bor-
rowed traditions, reactive or polemical trends, profoundly different beliefs and religious purposes motivated Jewish and Christian readings of the Hebrew Scriptures. These are the concerns

which dominate and separate rabbinic and patristic interpretations of Job, Jethro and Balaam.

Within this book, Job, Jethro and Balaam are treated respectively in their roles as righteous gentile, proselyte to Israel, and foreign prophet. After a short introduction, a major section of each chapter details, generally thematically, the rabbinic exegesis of the figure being considered. An effort is made to distinguish between specifically tannaitic and amoraic views, and to discuss progressions of attitudes, and changes in emphasis, from earlier to later generations of Sages. A major goal of the discussion, however, is to discover the consensus of rabbinic opinion: that is, the view of the figure and the body of tradition connected to him which would have been passed on to post-rabbinic generations. To aid in identifying authorities, all Rabbis are accompanied, when first mentioned, by the dates during which they flourished.

A third section of each chapter discusses the portrayal of the biblical figure in a range of late antique Jewish writings generally reckoned to have been produced outside of rabbinic circles. These include the writing of Philo of Alexandria and Josephus, and various sectarian and pseudepigraphical texts, in which the figure being considered happens to be mentioned or discussed. These writings are examined primarily because of their impact on Christian attitudes and writers, since they constitute another source of Jewish input into Christian exegesis. This book, however, is not a source study of the traditions about Job, Jethro and Balaam, and the commentary connected with them. It is not so much interested in development, as in the developed teachings of rabbinic Judaism and Latin Christianity, as they emerged into the Middle Ages. Thus, although a number of the works considered in the third section of each chapter can be dated before most of the rabbinic materials at our disposal, their relation to the rabbinic texts is not an issue which is considered here. They are discussed later, since their relevance in this study is to the succeeding texts, that is, to the patristic material, which is dealt with in a final section of each chapter. This segment, after a general survey of Christian opinion, focuses in each case on the remarks of three or four major exegetes whose writings on the particular figure had great influence on later Christian tradition.

Following the three chapters devoted to presentation and evaluation of the exegetical traditions about Pharaoh's counsellors, a brief conclusion summarizes the thematic issues raised by

the study, Jewish and Christian attitudes towards gentiles, and
rabbinic-patristic exegetical contacts in late antiquity.

A number of scholars have undertaken studies of individual
biblical characters in a range of late antique exegeses. Viktor
Aptowitzer, for example, studied Cain and Abel in aggadic,
Jewish-hellenistic, Christian and Islamic literatures, gathering a
full compendium of teachings on these primal brothers.[4] Samuel
Sandmel has examined the figure of Abraham in rabbinic and
Jewish-hellenistic traditions, primarily in an attempt to determine Philo's relationship to rabbinic literature.[5] Jack Lewis
gathered biblical and post-biblical Jewish and Christian materials
dealing with Noah and the flood, and commented, as well, on the
differing assumptions with which each group of exegetes approached
the biblical story.[6] Recent works by A. F. J. Klijn and Steven
Fraade have dealt with Seth, and with Enosh and his generation.[7]
This book is similar to these studies in its effort to be complete
in gathering all major traditions pertaining to Pharaoh's counsellors. It differs, however, in its thematic emphasis on views of
gentiles, and in its particular interest in comparing rabbinic and
patristic approaches to the same scriptural figures.

As for the three figures themselves, no similar study
exists for any of them. Surprisingly, a full compendium of rabbinic views of Job is not readily available. Herman Ezekiel
Kaufmann's nineteenth century work contains some of the aggadic
comments, but its concern is less with Job himself than with
exegetical traditions connected with the biblical book in its
entirety.[8] Nahum Glatzer, both in his *Dimensions of Job*, and in
an earlier article,[9] considers various exegetical perceptions of
Job among Jewish and Christian writers; his comments, however,
are regrettably brief. Two recent works, by Lawrence Besserman,[10]
and Günther Datz,[11] survey patristic materials on Job in the context of discussions of him in medieval literature, but neither is
primarily interested in Job as a gentile, or in Jewish-Christian
contacts.

Bernard Bamberger commented extensively on the figure of
Jethro as a proselyte in rabbinic literature, but concluded his
remarks with the wish that a more complete study of the figure
might be undertaken.[12] I am aware of no separate analysis of
Jethro in Jewish-hellenistic or patristic literatures.

The exegetical history of the Balaam of Numbers 22-24 has
been compiled in great detail by Geza Vermes.[13] Vermes, however,
is not interested in the figure of Balaam as it appears elsewhere

in rabbinic literature, nor in the Jewish-Christian discussion
generated by Balaam's prophecy of Numbers 24:17. E. Kirschbaum has
published a lengthy account of Balaam in patristic writings, but
his work is seriously marred by his untenable insistence that
Christian views of this foreign prophet were uniformly positive.[14]
Jay Braverman has touched briefly on some exegetical parallels on
Balaam in Jewish and Christian commentary; his study, however,
deals only with Jewish influences on patristic writings.[15]
Ephraim Urbach has written on rabbinic understandings of Balaam as
a prophet of the nations, especially in light of Christian claims,
and his study has been very helpful to this book.[16]

A number of books and articles have considered rabbinic
views of the gentile nations. Several of these works, particularly those written early in this century, have been apologetic
in their wish to show that Israel has always been appreciative of
gentile righteousness.[17] Such modern scholars as Samuel Hugo
Bergman,[18] Moshe Greenberg,[19] and Hans Joachim Schoeps[20] have also
dealt with this issue, to greater or lesser extent against the
backdrop of contemporary concerns. No other study that I am aware
of, however, has compared rabbinic and patristic views of specific
biblical gentiles with the goal of clarifying attitudes towards
the nations in general.

This book has its origins in my Medieval Studies doctoral
dissertation, *Reflections of Attitudes towards the Gentiles in
Jewish and Christian Exegesis of Jethro, Balaam and Job*, Yale
University, 1976. In its present form, however, it is substan-
tially different from the thesis. A research grant from the Amer-
ican Council of Learned Societies allowed me the time to begin the
long process of revision, new research and rewriting. I would
like to express my gratitude for the Council's support. A generous grant from the Hilles Fund of Yale University has subsidized
this manuscript's preparation for publication. I would like, too,
to thank Professor Jacob Neusner of Brown University for his help
in securing funding to pay the costs of publishing this book in
Brown Judaic Studies.

Professors Brevard Childs, Sid Z. Leiman and Jaroslav
Pelikan gave generously of their time and their learning during
the writing of the dissertation. The book in its current form has
benefited immensely from the readings of Professors Judah Goldin,
of the University of Pennsylvania; Robert Doran and Susan Niditch
of Amherst College; Jaroslav Pelikan of Yale University; and
Alexander Rofe of the Hebrew University. I express grateful

thanks to them all. The errors that remain, are, of course, my
own.

      I owe an enormous debt of love to my husband Warren
Ginsberg, for his constant support and for his editorial skill,
and to my son, Samuel Jonathan Ginsberg, for enriching my life
immeasurably. To my parents, Marjorie Shatz Baskin and Rabbi
Bernard Baskin, whose commitment to life and learning I can only
hope to emulate, I dedicate this book.

CHAPTER ONE

JOB : THE RIGHTEOUS GENTILE

i

Job is preeminent among righteous gentiles in Hebrew
Scriptures. While numerous individuals from among the nations,
figures such as Rahab the harlot (Josh 2), and the Aramean general
Naaman (2 Kgs 5), acknowledge the saving powers of Israel's God,
these characters appear only briefly, in short narrative se-
quences. Job alone dominates an entire book. So much have his
travails, his rebellion and his return to grace become part of the
biblical landscape that the very assertion of his gentile status
comes as a surprise. Yet nowhere in the book of Job is it stated
that Job was an Israelite; in fact, his location in the mysterious
land of Uz, and the striking lack of any genealogical data imply
that he was not.

The problem of Job's identity is inherent in the book itself. Other biblical narratives are rooted in time and place, but
Job seems to exist outside of time. And if there was a Job who
suffered cruelly for no apparent reason, where did he suffer? The
land of Uz, perhaps Hauran, possibly Edom, but certainly far away
and unspecific, serves only as the vague and misty setting proper
for a confrontation between man and God.[1] Nor is Job moored to
the rest of scriptural history; indeed, the book has no obvious
relation to the history of Israel at all. It transcends national
identity, proclaiming God's universality and omnipotence to all.

To the modern reader this lack of Israelite connection is
surprising in an anthology of national literature, but the Bible's
redactors were apparently not bothered by it. Generally, biblical
theology holds that all men, created by the hand of the Almighty
and descended from common ancestors, share in God-like qualities.
Israel owed its special position not to some inherent distinction,
but to its covenant with God, and could only remain a holy people
through observance of divine statutes and ordinances. Israel's
purpose in history, in fact, was to make God known to all nations:
God did not choose one people so that knowledge of Him would be
restricted to them alone. The Bible frequently insists that any
man may be aware of God's unique powers and act righteously in His
eyes, for God is everywhere accessible to all who seek Him. This
is why it is recounted that Jethro, a pagan priest, sacrificed to
the God of Israel (Exod 18), and that Balaam, a pagan seer, knew

the Almighty and obeyed Him (Num 22-24). This is why Job, a man
living far outside the boundaries of Israel could be a worthy worshipper of the one God.[2]

Biblical views of the nations, however, are not wholly
one-sided or unambiguous. The idealistic and universal utterances
of some of the prophets dwell side by side with long-standing traditions of hostility and mistrust. All nations will ultimately
live together, but whether in peace and harmony, or under Israel's
vindicated and vengeful domination is a matter of opinion.[3] Two
traditions, then, one which views the nations as potential converts and brothers, and another which sees the gentiles as malevo-
lent would-be architects of Israel's downfall, are passed on to
post-biblical Judaism, and both come into play in rabbinic interpretation of Job.

The structure of the biblical book of Job is also a major
factor in its interpretation. The book of Job is composed of two
separate elements. Within the frame of a simple prose folktale
there is a poetic dialogue between Job and his companions which
discusses the workings of God's justice in the world.[4] The Job of
the folktale (chs. 1 and 42) is righteous and God-fearing, a model
of piety. The Job of the rest of the book is defiant, even blasphemous. His disturbing theological debates are couched in
obscure language and filled with arcane allusions. It is not surprising that it was more often the pious Job, the Job of the prologue and epilogue who caught the ancient imagination, nor that
this Job became a popular model of piety and resignation in some
Jewish circles, and in Christian tradition.[5]

ii

The worth and potential righteousness of all human beings is
frequently acknowledged within the body of rabbinic literature.
According to one tradition, the most fundamental principle of
Judaism was the doctrine, indicated in the opening chapters of the
Torah, that all men share a common descent. The sage Ben Azzai
(fl. 110-135 CE) said: "'This is the book of the generations of
Adam' (Gen 5:1), is the most comprehensive rule of the Torah."[6]
The *Mishnah* at *'Abot* 3:14, quotes R. Akiba's (fl.110-135 CE)
dictum that "Every human being [and not only the Jew] is beloved
of God, since he is a creature God has made in his own image."
Rabbinic, as biblical Judaism, contains testimony that a man's
character was not determined by his birth or nationality; each man
was free to act rightly or wrongly. Nor did the Sages hold that

it was only through acceptance of Judaism's precepts and ordinances that a man could achieve righteousness. Obedience to the
universal or Noachite commandments assured the worthy gentile
divine approbation. These commandments, held by ancient tradition
to have been revealed to Adam and to Noah, are set forth in both
Talmud and midrash.[7] They consist of seven ordinances that forbid
idolatry, blasphemy, homicide, incest and adultery, robbery and
eating the flesh of a live creature, and they require the establishment of a system of justice. Although these commandments are
explicitly ordained, what they prohibit was thought to be self-
evident to any human mind and conscience.[8]

     The belief in a common descent and equal reward for all
righteous men, however, was often easier to maintain in theory
than in practice. Sharp distinctions between Jews and gentiles
were increasingly marked from the time of the Second Temple period. Social contacts with surrounding gentiles, often idolators,
were regarded as potentially damaging to proper conduct and worship. As the Jews chafed under harsh and insensitive foreign domination, the world seemed more and more divided: Israel stood
alone against the nations of the world.[9] It is not surprising
that many talmudic rulings discriminate against gentiles, nor are
hostile remarks uncommon. Still, amid such negative statements,
other voices speak of the salutary benefits and harmony which
result from fair dealings with non-Jews.[10] Both sides of an apparent controversy over the possibility of gentile merit are evident in a rabbinic discussion, recorded in the *Tosefta* to *M.
Sanhedrin* 13:2:

> R. Eliezer [fl. 80-110 CE] says: Gentiles have no place in the
> world to come, as it says, "Let the wicked go back to Sheol,
> all the nations who have forgotten God "(Ps 9:18) . . . R.
> Joshua [fl. 80-110 CE] replied: Had it said, "Let the wicked
> go back to Sheol, all nations," and stopped, I should agree.
> But since it adds, "Who have forgotten God," I infer that
> there are righteous among the nations who have a place in the
> world to come.

It is significant, moreover, that the majority of Rabbis apparently sided with R. Joshua, for *B. Sanhedrin* 105a states affirm-
atively that those righteous among the nations would have a place
in the world to come. Nevertheless, the minority view persisted,
and both attitudes are evident in rabbinic exegeses of Job.

     There are almost as many Jobs as Rabbis who speak about
him. This wealth of interpretation is due not only to theological
division over the merits of gentiles, but is also a result of
problems raised by the composite nature of the biblical book. The

contradiction between the pious and God-fearing Job of chapters 1
and 42, and the rebellious and contentious Job of the rest of the
book was difficult to resolve.[11] Since, in rabbinic terms, Job's
suffering must have been merited, his misdeeds also demanded clar-
ification. Some Rabbis chose to emphasize only the pious Job,
while others considered the reasons for his severe punishments.
Those exegetes who held high the ideal of the righteous gentile,
championed Job as its concrete example, while more sedulous Sages
attempted to undercut his achievement and reward. Still others
who recognized Job's virtues, yet hesitated to assign them to a
non-Jew, sought to prove that Job was not a gentile at all.

          Comments about Job are found throughout rabbinic litera-
ture.[12] These remarks differ in intent. Some deal with "whens"
and "wheres" in attempts to fill in narrative gaps in the folktale; they enlarge on Job's character and the details of his life.
Others use events from the experience of Job and his companions as
examples in the discussion of larger philosophical and ethical
questions. Only a very few statements about Job attempt to analyze the meaning of his behavior and experience, and most of these
barely touch the profound questions at the book's core.[13]

          The basic lines of rabbinic exegesis and debate over Job
are already well-established in remarks attributed to tannaitic
Sages. Thus, in M. Soṭa 5:5, Johanan ben Zakkai (fl. 40-80 CE) is
said to have taught that Job served God only out of fear, thereby
comparing him unfavorably with such Israelites as Abraham, while
Joshua b. Hananiah (fl.80-110 CE) insists that Job too served God
out of love. Most of the remarks attributed to Tannaim, however,
appear in post-tannaitic sources. Thus, R. Ishmael (fl. 110-135
CE) is said to have declared Job a gentile in J. Soṭa 20c, while
R. Eleazar (fl. 135-170 CE) is said to have maintained his Israelite origin in B. Baba Batra 15b. B. Baba Batra 15b also describes
a "difference among the Tannaim" on the question of Job's ultimate
end, R. Eliezer, not surprisingly, holding that Job has no place
in the world to come, and R. Joshua maintaining the opposite.[14]
In these sources, Amoraim then enlarge on the disputes attributed
to their predecessors. Although there are few novelties in
amoraic discussions of Job, insistence by some Palestinian Amoraim
on Job's Israelite origin appears to be directed against Christian
glorification of Job as a gentile witness to Christ.[15] Homiletical midrashim are mainly concerned with Job as a subject for consolatory sermonizing.[16]

          In virtually all rabbinic study of Job, the primary con-
cern is his origin, for on this all other considerations rest.

Much of the discussion on this point is related to when Job lived.
B.Baba Batra 15a-16b, for instance, in its examination of the
authors and the proper order of biblical books, contains a very
full discussion of Job's time and place. Moses is said to have
been the author of "his own book," and "the portion of Balaam and
Job" (14b), and this statement is then used to support the opinion
of R. Levi b. Laḥma (fl. 290-320 CE), that Job was a contemporary
of Moses (15a). This assertion is given substance by the similar-
ities of two verses: "O that my words were now written, would
that they were inscribed [ויחקו]" (Job 19:23), and "And he chose
the first part for himself, for a portion of a ruler [מחקק] [or
'inscriber'] was reserved" (Deut 33:21). Since Job asked that his
words be inscribed and Moses is called an inscriber, Moses must
have lived in the time of Job and written his story.

As a consequence, Job was thought to have lived in the
court of Pharaoh at the time of Israel's captivity in Egypt. In
J. Soṭa 20c, R. Ishmael teaches that "Job was one of the servants
of Pharaoh, and was one of the dignitaries of the household, as it
is written in Exodus 9:20, 'He that feared the word of the Lord
among the servants of Pharaoh made his servants and cattle flee
into the houses.'" "He that feared the word of the Lord" must
refer to Job because he is the only gentile whom Scripture called
a God-fearing man (Job 1:1). And once Job was associated with
Pharaoh, his later sufferings were no longer so inexplicable.[17]

Several related traditions teach that the span of Job's
life was from the time that Israel entered Egypt until they were
redeemed. *Seder 'Olam Rabbah*, which details Israel's chronology,
maintains that Israel's stay in Egypt was 210 years, just as Job's
lifetime was 210 years, and adds: "There are those who say that
when Israel went down into Egypt Job was born, and when they came
up he died."[18] Job's lifespan is reckoned at 210 years on the
basis of the biblical statement, "And after this Job lived a hundred and forty years "(Job 42:16). Since the Bible also says "The
Lord gave Job twice as much as he had before" (Job 42:10), the
Rabbis deduced that Job's age before his adversity must have been
70; thus the total of his years was 210. According to *Seder 'Olam
Rabbah*, then, Job's lifespan was a סימן, a "sign," pointing to the
number of years Israel spent in Egypt. It is symbolic evidence
that Job lived during the exact period of Israel's exile and servitude, and was in fact a contemporary of both Jacob and Moses.[19]

Another instance of this legend is found in *B. Soṭa* 35a,
which explains the verse, "It is a land which eateth up the inhabitants thereof" (Num 14:32), as follows:

Raba [fl. 320-350 CE] expounded: The Holy One, blessed be He, said, I intended this for good, but they thought it in a bad sense. I intended this for good, because wherever [the spies] came, the chief [of the inhabitants] died, so that they should be occupied [with his burial] and not inquire about them. Others say that Job died then, and the whole world was occupied with mourning for him. But they thought it in a bad sense, and said, "It is a land that eateth up the inhabitants thereof."

Elsewhere, too, Raba is quoted as maintaining that Job lived in the time of the spies Moses sent to investigate the land of Canaan. He points out that Scripture says in connection with Job, "There was a man in the land of Uz (עוץ)" (Job 1:1), and in connection with the spies, "Whether there be wood (עץ) therein" (Num 13:20). "Where is the parallel?" he asks. "In one place it is Uz (עוץ), in the other aẓ (עץ). What Moses said to Israel was this: See if that man is there whose years are as the years of a tree (עץ), and who shelters his generation like a tree (עץ)."[20]

This triple pun, Uz, aẓ ('wood'), and aẓ ('tree'), subtends a complicated legend: Moses' instructions to the spies to see "Whether there is wood therein "(Num 13:20), is said to refer to Job, a native of Uz. Moses had told the spies to inquire whether Job was still alive, for if he were dead, they assuredly had no reason to fear the Canaanites, since Job's merits alone were capable of shielding them from Israel's attack. This explains the third use of aẓ as 'tree,' for Job's virtue alone protected his Canaanite brethren as would a tree. When the spies reached Canaan, Job had just died, and all the inhabitants of the land were mourning him. Not being acquainted with the reason for this general grief, the spies exclaimed: "This is a land that eateth up the inhabitants thereof" (Num 14:32). Unstated, but implied in this story, is a strong defence of Job as a righteous and admirable gentile whose accrued merit would have been capable of protecting his people, even against Israel.

Final proof that Job was a gentile and a contemporary of Moses is that he was said to have been one of the seven prophets who preached to the gentiles. These seven were Balaam and his father Beor; Job; Eliphaz the Temanite; Bildad the Shuhite; Zophar the Naamathite; and Elihu son of Barachel the Buzite. *Seder 'Olam Rabbah* records the following tradition about these men:

Balaam and his father; Job from the land of Uz; and Eliphaz the Temanite; and Bildad the Shuhite; and Zophar the Naamathite; and Elihu the son of Barachel the Buzite: these are the prophets who prophesied to the nations before the Torah was given to Israel. From the time that the Torah was given to Israel, however, the Holy One, blessed be He, removed the Holy Spirit from the nations. Thus, Moses said, "For

wherein shall it be known that I have found grace in thy
sight, I and thy people? Is it not in that thou goest with
us, so that we are distinguished, I and thy people, from all
the people that are upon the face of the earth?" (Exod 33:16).
And from [what biblical verse] do we know that the Holy One,
blessed be He, followed Moses' will? For it is said, "And He
said, 'Behold I make a covenant: Before all thy people I will
do marvels, such as have not been wrought in all the earth,
nor in any nation: And all the people among which thou art
shall see the work of the Lord that I am about to do with
thee, that it is tremendous'" (Exod 34:10). And it was at
this moment that the Holy Spirit ceased among the nations.[21]

Since Job is a gentile and a prophet, he could have lived no later
than the period before the Torah was given to Israel, for immediately after Israel received the Torah, the gift of prophecy was
forever removed from the nations of the world.[22]

Although many Rabbis saw Job as a righteous gentile and a
prophet, a counsellor to Pharaoh and a contemporary of Moses, not
all concurred. We find many other suggestions for when Job lived,
ranging from the time of Abraham to the days of Ahasuerus.[23] *Genesis Rabbah* 57:4, for example, contends that Job lived in the days
of Abraham, comparing the similarity of "Uz (עוץ) his firstborn
[Abraham's nephew]" (Gen 22:21), and "There was a man in the land
of Uz (עוץ)" (Job 1:1). With similar reasoning one tradition,
recorded in *B. Baba Batra* 15b, declares that Job lived in the time
of Jacob, and married Jacob's daughter, Dinah. The proof again is
based on linguistic analogy: a word used by Job of his wife also
appears in the Genesis account of Dinah's rape by Shechem. In Job
2:10, Job says "Thou speakest as one of the foolish women [נבלות]
speaketh," and in connection with Dinah, Genesis 34:7 declares,
"Because he wrought folly[נבלה] in Israel."[24]

In virtually all the cases cited above, Job was considered
a gentile. Some rabbinic commentators, however, could not be persuaded that a man of his excellent qualities was not an Israelite.
To these Rabbis, Job was not a gentile prophet, but rather one of
the prophets of Israel who spoke primarily to the gentiles.[25]
These teachers hold that Job lived in a time when the gift of
prophecy had already been removed from the nations of the world.
In the context of discussing the possible times when Job could
have lived, *B. Baba Batra* 15b draws the following conclusion:

All these Tannaim agree that Job was from Israel, except those
who say [that he lived in the days of Jacob or Moses.] [This
must be so,] for if you supposed that [they regarded him as] a
heathen, [the question would arise] after the death of Moses,
how could the Divine Presence rest upon a heathen, seeing that
a master has said, Moses prayed that the Divine Presence
should not rest on heathens, and God granted his request, as

it says, "That we may be separated, I and thy people, from all the people that are upon the face of the earth" (Exod 33:16).

Accordingly, the same source relates that both R. Eleazar and R. Johanan (fl. 250-290 CE) stated that Job was among those who returned from the Babylonian Exile, and that his house of study was in Tiberias.[26]

The Rabbis were divided not only on the question of Job's origin and the time when he lived, but in their evaluation of his character and merits as well. This division of opinion stems first from the apparent contradiction between the pious and rebellious biblical Jobs, and secondly, from rabbinic responses to Job as a gentile. Urbach has shown that there was an effort among many of the Rabbis, as well as among those who translated the book in ancient times, to resolve the contradictions inherent in the biblical text by toning down Job's rebelliousness and contention.[27] Job, therefore, often appears in rabbinic literature simply in the role of a good and pious man. With Abraham and Joseph he is sometimes mentioned as one of the three men who were called "God-fearing."[28] Based on the description, "A whole-hearted and an upright man" (Job 1:1), he is said to have been born circumcised. Rabbinic exegetes believed that the use of two such similar adjectives could not be mere redundancy, but had to have some special significance. Accordingly, they sought another meaning for "whole-hearted," (תם). תם can also mean "perfect," and a perfect man is one who is born circumcised.[29] In a similar vein, Job is praised for keeping himself far from things which might lead to transgression.[30] He was frequently lauded for his generosity with money as well. In *B. Pesaḥim* 112a, R. Samuel b. Isaac (fl. 290-320 CE) said: "What is meant by the verse, "Thou hast blessed the work of his hands" (Job 1:10)? Whoever took even a small coin (פרוטה) from Job was blessed; even to buy or sell to him was advisable."[31]

Even those Rabbis who most praised Job, however, could not overlook biblical evidence that Job was a heretic and blasphemer; not only did he curse God, and deny the unswerving operation of divine justice, but he also refuted the rabbinic belief in the resurrection of the dead. In rabbinic eyes, these were Job's sins. In the rabbinic schema, suffering was either a punishment, satisfying the demands of justice, or an atonement, bringing pardon or forgiveness, and reconciling man with God. No man suffers gratuitously. This is not to say that the Rabbis ignored the evidence of their own experience. As one Sage admitted, "It is beyond our power to understand why the wicked are at ease, or why

the righteous suffer."[32] But who could doubt that all things had
a reason? The existence of evil in a world created by a merciful
and loving God posed a number of theological problems which the
Rabbis attempted to resolve in a variety of ways. All their solutions, however, were predicated on a conviction of the all-
encompassing nature of divine justice. Thus, the Rabbis insist,
indeed, had to insist, that Job's suffering was not without meaning. Even though God's ways may be beyond human understanding,
they are never without justice.[33] Granting these suppositions, it
was clear that Job must have done something to merit his suffering; his plight was comprehensible only as punishment or atonement
for some past misdeed.

      One tradition explained Job's plight as just deserts for
his role as one of Pharaoh's counsellors. According to rabbinic
accounts, Balaam, Jethro and Job were Pharaoh's advisors in Egypt
at the time of the Israelites' captivity. When Balaam persuaded
Pharaoh to decree that all male Israelite children be drowned,
Jethro fled, but Job remained silent and did not voice his dis-
approval. It was for this that he was afflicted with sufferings.[34] R. Ḥama b. Ḥanina (fl. 250-290 CE) is credited with the
following account:

> When Israel departed from Egypt, the angel Samael [Satan]
> arose to accuse them. R. Ḥama added the following explanation
> in the name of his father: It can be compared to a shepherd
> who was leading his sheep across a river when a wolf came to
> attack the sheep. What did the shepherd, who knew well how to
> deal with such emergencies, do? He took a large he-goat and
> threw it to the wolf, saying to himself, "Let him struggle
> with this till we cross the river, and then I will return and
> bring it back." So when Israel departed from Egypt, the angel
> Samael arose to accuse them, pleading before God: "Lord of the
> universe! Till now they have been worshipping idols, and now
> Thou dividest the sea for them?" What did God do? He deliv-
> ered into his hands Job, one of the counsellors of Pharaoh, of
> whom it is written, "And that man was whole-hearted and up-
> right" (Job 1:1), and said, '"Behold, he is in thy hands" (Job
> 2:6). While he is busily occupied with Job, Israel will go
> through the sea! Afterwards, I will deliver Job.' This is
> why Job said, "I was at ease, and he broke me asunder" (Job
> 16:12).[35]

This story furnishes a reason for Job's suffering (he was one of
Pharaoh's counsellors), and provides an explanation for God's
allowing Satan to torment Job (to turn his attention from Israel).
In this way Job received his deserved punishment, while, at the
same time, he helped preserve the children of Israel. This is a
fitting turn of events, since his offense was that he had previously done nothing to prevent their potential destruction.

Other Rabbis thought that acting as Pharaoh's counsellor was not Job's only misdeed. He was also accused of blasphemy and speaking against God in his heart. Raba, one of Job's severest critics, maintains that "In all this Job did not sin with his lips" (Job 2:10), implies that he did sin within his heart, saying, "The earth is given over into the hand of the wicked, He covereth the faces of the judges thereof: If it be so, where and who is He?" (Job 9:24). Raba's point is that even though Job did not utter any of his blasphemies until after his suffering had begun, God knew that he was harboring such impious thoughts in his heart, and was therefore compelled to punish him. Job's sin, in this instance, was that he doubted God's justice.[36] Several of Job's other remarks, such as "If a man died, may he live again?" (Job 14:14), were also seen as heretical by various Sages because they seemed to deny the rabbinic tenet of resurrection of the dead. In B. Baba Batra 16a, Raba is quoted as saying of the verse, "As the cloud is consumed and vanishes away, so he that goes down to Sheol shall come up no more" (Job 7:9), "This shows that Job denied the resurrection of the dead."

Another of Raba's charges against Job is based on a pun on his name:

> Raba said: Job blasphemed with the [mention of a tempest], "For He breaketh me with a tempest and multiplieth my wounds without cause" (Job 9:17), and with a tempest he was answered. Job said to God: Perhaps a tempest passed before Thee, and caused Thee to confuse איוב "Job," with אויב "enemy." He answered through a tempest, as it is written, "Then the Lord answered Job out of the whirlwind and said . . . Gird up thy loins like a man, for I will demand of thee and declare thou unto me" (Job 38:1,3). He said to Job, "I have created many hairs in man, and for every hair I have created a separate groove, so that two should not suck from the same groove, for if two were to suck from the same grove, they would impair the sight of a man. I do not confuse one groove with another, and shall I then confuse איוב with אויב?[37]

The passage continues by contrasting many examples of divine omniscience with Job's ignorance and insignificance. Could such a power, the text implies, ever have been mistaken in His purpose?[38]

Rabbinic ambivalence about Job stemmed not only from his questioning of God, but also from misgivings based on his apparent gentile origin. The Rabbis use Job as evidence of the eminence a gentile may attain, but wish as well to define the limits of his distinction. Thus, Job is often compared unfavorably with various Israelites. It is said, for example, that had Job borne his suffering without complaint he would have risen to great renown, equal to that of the patriarchs. Time and again the Rabbis ask a

lamenting Job to compare his sufferings with the greater tests the
patriarchs endured. A comment from *Pesiqta Rabbati* 47 is typical:

> The Holy One, blessed be He, said to Job: Why raisest thou a
> cry? Because suffering befell thee? Dost thou then perhaps
> consider thyself greater than Adam, the creation of my own
> hands? Because of a single command that he made nothing of, I
> decreed death for him and for his progeny. Yet he did not
> raise a cry. Or consider thyself greater than Abraham?
> Because he ventured to say "Whereby shall I know that I shall
> inherit it?" (Gen 15:8), I put him to trial after trial,
> saying to him, "Know of a surety that thy seed shall be a
> stranger" (Gen 15:13). Yet he did not raise a cry. Or con-
> sider thyself greater than Isaac? Because he persisted in
> loving Esau I made his eyes dim, "And it came to pass, that
> when Isaac was old, and his eyes were dim, so that he could no
> longer see" (Gen 27:1). Or consider thyself greater than
> Moses? Because he spoke in anger to Israel, saying, "Hear
> now, ye rebels" (Num 20:10), I decreed as punishment for him
> that he could not enter into the land. Yet he did not raise a
> cry . . .

A similar tradition in *Deuteronomy Rabbah* 2:4 commenting
on the verse, "And I besought the Lord" (Deut 3:23), also shows
Job at a disadvantage:

> R. Johanan said, "The poor useth entreaties" (Prov 18:23),
> this refers to the prophets of Israel. "But the rich answer-
> eth impudently" (Prov 18:23), this refers to the prophets of
> the other nations. R. Johanan said, There was no more right-
> eous man among the nations of the world than Job, and yet he
> addressed God with reproaches, as it is said, "I would order
> my cause before Him, and fill my mouth with arguments" (Job
> 23:4). There are no greater prophets than Moses and Isaiah,
> and yet both of them approached God with supplications.
> Isaiah said, "O Lord, be gracious unto us: We have waited for
> Thee" (Isa 33:2), and Moses said, "And I besought the Lord"
> (Deut 3:23).

According to these interpreters, even Job's connection
with the household of Israel does not redound to his credit. In
describing Job's marriage to Jacob's daughter Dinah, *Genesis
Rabbah* 80:4 offers the following exposition of "And Dinah the
daughter of Leah went out" (Gen 34:1):

> R. Huna [fl. 220-250 CE] commenced in the name of R. Abba
> Bardela the priest [late Tanna], "To him that is ready to
> faint, kindness is due from his friend" (Job 6:14). The Holy
> One, blessed be He, reproved [Jacob]: Thou hast withheld kind-
> ness from thy brother, when she married Job thou didst not
> convert him. Thou wouldst not give her in marriage to one who
> is circumcised [Esau]: lo! she is married to one who is uncir-
> cumcised [Job]. Thou would not give her in legitimate wed-
> lock; lo! she is taken in illegitimate wedlock; thus it is
> written, "And Dinah the daughter of Leah went out."

This tradition holds that on his return to Canaan, when he was
preparing to meet Esau, Jacob concealed his daughter Dinah in a
chest, lest his brother wish to marry her, and he be obliged to

give her to him. God spoke to him, saying, "Herein thou hast
acted unkindly toward thy brother, and therefore Dinah will have
to marry Job, one that is neither circumcised nor a proselyte."[40]
While this midrash does not deny Job's merits, it is clear that
Job, righteous gentile though he may be, is deemed inferior both
to descendants of Abraham, such as Esau, and to proselytes.

Job is also often compared, almost always to his disadvantage, with Abraham. Thus, in the *'Abot de Rabbi Nathan* 2, Job is
praised for his modesty:

> Lo! it says, "I made a covenant with mine eyes / How then
> should I look upon a maid?" (Job 31:1). This teaches that Job
> was particularly strict with himself and would not even look
> upon a maiden . . . and all the more in regard with another
> man's wife! And why was Job so strict with himself that he
> would not look upon a maiden? For Job said, If I should look
> upon her today, and on the morrow another man comes and weds
> her, it will turn out that I have been looking upon another
> man's wife.

Job's modesty, however, could not compare with Abraham's, of which
it is said: "Job refrained from looking at other men's wives.
Abraham did not even look at his own, as it is written [in reference to Sarah], 'Behold, now I know that thou art a fair woman to
look upon' (Gen 12:11), which shows that up to then he did not
know."[41]

Similarly, *'Abot de Rabbi Nathan* 7 comments on the greatness of Job's hospitality. "Nevertheless," the midrash continues,
"the Holy One, blessed be He, said to Job, 'Job, thou hast not yet
reached half the measure of Abraham . . . that is why delight of
spirit was vouchsafed to him.'" R. Levi is even recorded as having taught that Satan acted from pious motives in tormenting Job,
"for when he saw that the Holy One, blessed be He, was inclined to
favor Job, he said, 'Heaven forbid that He should forget Abraham's
love.'"[42]

From these comments we see that while some rabbinic exegetes would not deny the possibility of a righteous gentile,
clearly few could countenance the notion that a gentile was more
righteous than a father of Israel. In the same way, midrashim
contrast the prophetic gifts of Moses and Balaam in a fashion
unfavorable to Balaam.[43] Again, the gentiles are not denied their
prophet, but his inferiority to the visionaries of Israel is made
manifest.

In the comparison of Abraham and Job, a central question,
especially among the Tannaim, was whether it is more important to
serve God from love or fear. The difference between them is
revealed in a teaching of R. Simeon b. Eleazar (fl. 170-200 CE):

"Greater is he who acts from love than he who acts from fear, because within the latter [the merit] remains effective for a thousand generations, but with the former it remains effective for two thousand generations."[44] If it were established that Job served God only out of fear, then his behavior would appear far less praiseworthy.

Ephraim Urbach has shown that the impact of the personality of Abraham and his ordeal at the time of the *Aqeda* (the binding of Isaac), had a decisive influence on the conception of the terms "fear" and "love."[45] R. Meir's (fl. 135-170 CE) observation that the term "a God-fearing man" applied to Abraham because he feared God out of love was a generally accepted view. Yet, while no one could doubt that Abraham's fear of God was inspired by love, the Sages were also aware of the fear that stemmed only from dread or the possibility of losing one's reward.[46] This kind of fear is unable to stand the test of suffering and adversity. This was the type of fear many of the Rabbis attributed to Job, as we see in the following midrash attributed to R. Akiba:

> A certain king had four sons: One remained silent when punished; another protested when punished; another pleaded for mercy when punished; and another, when punished, said to his father, "Punish me (still more)." Abraham was silent when punished, as it is said, "Take now thy son, thine only son, whom thou lovest, even Isaac . . . and offer him there for a burnt-offering" (Gen 22:2). He could have answered, "Yesterday Thou didst tell me 'For in Isaac shall seed be called to thee'" (Gen 21:12). Yet it is stated "And Abraham rose early in the morning" etc. (Gen 22:3). Job remonstrated when punished, as it is said, "I will say unto God: Do not condemn me; make me know wherefore Thou contendest with me" (Job 10:2). Hezekiah begged for mercy when punished, as it is stated, "And he prayed unto the Lord" (2 Kgs 20:20) . . . David said to his father, "Punish me even more," as it is said, "Wash me thoroughly from mine iniquity, and cleanse me from my sin" (Ps 51:4).[47]

In accordance with this view of Job as rebel, Akiba grouped him with the generations of the Flood, Egypt, Gog and Magog, and with the wicked who are punished in Gehenna for twelve months.[48] Similarly, a Baraita that enumerates the various types of Pharisees distinguishes between "a God-fearing Pharisee," and "a God-loving Pharisee." A God-fearing Pharisee is exemplified by Job, a God-loving Pharisee is Abraham; the noblest of them all is the God-loving Pharisee like Abraham.[49]

Other Sages, however, defended Job. In *M. Soṭa* 5:5, for example, is the following comment:

> On that day R. Joshua b. Hyrcanus [fl.110-135 CE] expounded: Job only served the Holy One, blessed be He, from love, as it

is said, "Though he slay me, yet will I wait for him" (Job
13:15). And should it still be doubtful whether the meaning
is "I will wait for him לו " or "I will not לא wait" [as a
textual variant reads], there is another text to declare,
"Till I die I will not put away mine integrity from me (Job
27:5). This teaches that what he did was from love. R.
Joshua b. Ḥananiah said: Who will remove the dust from thine
eyes, R. Joḥanan ben Zakkai, since thou hast been expounding
all thy life that Job only served the All-Perfect from fear,
as it is said, "That man was perfect and upright, and one that
feared God and eschewed evil" (Job 1:1). Did not Joshua, the
pupil of thy pupil teach that what he did was from love?

Further testimony that Job served God out of love is found in *J.*
Soṭa 20c: "It was taught in the name of R. Judah [fl. 135-170
CE], "As God liveth, who hath taken away my judgement; and the
Almighty who hath vexed my soul" (Job 27:2); this teaches that no
man makes a vow by the name of a king unless he loves him." The
two opposing views are reconciled in *B.Soṭa* 31a. "It has been
taught," R. Meir (fl. 135-170 CE) said, "it has been declared of
Job, 'One who fearest God' (Job 1:1), and it is declared of Abraham, 'Thou fearest God' (Gen 22:21); just as 'fearing God' with
Abraham indicates from love, so 'fearing God' with Job indicates
from love."[50]

     One may partly account for the multiplicity of opinion
concerning Job's origin, the time in which he lived, and his character traits and ultimate righteousness, by the lack of consis-
tency and specific information in the book of Job itself. Some
views, however, would seem to have been prompted by particularistic or polemical considerations as well. The effort to represent
Job as an Israelite, or conversely, to compare him unfavorably
with Israelite sages because he was a gentile, is certainly evidence of contradictory Jewish attitudes towards gentiles in the
rabbinic period. Ginzberg has written that Job is claimed as an
Israelite because some commentators "could not allow that a man of
the kindness and piety of Job should be a non-Jew and therefore
make him a Jew."[51] Urbach, on the other hand, holds that the differing evaluations of Job's religious personality express only the
views of the Sages on the ways of fearing and loving God, and not
their attitude to the gentile world and its pious men. He writes
that "It would certainly be out of the question to represent the
polarity between the views of Jochanan ben Zakkai, R. Eliezer and
R. Ḥiyya (fl. 200-220 CE) on the one hand, and of R. Joshua b.
Hyrcanus, Ben Peturi (fl. 110-135 CE) and R. Joshua on the other,
as based on the antithesis between the particularistic notion that
a gentile saint like Job could not attain to the spiritual plane
of Abraham, and the universalistic conception that a Gentile could

likewise reach such heights."[52] Yet it seems likely that this is
exactly the case.

A number of particularly hostile comments on Job, in fact,
make just this point. *B. Baba Batra* 15b records a dispute between
R. Eliezer and R. Joshua on Job's merits. Seen in the light of
these Sages' exchange on whether or not a gentile could attain the
world to come, which is cited above, it is quite evident that the
issue is the possibility of gentile righteousness:

> There was a certain pious man among the heathen named Job, but
> he [thought that he had] come into this world only to receive
> [here] his reward, and when the Holy One, blessed be He,
> brought chastisements upon him, he began to curse and blas-
> pheme, so the Holy One, blessed be He, doubled his reward in
> this world so as to expel him from the world to come. There
> is a difference on this point between Tannaim, as it has been
> taught: R. Eliezer says that Job was in the days of "the judg-
> ing of the judges," as it says "Behold all of you together
> have seen it; why then are ye become altogether vain?" (Job
> 27:12). What generation is it that is altogether vain? You
> must say, the generation where there is a "judging of the
> judges." R. Joshua b. Korḥah says: Job was in the time of
> Ahasuerus, for it says, "And in all the land were no women
> found so fair as the daughters of Job" (Job 42:15). What was
> the generation in which fair women were sought out? You must
> say that this was the generation of Ahasuerus.

The juxtaposition of a vain generation and unfit judges, with a
time when beauty is sought out and found, provides a metaphorical
contrast of Job as best of a bad lot with Job as righteous and
godly gentile, each example chosen to express its author's view of
gentile salvation. In a similar vein, R. Ḥiyya is said to have
taught, "God said: One righteous man arose among the nations of
the world, and I gave him his reward and let him go. Who was
that? Job."[53] This negative comment, far from dealing with questions of love and fear, is anxious to establish the gentile's
essential inferiority. Thus, it also hastens to explain Job's
rich reward, virtually unequalled in biblical history, as a thing
of this world only. Israelite suffering will be rewarded in the
world to come. In such midrashim Job becomes symbolic of the way
gentiles fall short even in their apparent victories. Even Job,
the most righteous of biblical gentiles, forfeits his entry to the
world to come by his constant complaining and questioning of God.
Thus, the gentiles could not claim that they lacked the opportunity to achieve salvation; they were given it and fell short. Similar remarks, also reflecting hostility towards gentiles, justify
Balaam's prophetic powers: God made Balaam such a great prophet
that the nations of the world might not complain that had they

been given Israel's advantages they too would have been a righteous nation.[54]

In their hostile remarks about Job, such rabbinic writers
as Raba may also be responding to pietistic treatments of Job
which emerged from non-Pharisaic Jewish circles. Such texts as
the *Testament of Job* and a *Life of Job* written by a certain
Aristeas,[55] had glorified the pious sufferer of Job 1 and 42 as an
innocent and paradigmatic model of patience under duress. The
outraged and outspoken Job of the rest of the book is totally
ignored in these works, which had an immense impact on Christian
views of Job. The rabbinic respect for Scripture could not sanction so cavalier an approach to holy writ, and instead demanded
descriptions of Job's obvious wrongdoings, justifications of his
undoubtedly deserved punishment, and condemnations of his intem-
perate and occasionally blasphemous complaining. The flawed figure who thus emerged explains the hesitation some Rabbis felt to
grant Job full forgiveness and access to the world to come. At
the same time the rather one-dimensional Job, championed by the
authors of those pietistic texts, and their adherents, was also
disavowed.

A related reason for either denigrating Job, or claiming
him as an Israelite, has to do with Christian claims. Marcel
Simon, among others, has studied the fierce controversies which
raged between Jews and Christians in the first few centuries of
the Common Era.[56] Texts *adversus Judaeos* are common in patristic
literature,[57] but less obviously polemical patristic exegetical
writings, Jerome's works in particular, also show evidence of such
controversies.[58] Polemics as such are more difficult to find in
rabbinic literature, given its comprehensive nature, but here too
traces of such disputes can be discerned, especially where discussions of similar import, based around the same biblical verse or
biblical figure can be found in both literatures.[59] Such a controversy appears to have centered around Job.

One of the major areas of Jewish-Christian contention was
the primacy of Israel in God's dispensation following the appearance of the man Christianity believed to be the Messiah. A popular and effective Christian argument proclaimed that with the
Incarnation, Israel had been displaced by the new Israel, the community of Christian believers. The destruction of the Temple in
70 CE, and Israel's further debasement after the failed rebellion
of 132-136 CE, seemed to support this position. Christian claims
of a preexistent community of believers outside the nation of
Israel, one which took precedence over the Levitical priesthood,[60]

only lent fuel to the fire. Prominent among these saintly pagans
who are said to have formed a true Christian community, even
though they lived before the birth of Jesus, is Job.[61]

The Rabbis responded to these claims of succession by re-
iterating proofs of divine love for Israel. Rabbinic insistence
that prophecy ceased among the gentiles after the death of Moses
constituted one line of response.[62] A midrash in *Song of Songs
Rabbah* on Song of Songs 1:14, "My beloved is to me a cluster of
henna blossoms / in the vineyard of En-gedi," makes a similar
point about the primacy of Israel in God's affections:

> Abraham, whose covenant with God had cancelled the previous
> covenant God had made with Noah, was anxious lest his covenant
> in turn be annulled in benefit of a man more deserving than
> himself in terms of observance and good deeds. "Do not fear,"
> God responded, "I will not raise from among the descendants of
> Noah any pious man worthy of serving as an Intercessor for
> other people. I will raise such men only from among your de-
> scendants. Even if your sons fall into sin, I will choose
> among them one man capable of putting a curb on [my] punishing
> justice by saying 'Enough.' He will redeem their faults. He
> will be surety to me for them."[63]

As Simon comments, the anti-Christian implications of this tradition are perfectly clear, for at the same time that the midrash
affirms the immutable character of the alliance between God and
Israel, it implicitly refutes the Christian dogma of the redemp-
tive power of Jesus' death.[64] Further lines of attack would
insist that such "saintly pagans" as Job and Melchizedek were
actually Israelites.[65]

The texts reveal that debates over Job's origins, virtues
and final fate were already developed in Tannaitic times. Whether
their original intent was polemical in any aspect is difficult to
determine. But certainly the comments of such Palestinian Amoraim
as R. Johanan on Job may be seen in a polemical context. R.
Johanan was the head of a studyhouse in third century Tiberias.
Tiberias was also a Christian center, and it seems likely that
R. Johanan had contact with Christian scholars, or at least was
aware of some Christian teachings. R.R. Kimelman, who has studied
R. Johanan and his setting, writes: "A number of scholars have
focused attention on the metamorphosis of traditional agadic
themes in the amoraic period, attributing this change to rabbinic
responses to anti-Jewish, Christian polemic. In several of these
developments a discernible role is played by Rabbi Yohanan."[66] A
Church Father who was a contemporary of Johanan, and whose exegesis shows knowledge of Jewish traditions, is Origen (d. ca.
253).[67] The two scholars appear to have been aware of and

responded to each other's "exegetical tendencies," at least in the
case of the Song of Songs.[68] In light of Joḥanan's determined
advocacy of Job as an Israelite who lived at the time of the
return from Babylon, it is interesting to find that Origen, who
glorifies Job as a model of Christian patience,[69] maintains the
view, cited by various Tannaim, that Job spanned the period between Jacob and Moses.[70] In his championing of Job as a Jew, it
seems likely that Joḥanan is responding to such Christian appro-
priation and adaptation of Jewish traditions for polemical use.

     Further indications that Job was a subject of discussion
between Jews and Christians are found in the writings of Jerome.
Again the disputed question is Job's origin. Jerome was one with
Christian tradition in placing Job in the tradition of pagan
priests, outside of the Levitical priesthood. In a letter, he
describes, with apparent approval, the traditions of his predecessors, Hippolytus, Irenaeus and Eusebius of Caesarea, concerning
Melchizedek and his spiritual descendants:

> They add that it is not astonishing that he is represented as
> a priest of the Most High, since he lived before the covenant
> demanding circumcision, and the institution of the legal rit-
> uals of the race of Aaron. For Abel, also, and Enoch and Noah
> were agreeable to God, and offered sacrifices to Him; and in
> the book of Job, we read that he too was one who sacrificed,
> and a priest, and each day offered sacrifices on behalf of his
> children. *They say too that Job himself was not of the race
> of Levi, but of the descendants of Esau; although the Hebrews
> declare the contrary.*[71]

Jerome most probably learned of Jewish views about Job's origin
from the Jewish teacher he hired to instruct him on difficulties
in the text of Job,[72] rather than from Jewish-Christian disputation, but it is significant that the issue remains a live one in
fifth century Palestine, and that the Jewish point of view made
known to Jerome is that Job was an Israelite.[73]

     The Rabbis were aware of the happy sequel to Job's suffer-
ing, and saw his restoration to prosperity as a symbol of hope to
sufferers in all times. Job's death, when he was "Old and full of
days" (Job 42:17), was seen as an enviable one, the death of a man
who had maintained his good name. R. Joḥanan, who glorified Job
as an Israelite, believed that Job could serve as a model for all
Jews:

> When R. Joḥanan finished the book of Job, he used to say the
> following: The end of man is to die, and the end of a beast
> is to be slaughtered, and all are doomed to die. Happy is he
> who was brought up in the Torah, and who has given pleasure to
> his Creator, and who grew up with a good name; and of him

Solomon said, "A good name is better than precious oil, and the days of death than the day of one's birth" (Eccl 7:1).[74]

Just as Job symbolized individual suffering and redemption, so his travails are occasionally compared with the trials of Israel. *Pesiqta Rabbati* 26:7, for example, contrasts the chastisements of Zion with the chastisements of Job; both lost sons and daughters, both were robbed of gold and silver, and both were cast upon a dungheap. The intention of these parallels is to reassure Israel that just as Job was comforted for his suffering, even more will Israel be consoled for the miseries she has endured. In *Pesiqta Rabbati* 29/30, Job and Israel are explicitly linked:

> All thy lovers have forgotten thee, O Israel, they seek thee not: For I have wounded thee with the wound of an enemy"(Jer 30:14). The words, "the wound of an enemy [אויב,"
> are to be read "the wounds of Job [איוב] ."
> Of Job it is written, "The Chaldeans set themselves in three bands" (Job 1:17), and of Jerusalem it is written, "From on high he sent fire" (Lam 1:13). Of Job it is written, "And he took a potsherd [חרש]" (Job 2:8); and of Jerusalem it is written, "The precious sons of Zion . . . How they are esteemed as earthen pitchers [נבלי-חרש]" (Lam 4:2).
> Of Job it is written, "Have pity upon me, have pity upon me, O ye my friends"(Job 19:21), and of Jerusalem it is written, "Forasmuch as I will show you no pity" (Jer 16:13). Of Job it is written, "For the hand of God hath touched me" (Job 19:21); and of Jerusalem, "That she hath received of the Lord's hand double for all her sins" (Isa 40:2).
> Now, taught R. Joshua the son of R. Neḥemiah [fl. 320-350 CE], if Job, who sinned, eventually had given to him a double recompense, so Jerusalem will eventually be given a double recompense of comfort. [Thus Scripture says] "Comfort ye, comfort ye my people" (Isa 40:1).[75]

The repetition of "comfort" is understood as proof that Jerusalem's recompense, as Job's, will be a double one. Jerusalem's destiny, as the midrash shows, has been presaged in every particular by Job's; surely the final boon will not be lacking.

There is no rabbinic consensus on Job. Even those who grant his good qualities cannot deem him, a gentile and a blasphemer, the equal in righteousness with an Israelite. Some Sages, out of a general sense of hostility towards perceived sectarians as well as the gentile nations, do their best to stress his iniquities and denigrate his rewards. Even the glorification of Job as a model Israelite by such Rabbis as Joḥanan may have as much to do with scoring points against Christian argument, as genuine esteem for the character himself. The problems caused by Job's claims to righteousness as opposed to his gentile origin and violent complaints are not resolved by the Rabbis. It is only in such pietistic works as the pseudepigraphical *Testament of Job*, produced

outside rabbinic circles, or the writings of the Church Fathers,
that an unambiguous, if single-faceted, figure emerges.[76] For the
Rabbis, the quandary of the gentile's place in creation remains in
all its complexity. Job as "fearer of God" has come as close to
divine approbation as a gentile can, but for most of the Rabbis it
will be his contemporary, Moses' father-in-law, Jethro, who takes
the ultimate step towards righteousness by becoming a convert to
the religion of Israel.[77]

iii

The dilemma posed by Job's claims to righteousness on the
one hand, and his gentile origin and the apparent misdeeds which
necessitated his severe punishments on the other, is not resolved
in rabbinic literature. As conscientious exegetes, the Rabbis had
perforce to read the Hebrew book of Job as it stood. In their
homilies, however, some Rabbis did concentrate on the patient and
God-fearing Job who experienced such a generous restoration.
Certainly it is this pious sufferer who was popularly known and
remembered in other Jewish texts of late antiquity, sources such
as the Septuagint version of the book of Job, and the pseudepigraphical *Testament of Job*.

The book of Job was problematic to translators as well as
to exegetes. The book's content was not easily accessible to a
general audience, and Job's anguished complaints and accusations
would surely not bring comfort to the untutored. There seems,
accordingly, to have been an early trend to mitigate Job's apparent blasphemies and to soften and explain his rebukes against God
in the various translations which were made of the book. Not only
is this the case in the Septuagint translation, discussed below,
but it also was operative in versions which were sanctioned and
disseminated by rabbinic circles. The following tradition bears
witness to rabbinic concerns:

> R. Jose (fl. 135-170 CE) relates: 'Once R. Ḥalafta (fl. 110-
> 135 CE) visited Rabban Gamliel(fl. 80-110 CE) at Tiberias. He
> found him sitting at the desk of R. Joḥanan b. Nazif and in
> his hand was a *Targum* of the Book of Job, which he was read-
> ing. Said R. Ḥalafta to him: I remember that Rabban Gamliel
> the Elder (first half of first century CE), your grandfather,
> was sitting on a step on the Temple Mount, when a *Targum* of
> the Book of Job was brought to him, and he ordered the builder
> to build it into the wall. At that time Rabban Gamliel (II)
> sent instructions to withdraw it from circulation.'[78]

As Urbach notes, we do not know what translation was brought to
Rabban Gamliel the Elder--whether Greek or Aramaic, nor to his

grandson for that matter. "But," he continues, "whether this was the Septuagint, or a translation that rendered the Book quite literally, the reason for its suppression is to be found in the very fact of its translation--on the same principle as 'The incident of Reuven is read [in Hebrew], but is not translated' (M. *Megilla* 4:9)--or at most in the manner of the rendition which did not find favor with Rabban Gamliel."[79] In other words, the Rabbis did not want the difficult and apparently blasphemous Book of Job translated and widely disseminated among those most likely to misconstrue it. The translations which finally were allowed seem to have been those which attempted to explain away Job's harsh charges and cast his personality in a favorable light.[80]

The Rabbis had several reasons for wishing to encourage the representation of a self-effacing and humble Job in translations meant for popular audiences. Perhaps the most important of these were theological. As Gordis points out, all ancient versions of Scripture were prepared for the uneducated masses, and therefore sought to transmit acceptable religious ideas to their readers and to exclude heretical notions.[81] The Book of Job appeared to deny two doctrines which had become central to rabbinic Judaism: the operation of divine justice in the world, and the future resurrection of the dead. Both in their exegesis, and in the translations of the Book of Job they sanctioned, the Rabbis sought to eliminate or render innocuous any of Job's assertions which disagreed with their tenets. Moreover, it was the simple Job of the Book's prologue and epilogue who was best known and loved by the people. It was this Job who provided a salutary and consolatory model of endurance and reward to a downtrodden people; this Job was an inspirational figure worth preserving and promoting. It was this subdued and unquestioning Job who also appeared in the Septuagint version of the book.

The Septuagint is the oldest of the surviving ancient versions of the Book of Job. The present Greek text is largely co-extensive with the Hebrew, but it is clear that the original Septuagint of Job was between a quarter and a sixth shorter. In the third century of the Common Era, for example, the current Greek version had some four hundred fewer lines than the Hebrew, for when Origen compiled his *Hexapla* he supplied the lines he found missing from Theodotion's translation of the Hebrew, marking them with an asterisk.[82] It seems likely that the original translator perplexed by the difficult language of the Hebrew Book, simply omitted those passages he was unable to understand.[83]

In a number of passages the Septuagint version of Job
should be regarded more as a paraphrase than as a translation.[84]
Many students of this version of Job have thought theological
biases on the part of the Greek translator led him to obscure or
alter the sense of the Hebrew.[85] The biblical Job, for example,
is skeptical about the doctrine of man's resurrection, a belief
which had come to be accepted popularly, as well as in rabbinic
circles. So, where the Hebrew Job asks, "If a man dies, can he
live again?" (Job 14:14), the Greek Job eliminates the doubt and
the heresy by the simple device of changing the interrogative into
a declarative, "If a man dies, he will live again."[86] The Job of
the Septuagint also possesses a new humility and patience; many of
his accusations have been rendered less harsh. As Urbach says,
"In not a few passages the Greek Job speaks almost with composure,
and his words lack that quality of self-assurance and protest
found in the Hebrew original."[87] The indictments have been converted into statements of resignation by means of interpretations,
omissions and interpolations.

In addition to subtle redirections in the body of the
translation, the Septaugint version of Job contains two passages
which do not appear in the Hebrew text. The first of these is a
long addition made to Job 2:9, in which Job's wife urges her husband to "Curse God and die." The Greek expands this simple suggestion considerably:

> After a long time had passed, his wife said to him: "How long
> will you endure and say, 'See, I will wait a bit longer, look-
> ing for the hope of my salvation.' Look, your memory is
> already blotted out from the earth [along with] the sons and
> daughters, the travail and pangs of my womb, whom I reared in
> toil for nothing. And you, yourself, sit in wormy decay,
> passing the nights in the open, while I roam and drudge from
> place to place, and from house to house, waiting for the sun
> to go down, so that I may rest from my toils and the griefs
> which now grip me. Now say some word against the Lord and die
> . . ."[88]

The intent of the Greek seems to be to enlarge on the words of
Job's wife to explain her meaning more fully. In the biblical
context, Pope has pointed out, death is not necessarily the immediate consequence of cursing God: "[Job's] wife, perhaps, meant to
suggest that since he was not long for this world, he might as
well give vent to his feelings, or hers, and curse God."[89] In the
Greek, however, Job's wife believes that Job has no rational hope
of salvation; their suffering is now so enormous that death would
be welcome in the face of enduring such a miserable life. Thus,

she urges her husband to speak such words against God as will
cause their immediate deaths.

The second, and for our purposes, the more significant
addition, is an addendum to the book which again clearly diverges
from the Hebrew account. Although Pope notes that the traditions
recorded here are garbled and of dubious value as witnesses to the
original Septuagint text of Job,[90] they are of cardinal importance
in documenting the growth of the figure in popular legend. This
addendum, attached at Job 42:17, begins by affirming the commonly
accepted belief in the resurrection of the dead: "And Job died,
an old man and full of days; and it is written that he will rise
again with those whom the Lord raises up."[91] In one sentence the
central issue of the Book of Job, the existence of unjustified
suffering in the universe of a just God, is neatly vitiated. All
present wrongs will be righted when we rise again. One is reminded of the "pious editor's" palinodic addition to the end of
Ecclesiastes and rightly so, for both these final words deny all
that has gone before at the same time as they ordain currently
acceptable doctrine.

The addendum to Job continues by dealing with another difficult question, that of Job's origin. Job is identified as the
Jobab of Genesis 36:33-34, and his genealogy is given in detail:

> This [man] is explained from the Syriac Book as living in the
> land of Ausis, on the borders of Edom and Arabia; formerly his
> name was Jobab. He took an Arabian wife and sired a son whose
> name was Ennon. But he himself was the son of his father
> Zare[th], one of the sons of Esau, and of his mother Bosorra,
> so that he was the fifth from Abraham.

This genealogy, which is not found in any rabbinic source,[92] also
appears in the *Testament of Job*, and a *Life of Job*, cited in
Eusebius and attributed to a certain Aristeas.[93] Its origin seems
to lie in the similarity of the names "Job," and "Jobab," as well
as in well-established traditions that Job lived in patriarchal
times. It may also reflect ancient lore linking the legendary Job
to the land of Edom, which was believed to be the habitation of
Esau's descendants. It is significant that this genealogy does
not appear in rabbinic texts. That the tradition was known to
some Rabbis is clear from Jerome, who recounts that the Hebrews
strongly deny that Job was a descendant of Esau.[94] Rabbinic disavowal of this theory of Job's origin most likely has to do with a
rabbinic horror of Esau and his progeny, for in rabbinic literature Esau and his descendants, the Edomites, became synonymous
with Israel's greatest enemy, Rome, whether pagan or Christian.[95]
Regardless of his faults, the Rabbis were not prepared to admit

that a man of Job's evident merits was a member of such a race.
It seems apparent that to the Rabbis, a descendant of Esau would
have been a gentile. This may also have been a factor in the
vehement denials Jerome encountered. Whether this is the case as
far as the Septuagint addendum is concerned is not clear. Certainly, in patristic exegesis derived from this tradition, and
discussed below, it is assumed that a descendant of Esau would be
a gentile. All that can be said is that in this text the important point is that Job is fifth in descent from Abraham, a relationship which automatically establishes his righteousness.

Job's righteousness is also unquestioned in the *Testament
of Job*, This Job, in fact, differs from all his known precursors
in the degree of his virtue, and beyond bearing his woes patiently
and without complaint, he also knows why he suffers. The *Testament of Job* exists in two Greek versions, both rediscovered in the
nineteenth century. Some scholars believe the Greek may be based
on a lost Hebrew or Aramaic original.[96] There is no scholarly
agreement on either the book's date, or the milieu in which it was
written,[97] and certainly the book combines many diverse elements.
The author of the *Testament* was clearly familiar with the Septuagint version of Job, for he reproduces much of the speech uttered
by Job's wife in the Septuagint at Job 2:9. Similarly, he knew of
the traditions recorded in the addendum to the Septuagint version
of Job, for he too identifies Job with Jobab of Genesis 36. He
also parallels midrashic material on Job, identifying Job's second
wife with Dinah,[98] and linking him with Abraham as one of the men
who discovered the true God and abandoned idolatry on his own.[99]
The description of Job's great hospitality and charity to the
destitute are also reminiscent of many remarks about Job in rabbinic literature.[100]

The book takes the form of a farewell address to Job's
seven sons and three daughters, in which their father reviews his
life. As Jobab, a descendant of Esau (Gen 36:33), Job was a rich
ruler of the land of Uz (Ausitis). Like Abraham, he abandoned
idolatry for the worship of the true God, the Maker of heaven and
earth.[101] Job voluntarily set out to destroy the idols of his
land, the works of Satan. An archangel of the Lord told him that
he must therefore prepare for a life-long battle with Satan; if he
were steadfast, however, he would achieve lasting renown as a
great spiritual athlete, and would bear a crown of amaranth in the
world to come.

The *Testament of Job* chronicles the suffering Satan brings
upon Job, yet in the face of all afflictions Job remains unbroken.

In the end Satan is abashed; he breaks into tears and leaves Job, yielding as if to a greater wrestler (27:3-9). Job's friends, now, not Job himself, lament and complain about his bitter fate; but Job withstands the trial and cries, "Shall I sin with my lips against the Lord? It shall not come to pass!" (38:2).

Elihu too acts far differently in this book than he does in the biblical story. Here he is imbued with the spirit of Satan and speaks hard words to Job, accusing him of having committed terrible sins. He does not speak sincerely, for afterwards God shows Job that Elihu was a wild beast (a "serpent"), not a man. When at last the three friends confess their error to Job, bringing animals to be sacrificed as sin-offerings to the Lord, and obtaining their pardons through Job, Elihu, unlike the others, is not forgiven.[102]

Job returns to his city and holds a feast of thanksgiving. Taking up his former words of charity, he soon becomes rich, marries Jacob's daughter Dinah, and becomes the father of ten children as before. At the end of his recitation, Job admonishes his sons, rehearsing his beliefs and religion in these precepts: "Forsake not the Lord! Be charitable to the poor and do not disregard the feeble. Take not unto yourselves wives from strangers" (*Test. Job* 45:1-4). This last command, according to at least one commentator, proves beyond possibility of doubt that the book is Jewish in character and conception.[103]

Certainly Job's origin is not an issue to the author of the *Testament*. Job identifies himself to his children as of the sons of Esau (1:4). Their mother and Job's wife is Dinah, the daughter of Jacob: "For I am your father Job, who exhibits complete endurance: and you are a chosen and honored race from the seed of Jacob, your maternal grandfather" (1:3). The implications of Job's descent, however, are not clear. Given the lack of scholarly consensus on the setting in which this book was written, it is impossible to say if this Job is meant to be seen as a Jew, a convert to Judaism, or a righteous gentile. Certainly, this Job is proud of his own and his wife's descent from Abraham, and there is no doubt that he is perceived as a fitting worshipper of Abraham's God. All that can be said is that this book emerged from a community which saw Job as an exemplar of spiritual strength, and fortitude in suffering.

By the end of the *Testament* Job has become a virtual personification of righteousness. This is manifest in the eulogy which follows his death:

> Woe to us today, for today there has been taken away the
> strength of the helpless, the light of the blind, the father
> of the orphans. Taken away is the host of the strangers, the
> path of the weak. Taken away is the clothing of the naked,
> the protector of the widows. Who then will not weep for the
> man of God?[104]

The hero of the *Testament*, the "man of God," is a Job both more
humble and more accepting than his biblical namesake; he is the
innocent Job of the biblical book's prologue and epilogue. The
culmination of this folklore tradition will be found in the Job of
the New Testament and later Christian tradition.[105]

Although the *Testament* may have originally been intended
for the edification of a small ascetic community, its influence
was far more pervasive, entering even into some late rabbinic
texts.[106] It is reflected too in the New Testament where James
5:11 proclaims: "Behold, we call those happy who were steadfast,
you have heard of the steadfastness of Job, and you have seen the
purpose of the Lord, how the Lord is compassionate and merciful."
Even though Pope Gelasius (482-496) removed the *Testament of Job*
from the Apocrypha, that book's patient Job, far more than the
complaining and fractious biblical Job, became the model for subsequent Christian interpretation.[107] The possibility of Job's
gentile origin, moreover, so much a problem to the Rabbis, so
expeditiously dealt with by the Septuagint and the *Testament*,
rises again in Christian exegesis, but this time triumphantly, as
Job takes his place among the gentile prophets of Christ to the
nations.

iv

Job occupies an important place in patristic biblical
exegesis. As a righteous gentile, he symbolized all saintly
pagans who formed a part of the true Christian community, even if
they lived before the birth of Jesus. As a man who bore his
cruel sufferings patiently, he was a model of Christian fortitude
and faith. And as a virtuous individual who experienced pain,
humiliation and final restoration, Job also became a type and
prefiguration of the crucified and resurrected Christ.

Patristic exegetes are unanimous that Job was a gentile;
most writers agree that he was an Idumean, a descendant of Esau,
and identical with Jobab of Genesis 36:33. In this they follow
the traditions present in the addendum to the Septuagint version
of Job.

Since Christianity was a religion which sought to encom-
pass all peoples, the portrayal of saintly pagans, biblical and

non-biblical, as gentile witnesses to the coming Incarnation of Christ played an important part in the early theology of the Church, which commonly found adherents, not by destroying what had gone before, but by building on the bases of entrenched pagan beliefs.[108] The pagan religions that Christianity believed it had come to supplant and fulfill, then, were not thought to be totally without truth; rather, even as the Jews had received a revelation of God's law, so many pagans had received a revelation of cosmic or natural religion. The coming of Christ was the last and greatest revelation of the will of God, but as Jaroslav Pelikan writes, that did not mean the previous partial visions of divine truth should be denied their importance:

> The missionary practice of the church was constrained to recognize from the outset that "God shows no partiality, but in every nation any one who fears him and does what is right is acceptable to him," and that therefore the Greek did not have to become a Jew en route to the gospel. From this premise it appeared to follow that Christian missionaries should affirm whatever could be affirmed of the religion prevailing in the nations to which they came and should represent Christianity as the correction and fulfillment of the expectations at work in those nations.[109]

The conviction that "Jesus Christ was the divinely ordained answer to the needs and aspirations of the gentiles as well as the fulfillment of the messianic hopes of Israel,"[110] is implicit in the Epistles and Acts of the Apostles. In the Epistles, Paul affirms again and again the existence of a continuous revelation of God made through the natural order and directed to all mankind. He affirms that every man will be judged in accordance with the revelation he has known; the pagan who knows only the interior law of conscience will be judged according to that.[111] In this Paul seems to echo the rabbinic notion of the righteous gentile, who had only to follow the Noachite commandments to be worthy of salvation. The Rabbis believed that even if these commandments had not been written down, they would still be in force, for they were moral laws evident to any rational human being.[112] Paul's remarks in Romans 2:14-16 seem to reflect this concept:

> When gentiles who have not the law do by nature what the law requires, they are a law to themselves, even though they do not have the law. They show that what the law requires is written on their heart, while their conscience also bears witness and their conflicting thoughts accuse or perhaps excuse them when on that day, according to my gospel, God judges the secrets of men by Jesus Christ.

The Church after Paul continued to affirm respect for the
religious values of the pagan world, believing that wise and
righteous men among the gentile nations typified the advent of
Christ to the pagan soul. Irenaeus (d. ca. 200), for example,
echoes the Apostle: "The word of God has never ceased to be present in the race of man,"[113] and later writers went so far as to
canonize wise and worthy men from among the gentiles as saints of
the Church. Augustine's (d. 430) view of human history as the
parallel chronicles of the deeds of the "City of Men," and the
"City of God," is based on similar assumptions. "It is necessary," Augustine writes, "to include within the Church, all the
holy people who lived even before the coming of Christ and
believed that he would come, just as we believe he has come."[114]

Justin Martyr (d. ca. 165), explained this coincidence of
beliefs by the eternal presence of the Word:

> All men who have lived according to the Word, in Whom all men
> have part, are Christians, though they may have passed for
> atheists, men such as Socrates, Heraclitus, and others like
> them amongst the Greeks[115] and Abraham, Elias and many others
> amongst the barbarians.

Justin included two biblical figures, Abraham and Elias, with
Greeks such as Socrates and Heraclitus, since Christianity held
that many of the righteous figures mentioned in the Hebrew Bible,
whether Israelite or non-Israelite, together with righteous men
among the pagans, had some partial revelation of the true religion
of Christ.

In fact, in its efforts to dissociate itself from the tradition of the Levitical priesthood, which insisted on the preser-
vation of Mosaic law, Christianity preferred to trace its heritage
to non-Levitical biblical priests such as Melchizedek. Biblical
gentiles such as Abel, Enoch, Noah and Job also find a place in
this tradition, as in the sixth book of the *Constitution of the
Holy Apostles*, a Syrian document probably no later than the fourth
century. A portion of the prayer for the ordination of a bishop
reads:

> Thou who didst appoint the rules of the Church, by the coming
> of Thy Christ in the flesh; of which Thy Holy Ghost is the
> witness, by Thy apostles, and by us the bishops, who by Thy
> grace are here present; who hast foreordained priests from the
> beginning for the government of Thy people: Abel in the first
> place, Seth and Enos, Enoch and Noah, and Melchizedek and Job;
> who didst appoint Abraham and the rest of the patriarchs, with
> Thy faithful servants Moses and Aaron, and Eleazar and
> Phineas; who didst choose from among them rulers and priests
> in the tabernacle of Thy testimony.[116]

It is interesting that the priestly line begun by Abel, the first
man to offer sacrifices to God, is quite distinct from that de-
scending from Aaron, and that this original line represents God's
initial establishment of order among men, a revelation before the
revelation to Israel. Thus, in the prayer for ordination of a
bishop, this line of tradition is given precedence over the
priesthood of Israel.

For many patristic writers, the existence of holy biblical
pagans such as Job was proof that Christ had indeed come to redeem
not only the Jews but all mankind. Gregory the Great (d. 604), in
his exhaustive *Moralia on Job*, comments on Job's gentile origin in
a typical way: "It is not without cause that the life of a just
pagan is set before us as a model side by side with the life of
the Israelites. Our Savior, coming for the redemption of Jews and
gentiles, willed also to be foretold by the voices of Jews and
gentiles."[117]

The tradition of Job's great patience in adversity, as
well as the belief that Job was a prophet of God, is echoed in
James 5:7-11. It is this saintly Job of the prologue and epilogue
of the biblical book, the Job of Ezekiel 14 and of such works as
the *Testament of Job*, to whom both the New Testament and most
patristic writers refer; the rebellious and blasphemous Job is
virtually unmentioned in Christian commentary. Indeed, when James
advises his Christian reader to look to the prophets who spoke in
the name of the Lord for his models of virtue, he numbers Job
among them because of his forebearance: "As an example of suffering and patience, brethren, take the prophets who spoke in the
name of the Lord. Behold, we call those happy who were steadfast.
You have heard of the steadfastness of Job, and you have seen the
purpose of the Lord, how the Lord is compassionate and Merciful"
(Jas 5:10-11). Job's was a special order of patience, then, one
predicated completely on trust in God and his purposes. "In the
Christian view," writes Daniélou, "it is not a question of stoical
patience, of pure resignation bearing witness to the greatness of
the soul. It is patience linked with hope, founded on the certainty of the happiness promised by Christ; and this certainty
gives strength to endure the trials of earthly life. This is a
new picture of Job, bound up with the faith in eternal life."[118]

Following the example of James, many Christian writers
exalted Job for his special patience. The *First Epistle of
Clement*, written about 100, refers to Job as the "righteous and
blameless true worshipper of God," and places him in the company
of Abraham, Moses, Elijah, Elisha, Ezekiel and the other prophets

who were "heralding the coming of Christ," and whose piety and
humility is to be imitated by the faithful.[119] In his *Treatise on
Patience*, Tertullian (d. ca. 220) says of Job: "Oh, happy also he
who met all the violence of the devil by the exertion of every
species of patience":

> For by all his pains [Job] was not drawn away from his rever-
> ence for God; but he has been set up as an example and testi-
> mony to us, for the thorough accomplishment of patience as
> well in spirit as in flesh, as well in mind as in body; in
> order that we succumb neither to damages of our worldly goods,
> nor to losses of those who are dearest, nor even to bodily
> afflictions. What a bier for the devil did God erect in the
> person of that hero![120]

In the *Apostolic Constitutions* (ca. 380) the example of Job is
exalted as well: "Accept undisturbed the misfortunes which come
to thee and bear contradictions without vexation knowing that
recompense will be given thee by God, as it was given to Job and
Lazarus."[121] The apocryphal *Apocalypse of Paul* (dated in the late
fourth century)[122] numbers Job among those saints who have given
hospitality to strangers (v. 27), and describes Job as a model of
piety and silent endurance. Job himself recounts his expression
of patience when tempted by the Devil to speak a word against the
Lord and die:

> If it is the will of God that I continue in affliction all the
> time I live until I die, I shall not cease to praise the Lord
> God and shall receive greater reward. For I know that the
> trials of this world are nothing in comparison to the consola-
> tion that comes afterwards.[123]

And Gregory summarized these lessons in his *Moralia* when he wrote
of the biblical pagan saints: "Abel came to exhibit innocence,
Enoch to give a lesson in the integrity of morals, Noah to teach
perseverance in hope, and Job to exhibit patience in the midst of
trials."[124] The steadfast Job was to remain an important model
for Christian sufferers.

Christians saw in Job not only an ideal of virtue, but
also a figure of the Christ who was to come. Zeno, Bishop of Vero
(d.491), established the parallels between Job and Christ: Job,
rich in the goods of this earth and then reduced to poverty, pre-
figures Christ, "leaving for love of us the goods of heaven, and
making himself poor to make us rich." Job's temptations prefigure
those of Christ, who "by taking flesh takes upon himself the blem-
ishes of all humanity." Job is insulted by his friends, and Jesus
is insulted by the priests. Job upon his dunghill represents
Christ in the aftermath of sin.[125] It is noteworthy that Zeno
underlines especially the parallel between Job's abjection and the

kenosis of Christ: it is the Incarnation even more than the Passion that is emphasized in this comparison. Gregory spoke in the same vein: "It was necessary, therefore, that the blessed Job, who foretold the greatest of the mysteries, the Incarnation, would prefigure by his life Him whom he described in words."[126]

The implications of this comparison between Job's ordeal and the Incarnation of Christ are far-reaching. No particular aspect of Job's life, such as his temptation, patience or suffering, is singled out for comment; instead, as Daniélou notes, man's very humanness is redeemed: "Christ in this comparison is mankind itself reduced to the nakedness of its tragic condition, of which Job was its most perfect prefiguration."[127]

To the early Fathers of the Church, then, Job was saintly and righteous, a model of the pagan who awaited the coming of Christ, an example of patience to all present-day Christians, and a prefiguration of Christ. Each subsequent commentator drew from this repository of tradition to recreate Job according to his own purposes. The comments of three Latin Fathers, Jerome, Augustine and Gregory, are of particular interest to the study of perceptions of Job as a gentile.

Jerome (d. 420) was unique among his contemporaries in the Church for his interest in literary and linguistic problems in the biblical text. His desire to prepare a new and accurate Latin translation of the Hebrew Scriptures, the Vulgate, led him to learn Hebrew and to consult Jewish teachers about difficult words and passages.[128] Jerome was particularly conscious of the failings and omissions in the various versions of the Book of Job available in his time; in his Preface to his own translation of that book he details their deficiencies:

> . . . those translators, who it is clear have left out numerous details, have erred in some points; especially in the book of Job, where, if you withdraw such passages as have been added and marked with asterisks, the greater part of the book will be cut away. This, at all events, will be so in the Greek. On the other hand, previous to the publication of our recent translation with asterisks and obeli, about seven or eight hundred lines were missing in the Latin, so that the book, mutilated, torn and disintegrated, exhibits its deformity to those who publicly read it.[129]

Jerome notes that in his own new translation he followed no ancient translator, "but attempted to reproduce now the exact words, now the meaning, now both together, of the original Hebrew, Arabic, the Greek, and occasionally the Syriac."[130]

Alone among patristic, or for that matter, among rabbinic exegetes, Jerome comments on the differences of style within the

Book of Job. He noticed that from the beginning of the book to
the first words of Job, the Hebrew version is in prose, but from
that point on until "Therefore I blame myself and repent in dust
and ashes" (Job 42:6), the book is in poetry: "We have hexameter
verses running in dactyl and spondee; and owing to the idiom of
the language other feet are frequently introduced not containing
the same number of syllables, but the same quantities . . . But
from the aforesaid verse to the end of the book the small remain-
ing section is a prose composition."[131] Jerome goes on to defend
biblical poetry against those who claim that the Hebrews possesses
no metres or rhythms, and grudgingly excuses those earlier translators of the book who failed to recognize its poetic nature.

Jerome himself was well aware of the difficulties presented by the Book of Job, writing in his Preface that an indi-
rectness and slipperiness attaches to the whole book, even in the
Hebrew: "It is tricked out with figures of speech, and while it
says one thing, it does another." He compares the book's meaning
to an eel or a *muraena* (a seafish), "the more you squeeze it, the
sooner it escapes."[132] In his efforts to discover the book's
mysteries, Jerome relates that he paid a "not inconsiderable sum"
to a Jew, "a native of Lydda, who was amongst the Hebrews reckoned
to be in the front rank."[133] He is uncertain, however, how much
he profited from this instruction, concluding, "Of this one thing
I am sure, that I could not have translated that which I had not
previously understood." It is clear that Jerome did assimilate
certain elements of rabbinic teachings about Job from his Jewish
teacher. Thus, Jerome disagrees with most other Christian writers
who followed the Septuagint and the *Testament of Job* on Job's origin, and thought he was Esau's descendant Jobab of Genesis 36:33.
Jerome, rather, follows a rabbinic view, that Job was a descendant
of Abraham's brother Nahor.[134] Commenting on "Now after these
things it was told Abraham, 'Behold Milcah also has borne children
to your brother Nahor: Uz the firstborn, Buz his brother, Kemuel
the father of Aram'" (Gen 22:20), Jerome says:

> The firstborn of Nahor, the brother of Abraham, by his wife
> Milcah, was Uz; from his stock Job descended, as it is written
> in his book, "There was a man in the land of Uz, whose name
> was Job" (Job 1:1). Therefore, they are wrong who judge Job
> to be one of the offspring of Esau as it is written at the end
> of the Septuagint [in the portion] not found in the Hebrew
> version.[135]

Jerome also preserves a second rabbinic tradition, this
time having to do with Elihu. He relates that Balaam, "the

divinely inspired," was descended from Milcah's second son, Buz, and that Balaam appears in the Book of Job in the person of Elihu:

> This Elihu, the Hebrews relate, was at first a holy man and prophet of God, but afterwards through disobedience and desire for reward, and wishing to curse Israel, he lost the divine voice, as it is said in that Book: "Then Elihu, the son of Barachel the Buzite, of the family of Ram, became angry" (Job 32:2).[136]

Jerome agrees with his co-religionists, however, when he sees Job in the tradition of pagan priests, outside of the Levitical priesthood. In a letter he describes, with apparent approval, the traditions of his predecessors, Hippolytus, Irenaeus and Eusebius of Caesarea concerning Melchizedek and his spiritual descendants:

> They add that it is not astonishing that he is represented as a priest of the Most High, since he lived before the covenant demanding circumcision, and the institution of the legal rituals of the race of Aaron. For Abel also, and Enoch and Noah were agreeable to God, and offered sacrifices to Him; and in the book of Job, we read that he too was one who sacrificed, and a priest, and each day offered sacrifices on behalf of his children. They say too that Job himself was not of the race of Levi, but of the descendants of Esau; although the Hebrews declare the contrary.[137]

Jerome extols Job as an example of steadfastness in adversity. In his commentary on the Epistle to the Ephesians, he recommends Job as an example of patience, and of hope, for all his bad was changed by God to good.[138] Jerome also believed that Job was a prophet of Christ. In a letter to Pammachius against John of Jerusalem, he says that Job solaced his miseries with the hope and reality of the resurrection:

> "Oh that my words were written," [Job] says, "Oh, that they were inscribed in a book with an iron pen, and on a sheet of lead, that they were graven in the rock forever. For I know that my redeemer liveth, and that in the last day I shall rise from the earth, and again be clothed with my skin, and in my flesh shall see God" (Job 19:23-26).[139] What can be clearer than this prophecy? No one since the days of Christ speaks so openly concerning the resurrection as he did before Christt. . . He hopes for a resurrection; nay, rather he knew and saw that Christ, his redeemer, was alive, and at that last day would rise again from the earth. The Lord had not yet died, and the athlete of the Church saw his redeemer rising from the grave.[140]

Encomia to Job's steadfastness and prescience, however, do not set Jerome's comments on Job apart from other patristic writers' as much as his interest in the Hebrew text of the book, and his reflection of rabbinic exegesis of it. His consulting a rabbinic Sage, and what he learned from that Sage, indicate that

the question of Job's origin was not only a rabbinic concern but
had become a matter of Jewish-Christian dispute.

Jerome's interests in Jewish exegesis of biblical verses,
and the literary integrity of Scripture, were of little concern to
his contemporary, Augustine of Hippo (d. 430). Although Augustine
upheld the historical truth of the letter of Scripture, maintaining that scriptural meaning could be discovered only through an
understanding of biblical fact, he was more concerned to find in
the Bible's characters and narratives the stuff of Christian life.
Through his wide view of human history as the story of two cities,
the godly and the ungodly, Augustine sought to demonstrate that
the christological implications of biblical personages and situations were implicit on the literal level. The lessons that Job,
for instance, teaches the Christian emerge not only through complicated exegesis; they are present and intended to be present in
the scriptural account of Job's life.

Augustine reiterates many of the patristic teachings about
Job found in his predecessors' writings. He praises his faith
despite torment, and sees him as an exemplar of the crucified
Christ.[141] Of greatest interest, here, however, are his remarks
on Job as gentile. In the eighteenth book of the *City of God*,
Augustine asks "Whether before Christian times there were any outside of the Israelite race who belong to the fellowship of the
heavenly city." He responds as follows:

> Wherefore if we read of any foreigner--that is, one neither
> born of Israel nor received of that people into the canon of
> the sacred books--having prophesied about Christ, if it has
> come or shall come to our knowledge, we can refer to it over
> and above; not that this is necessary, even if wanting, but
> because it is not incongruous to believe that even in other
> nations there may have been men to whom thy mystery was re-
> vealed, and who were also impelled to proclaim it . . . [142]

Should the Jews deny this, Augustine continues, they might be easily refuted by the case of the "holy and wonderful man, Job,"

> who was neither native nor a proselyte, that is a stranger
> joining the people of Israel, but being bred of the Idumean
> race, arose there, and died there too, and who is so praised
> by the divine oracle, that no man of his time is put on a
> level with him as regards justice and piety. And although we
> do not find his date in the chronicles, yet from his book,
> which for its merit the Israelites have received as of canon-
> ical authority, we gather that he was in the third generation
> after Israel. And I doubt not that it was divinely provided,
> that from this one case we might know that among other nations
> also there might be men pertaining to the spiritual Jerusalem
> who lived according to God and have pleased Him.[143]

Augustine was convinced that Job must have had a revelation of the coming of Christ to be included in this august company:

> And it is not to be supposed that this was granted to anyone, unless the one Mediator between God and men, the man Jesus Christ, was divinely revealed to him; who was pre-announced to the saints of old as yet to come in the flesh, even as He is announced to us as having come, that the self same faith through Him may lead all to God who are predestined to be the city of God, the house of God, and the temple of God.[144]

Augustine affirms Job's place among the elect in other writings as well. In his *Questions on the Heptateuch*, Augustine wonders if Jethro, who was not an Israelite, ought to be included among those religious and wise men who honor the true God outside of Israel as Job did, "although he was not one of the people of God."[145]

Related to Augustine's conviction that the righteous of all nations were granted a revelation of Christ, is his belief that all good and right things that come from men are prompted by divine inspiration. In *On Christian Doctrine*, Augustine inquired how Moses could accept counsel concerning the governance of Israel from Jethro, a gentile and a stranger, and concluded: "Moses know that, from whatever mind true counsel might proceed, it should not be attributed to that mind but to Him who was the truth, immutable God."[146] In one of his sermons, Augustine comes to a similar resolution about Job:

> For that law on tables was not yet given to the Jews in the time of Job, but in the hearts of the godly there remained still the eternal law, from which that which was given to the people was copied.[147]

Thus, as Jethro, Job did not need the written law for he was privy to God's eternal law, which is the possession of all godly men. Again the levitical priesthood is put aside, and the true and pre-existant priesthood revealed.

The standard views of Job as they developed and were preserved in Christian tradition can be found in the monumental *Moralia on Job* of Gregory the Great (d. 604). It was Gregory's aim to explicate the Book of Job, chapter by chapter, verse by verse, explaining not only its literal, surface meaning, but making clear as well the Book's deeper spiritual and moral significance. The methods he adopted in discovering his text's true meaning were various:

> Be it known that there are some parts, which we go through in an historical exposition, some we trace out in allegory upon an investigation of the typical meaning, some we open in the lessons of moral teaching alone, allegorically conveyed, while

there are some few which, with more particular care, we search
out in all these ways together, exploring them in a three-fold
manner.[148]

Although he never denies its value, Gregory reduces his
literal exposition of Job to a bare minimum. It consists mainly
of doctrinal discussions, such as how to excuse the curses uttered
by Job, or of disquisitions on subjects dealt with in the book,
such as the nature of prophecy. The question of the authorship of
Job, for example, was of little moment, for in Gregory's view all
scriptural books were the creation of the Holy Spirit: "If we
were reading the words of some great man with his epistle in our
hand, yet were to inquire by what pen they were written, it would
be an absurdity."[149] The result of Gregory's exegesis in the
Moralia, then was not so much an explication of the sense of the
Book of Job, as an exposition on Christian doctrine and a compendium of moral exhortation, both often far removed from the text
itself. As Beryl Smalley has noted of Gregory, the function of
his exegesis was largely educative: The finding of types "enabled
him to connect a resumé of some doctrinal point to each passage,
and to refute heresies." The moral sections contain his teachings
on the religious life and ethics."[150] The *Moralia* itself has little to say about Job that is new. Gregory drew much of his material from the great figures of the past, Origen, Ambrose and
especially Augustine; from their works he passed on to the Middle
Ages much of what was of permanent worth in his predecessors'
writings.[151]

Gregory speaks of Job's gentile origin in the Preface to
the *Moralia*, and suggests that he was intended as an example to
those who do not obey God's law: "A gentile, one without the Law,
is brought forward to confound the iniquity of those that are
under the Law."[152] This is the import of "Be thou ashamed Oh
Sidon, saith the sea" (Isa 23:4):

> For in Sidon we have a figure of the steadfastness of those
> settled upon the foundation of the Law, and in the sea, of the
> life of the gentiles; accordingly, "Be thou ashamed, Oh Sidon,
> saith the sea," because the life of those under the Law is
> convicted by the life of the gentiles, and the conduct of men
> in a state of religion is put to confusion by the conduct of
> those living in the world.[153]

As for Job's righteousness, Gregory repeats Augustine's explanation from the *City of God* 18:47: "That in the midst of Hebrew
lives, that of a righteous gentile is placed in that authority
which commands the reverence of men; because as our Redeemer came

to redeem both Jews and gentiles, so He was willing to be prophesied by the lips both of Jews and gentiles, that He might be named
by either people, Who was at a future time to suffer for both."[154]

Augustine is the source as well of Gregory's conviction
that Job was stricken so that his righteousness might be made
known to all men. In his usual manner, Gregory first details the
various reasons why a man might be stricken with suffering, and
then concludes that Job was so afflicted that "by that scourge the
excellence of his merits might be increased, and while there is no
past transgression wiped away, the patience may engender a mighty
fortitude."[155]

For Gregory, all the virtues have been personified in biblical figures; each scriptural paragon is a star appearing in the
face of heaven, "until that towards the end of the night, the Redeemer of mankind ariseth like the true Morning Star."[156] Job
demonstrates the virtue of patience amid afflictions among these
luminaries, yet as each of these virtues symbolizes Him who would
unite them all, Job is also a type of Christ:

> And therefore it behoved that blessed Job also, who uttered
> those high mysteries of His Incarnation, should by his life be
> a sign of Him, Whom by voice he proclaimed, and by all that he
> underwent should show forth what were to be His sufferings;
> and should so much the more truly foretell the mysteries of
> His Passion, as he prophesied them not merely with His lips,
> but also by suffering.[157]

In Gregory's hands, then, the Book of Job becomes pre-
eminently a vehicle for teaching the doctrines of the Church and
the proper modes of Christian conduct. As Job, the suffering man
of the nations, is a lesson in patience and steadfastness in
adversity to all men, so is his book a guide to Christian conduct
and eternal salvation. Gregory's *Moralia* represents the sum and
culmination of patristic exegesis of Job, and through this work in
particular, the patient Job, stoically sitting on his dunghill,
became the standard Christian representation of this righteous
gentile.

CHAPTER TWO

JETHRO: THE PROSELYTE TO ISRAEL

i

The existence of righteous gentiles like Job, who lived praiseworthy lives outside the boundaries of Israel and her laws, provided one solution to the problem of Israel's election as the special people of a universal God. A far more satisfying theology, however, not only approved of the meritorious non-Jew, but crowned that regard with his conversion to the precepts and life of Israel. As a "light unto the nations," Israel could only fulfill its special role by bringing others to the worship of the one God. This was, in fact, the single goal of history.[1]

As conversion became common in the centuries after the Babylonian Conquest, exegetes turned to Scripture to search out, not only prophetic exhortations to universal and uniform worship, but also examples of likely gentiles who seemed to have recognized the ubiquity and potency of Israel's God. Such figures as the Moabite Ruth, Rahab the harlot (Josh 2), and Moses' father-in-law, Jethro (Exod 2,18), all biblical gentiles who acknowledged God's saving powers, were ideal candidates for models to aid contemporary missionary efforts.

Jethro first appears in Exodus 2, when Moses, having slain an Egyptian taskmaster, flees the wrath of Pharaoh and comes to Midian. There, by a well, Moses encounters and protects the daughters of Jethro (called Reuel in Exod 2:18), the priest of Midian. So grateful is this worthy for Moses' aid to his daughters, that he gives Moses one of them, Zipporah, for his wife. In Exodus 4:18, after the death of Pharaoh, and the revelation at the burning bush, Moses leaves Midian to return to his people in Egypt and receives his father-in-law's blessing.

Jethro reappears in Exodus 18, after the delivery of Israel from Egypt, and it is this chapter which provides the fullest picture of Moses' father-in-law, the priest of Midian. Having heard, "How the Lord had brought Israel out of Egypt" (Exod 18:1), Jethro took Zipporah, Moses' wife and their two sons, and came to Moses in the wilderness, where he was encamped at the mountain of God. After a brief reunion in which Moses repeats for his father-in-law all that God had done for Israel, Jethro blesses the Lord, and offers a sacrifice and burnt offering to Him. He then

45

partakes of a festive meal, breaking bread with Aaron and the -
elders of Israel before God.

On the following day, when Moses is hearing the disputes
of the people, Jethro sees the great strain to which his son-in-
law is put by this task, and suggests that Moses might lighten his
load by appointing other judges for minor cases:

> Moreover thou shalt provide out of all the people able men,
> such as fear God, men of truth, hating unjust gain, and place
> such over them, to be rulers of thousands, rulers of hundreds,
> rulers of fifties, and rulers of tens. And let them judge the
> people at all seasons: And it shall be, that every great mat-
> ter they shall bring unto thee, but every small matter they
> shall judge themselves: so shall they make it easier for
> thee, and bear the burden with thee (Exod 18:21-22).

Moses listens to this advice and puts his father-in-law's suggestions into effect. The chapter ends with Jethro's departure from
his son-in-law and the people of Israel, and his return to his own
land.

There is further pentateuchal reference to Moses' father-
in-law in Numbers 10 where Moses invites a certain Hobab to serve
the Israelites as their guide in the wilderness, and share, in
return, in Israel's destiny:

> And Moses said unto Hobab, the son of Reuel the Midianite,
> Moses' father-in-law: We are journeying unto the place of
> which the Lord said: I will give it you: Come thou with us,
> and we will do thee good: For the Lord hath spoken good con-
> cerning Israel (Num 10:29).[2]

Whether or not Hobab decided to accompany Moses is not made clear
by the passage, which ends with an iteration of Moses' entreaty.[3]

All of these elements, Jethro's several names, his sacrifice to and acknowledgement of Israel's God, his part in shaping
Israel's judicial system, and the fact that a weekly portion of
the Pentateuch (Exod 18-20) is called by his name, provided the
grist for later interpreters. And, although no conversion was
explicitly described in Scripture, rabbinic exegetes assumed its
occurrence. That this conviction of Jethro's conversion was
limited to the Rabbis, however, is evidenced by the commentary on
Jethro, and the episodes in which he appears, in Philo, Josephus
and the early Church Fathers. These interpreters' very different
approaches to the same biblical texts illuminate the disparate
goals which inspired the various practitioners of scriptural
exegesis.

ii

Since the ideal gentile was the convert, it is not surprising that of Pharaoh's counsellors, the three prototypical
gentiles cited in rabbinic literature,[4] one should figure in rabbinic tradition as a proselyte. As Moses' father-in-law, the con-
tributer of a section to the Torah, and the ancestor of worthy
Israelites, Jethro was an excellent example of the prestige and
rewards available in Israel to the worthy convert. The favorable
rabbinic attitude towards proselytes, even after the disastrous
second revolt against Rome of 132-136 CE, has been well-
documented.[5] Rabbinic literature is replete with both legal ordinances and ethical maxims regarding the acceptance and reverence
due the proselyte to Israel. To attract gentiles to God's unique
people was a manifestation of love for fellow man: Hillel (fl.
ca. 30 CE), for example, urged his students to "love mankind and
draw them to the Torah,"[6] and R. Jose ben Ḥalafta (fl. 135-170 CE)
expressed the hope that in the time to come all the nations of the
world would come freely to convert to Judaism.[7]

In theological terms proselytism was viewed as part of
Israel's obligation to bring knowledge of the God of Israel to the
nations of the world.[8] R. Eleazar (fl. 135-170 CE) echoes numerous traditions when he says that "the Holy One, blessed be He,
exiled Israel among the nations only to the end that proselytes
might join them."[9] A homily dated at the end of the fourth century couches this teaching in sterner terms in a comment on "If he
does not declare it, then he shall bear his iniquity" (Lev 5:1):

> The Holy One, blessed be He, said to Israel, If you will not
> declare my Godhood among the nations of the world, I shall
> exact retribution from you.[10]

According to R. Berechiah (fl. 320-350 CE) the very election of
Israel demanded the continued attraction of proselytes. According
to one of his teachings, in fact, Israel's merit might be measured
by the number and quality of converts attracted at any given time:

> So long as they [Israel] do the will of the Holy One, blessed
> be He, then whenever he sees a righteous person among the
> nations of the world--like Jethro, Rahab and Ruth, and Anton-
> ius--He makes them come and join Israel.[11]

The clear implication that Israel, as much as the proselyte, is
enriched by conversion, is a thought often expressed in rabbinic
writings.

Practically, of course, complications connected with the
acceptance of converts were not infrequent. According to

tradition a non-Jew was accepted into the Jewish faith only after
a deep questioning of his or her sincerity:

> In our days, when a proselyte comes to be converted, we say to
> him: "What is your objective? Is it not known to you that
> today the people of Israel are wretched, driven about, exiled
> and in constant suffering?" And if he says: "I know of this
> and I do not have the merit," we accept him immediately and we
> inform him of some of the lighter precepts and of some of the
> severer ones . . . we inform him of the chastisements for the
> transgressions of these precepts . . . and we also inform him
> of the reward for observing these precepts . . .[12]

Fully accepted proselytes were required to accept all of Jewish
law. Thus, the *Sipra* dictates:

> As the native born Jew takes upon himself all the words of the
> law, so the proselyte takes upon himself all the words of the
> law. The authorities say, if a proselyte takes upon himself
> to obey all the words of the law except one single command-
> ment, he is not to be received.[13]

Of course, distrust and snobbism towards converts were
present in the Jewish community. Native Jews are frequently ad-
monished to refrain from harming or shaming proselytes in any way.
This is a matter of legal import, and is mentioned in *M. Baba
Meṣiʿa* 4:10: "No one should say to a son of converts: Remember
the deeds of thy fathers, as it is said, "And a stranger (גר) [to
the Rabbis, 'convert'][14] thou shalt not oppress" (Exod 23:9). In
a similar spirit a midrash asks:

> Why was the Torah given in the wilderness? To say that just
> as the wilderness is free to all men, so the words of the
> Torah are free to anyone who wishes to learn. Let no one say:
> "I am a son of the Torah, for the Torah was given to me and my
> fathers, but you and your fathers are not sons of Torah, your
> fathers were converts." Therefore, it is written, "The inhab-
> itants of the congregation of Jacob" (Deut 33:4)--that is, all
> who congregate in Jacob.[15]

On the other hand, it is clear from negative remarks about
them, that converts caused difficulties in the Jewish community
from time to time.[16] As Moshe Greenberg notes: "Pagan Rome spor-
adically, Christian Rome persistently, persecuted Jews, forbidding
proselytizing on pain of death. Hard times impelled some converts
to relapse, and some of these betrayed the resistance and disobedience of the Jews to their hostile governments."[17] Hostility
expressed towards converts, then, was usually the result of differing contemporary conditions and the personal experiences of
specific Rabbis.[18] Despite individual disillusionments, and
occasional personal danger, Jews continued to accept sincere converts throughout the rabbinic period. Urbach writes that "The
hope for conversion did not cease so long as the belief in

Israel's election and in the power of the Torah was a living and
dynamic faith that deemed its purpose to be the perfection and
removal of the world. This faith was shared by both the first and
last of the Amoraim, both in Babylonia and in Eretz-Israel."[19]

Rabbinic literature reflects this generally well-disposed
attitude towards converts in numerous comments on proselytes of a
non-legal nature. A tendency to increase the honor of the proselyte and to glorify conversion, for example, is found in the
traditions which trace the origins of such great personalities as
R. Meir (fl. 135-170 CE), R. Akiba (fl. 110-135 CE), and Shemaiah
and Avtalyon (both 2nd century BCE), to such wicked gentiles as
Sisera, Sennacherib, Haman and Nero.[20] There are two general
trends in this aggadic material, as Bamberger has pointed out:
those traditions which directly express opinions about conversion
and converts pro and con, and those which are elaborations of biblical stories about converts, or about biblical characters whom
the Rabbis wished to represent as converts. Of this second category, he remarks:

> In many cases the Rabbis represented as converts biblical fig-
> ures concerning whom Scripture does not give the slightest
> hint of the sort. The volume of this material is so amazingly
> large and its general tone so unmistakable, that it consti-
> tutes an important factor in the proof that the rabbinic atti-
> tude toward conversion was highly favorable.[21]

Rabbinic comments on Jethro fit this description well, for while
the Rabbis were confident that Jethro was a proselyte to Judaism,
and champion him as a model convert, their portrayal of him is
difficult to justify from accounts of Jethro in the biblical text.

As with Job, there is very little divergence in tannaitic
and amoraic conceptions of Jethro. The basic traditions about him
are already highly developed in such tannaitic texts as *Sipre* on
Numbers, and the *Mekiltas*. These are the main sources cited in
the discussion below. Amoraic commentary on Jethro, such as the
instances quoted here from *Exodus Rabbah*, does little more than
elaborate the themes already laid out by the Tannaim. In some
homiletical texts, such as *Pesikta de-Rab Kahana*, an element of
hostility towards Jethro is introduced. Here he is no longer the
welcome convert but the intrusive alien. This shift appears to
reflect changed circumstances, and changing attitudes towards proselytes.

On the basis of biblical accounts, there seems to be little warrant for assuming Jethro's conversion or even continuing
contact with the Israelites. Although the Rabbis thought Jethro's

declaration of faith, "Now I know that the Lord is greater than
all gods" (Exod 18:11) proved his acceptance of Judaism, it seems
an ambiguous statement of conversion: Jethro does declare the
preeminence of God, but he does not deny the existence of other
deities.[22]   The Rabbis, however, took into account not only Exodus
and Numbers, but all biblical references which could be linked to
Moses' father-in-law before drawing their conclusions.   Thus, on
the basis of several post-pentateuchal verses they maintained that
regardless of whether or not Jethro/Hobab accompanied Moses and
the Children of Israel to the Promised Land, his descendants certainly ended up there and lived among the people of Israel.
Judges 1:16, for example, establishes that the offspring of Moses'
father-in-law dwelt among the tribe of Judah at Arad:

> And the children of the Kenite, Moses' father-in-law, went up
> out of the city of palm-trees with the children of Judah into
> the wilderness of Judah, which is in the south of Arad; and
> they went and dwelt with the people.

Another verse, "These are the Kenites that came of Ham-
math, the father of the house of Rechab "(I Chr 2:55), provided
the necessary link to connect Jethro's offspring with the famous
family of pious ascetics, the Rechabites, described in Jeremiah
35,[23] and to establish their professions as scholars and
scribes.[24]

These traditions concerning Moses' father-in-law are puz-
zling for the many names he bears.   In Exodus 2, the priest of
Midian and father of the seven maidens is Reuel.   His name is
Jethro in Exodus 3-4 (although in Exod 4:18 he is called Jether).
In Exodus 18, he is again called Jethro, but in Numbers 10 and
Judges 4:11 we read that Hobab, the son of Reuel the Midianite, is
Moses' father-in-law.   For modern scholars, this embarrassment of
appellations presents a variety of problems,[25] but for the Rabbis
these numerous names provided fortuitous opportunities for praise
of the convert.   While some sources simplify the muddle by making
Reuel Jethro's father, others discussed below, increase it by ad-
vancing Keni, Heber and Putiel as additional names for Moses'
father-in-law.   For the Sages, this variety of designations was no
contradiction: several biblical characters, Jacob among them, had
more than one name.   Rather, the Rabbis used these many denomina-
tions as pegs for their homiletical remarks.   Thus, the *Mekilta*
explains: "Jether, because he caused an additional portion to be
put into the Torah; Jethro, because he abounded in good deeds."[26]
Both of these interpretations are based on puns on the Hebrew root

יתר , which in the intensive conjugation of rabbinic Hebrew, means
"to add," or "to do much."

The *Mekilta* also records that Jethro was called Heber,
from "Now Heber the Kenite severed himself from the Kenites, even
from the children of Hobab, the father-in-law of Moses" (Judg
4:11), because "he associated himself with God," from the root
חבר, "to join, befriend"; Hobab, because he was beloved of God,
from חבב , "to love, cherish"; Reuel, "because he was like a friend
to God," from ריע אל, "God's friend"; Putiel, "because he freed
himself from idolatry," perhaps from פטר, "to set free"; and Keni,
"because he was zealous for God," from the root קנא , "to be zealous," and also, "because he acquired the Torah for himself," from
קנה , "to acquire."[27]

This series of puns and word-plays is expanded even further in the *Sipre* to Numbers. Here an appropriate biblical verse
reproduces the word-play used to explain each particular name:

> Was Hobab his name or was Reuel his name? It says, "And when
> they came to Reuel their father" (Exod 2:18), but it also
> says, "Now Heber the Kenite severed himself from the Kenites,
> even from the children of Hobab, the father-in-law of Moses"
> (Judg 4:11). [Therefore] Hobab was his name, and not Reuel.
> But if this is so, how are we to understand, "And when they
> came to Reuel their father?" This teaches that young children
> call their grandfather "daddy" (אבא).
>
> R. Simeon ben Menasia [fl. 170-200 CE] says: Reuel was his
> name for he was a friend (ריע) to God, as it says, "And Aaron
> came and all the leaders of Israel, to eat bread with Moses'
> father-in-law before God" (Exod 18:12).
>
> R. Dostai [fl. 170-200 CE] says: Keni was his name and why
> was he called Keni? Because he separated himself from the
> idolatry of the Kenites who made the Lord jealous (קנא), as it
> is said, "They have roused me to jealousy with no god" (Deut
> 32:21), and "Wherein was the seat of the image of jealousy
> which provoketh to jealousy" (Ezek 8:3).
>
> R. Jose [fl. 135-170 CE] says: His name was Keni; and why was
> he called Keni? Because he acquired (קנה) heaven and earth
> and the Torah by becoming a proselyte.
>
> R. Samuel [fl. 220-250 CE] said in the name of R. Jose, his
> name was Reuel; and why was he called Reuel? Because he was a
> friend to God, as it says, "Thine own friend and thy father's
> friend forsake not" (Prov 27:10).
>
> R. Simeon b. Yoḥai [fl. 135-170 CE] says: He had two names:
> Hobab and Jethro. Jethro because he added (יתר) a section to
> the Torah, as it is said, "Moreover thou shalt provide out of
> all the people able men" (Exod 18:21). [This is the sugges-
> tion Jethro made to Moses on the appointing of judges.]
>
> He was called Hobab, because he loved (חבב) the Torah, for we
> do not find in all proselytes any who loved the Torah as did
> Jethro, and as Jethro cherished the Torah, so his sons

cherished it, as it is said, "Go into the house of the Rechabites, and speak unto them, and bring them into the house of
the Lord (Jer 35:2). [According to the Rabbis, the Rechabites
were Jethro's descendants.][28]

In his many guises, then, Jethro served as a model and example
for converts. Rabbinic literature contains innumerable brief
references to him. As a rule, in fact, when proselytes are
mentioned, Jethro together with Rahab (the heroine of Josh 2),[29]
are the exemplars presented. The *Mishnat R. Eliezer*, for example,
declares:

> Beloved are the proselytes, whose name the Holy one, blessed
> be He, enlarges. Of this Jethro is an example; his name was
> originally called Jether [Exod 4:18], but after he became a
> proselyte [Exod 18:11], it was enlarged to Jethro.[30]

Similarly, in *Exodus Rabbah* 27:2, Jethro is set in contrast to
Esau, who was born into Israel but chose to abandon his heritage:

> It is written, "Thine own friend, and thy father's friend for-
> sake not: Neither go into thy brother's house in the day of
> thy calamity: Better is a neighbor that is near than a bro-
> ther that is far off" (Prov 27:10). "Better is a neighbor
> that is near" refers to Jethro, who was "far" from Israel yet
> was better than Esau the brother of Jacob. For what does it
> say of Jethro? "And Saul said unto the Kenites . . . For ye
> showed kindness to all the Children of Israel when they came
> out of Egypt" (I Sam 15:6), and of Esau it was written, "Re-
> member what Amalek did unto thee" (Deut 25:17). You will find
> many things written of Esau to his discredit, but of Jethro
> many in praise . . . Of Esau it says, "And he feared not God"
> (Deut 25:18), but of Jethro is written, "And God command thee
> so" (Exod 18:23). Esau put a stop to sacrifices [by destroy-
> ing the Temple], but "Jethro, Moses' father-in-law, took a
> burnt offering and sacrifices for God" (Exod 18:12). When
> Esau heard of Israel's departure, he came to do battle with
> them, for it says, "Then came Amalek" (Exod 17:8), but when
> Jethro heard Israel's praises sung, he joined them, as it is
> said, "Now Jethro heard" (Exod 18:1).

And, as with other proselytes, Jethro is credited with outstanding
descendants: he was the progenitor of great sages of Israel who
sat in the Sanhedrin.[31]

Many references to Jethro in rabbinic literature are brief
and random; his history as a proselyte, however, unfolds in greatest detail in the midrashic expositions of the biblical chapters
in which he appears. The Tannaim were especially interested in
his story. As Bamberger notes, this might be explained as far as
the *Mekiltas* are concerned by the fact that a whole chapter of
Exodus is devoted to Jethro, but it is more difficult to account
for the voluminous material about him in the *Sipre to Numbers*, and
Sipre Zuta, since Jethro/Hobab commands but four verses in Numbers
10.[32] The Tannaim were obviously very interested in the Jethro

narratives and what they had to say about the welcome a proselyte should receive. As the Sages comment on verse after verse, it becomes clear how glad they were for the opportunity to sing the praises of a model proselyte.

This trend is apparent in rabbinic comments on Exodus 18:5, "And Jethro, Moses' father-in-law, came with his sons and his wife unto Moses into the wilderness where he was encamped at the mountain of God."[33] Since the phrase, "into the wilderness," seems redundant in the context of the chapter, the Rabbis sought a more subtle meaning. They declared that for Jethro to journey to Moses over such a distance showed the humiliation Jethro was willing to undergo in order to become a convert: "Behold! Scripture expresses surprise at him [by emphasizing the place to which he came]. He was dwelling in the midst of the splendor of the world, and yet was willing to go out to the desert, a place of desolation where nothing[34] is to be had. In this sense it is said, "Into the wilderness."

It appears from Exodus 18:6, "And he said unto Moses," that Jethro sent a message to Moses asking to be received, before he approached the camp. The *Mekilta* explains that in this letter, Jethro announced his intention to convert:

> "And he said unto Moses." R. Joshua [fl. 80-110 CE] says: He wrote it to him in a letter. R. Eleazar of Modi'im [fl. 110-135 CE] says: Through a messenger he sent him a message, saying to him: Do it for my sake [come out and meet us]. If you do not care to do it for my sake, do it for the sake of your wife. And if you do care to do it for your wife's sake, then do it for the sake of your children. Therefore, it is said, "And He said unto Moses: I thy father-in-law Jethro am coming unto thee, and thy wife, and her two sons with her" (Exod 18:6).[35]

R. Eleazar's comment explains the apparent repetitions of Exodus 18:6. Why should Jethro have to repeat the names of his entire party unless Moses was at first hesitant to come out and meet them: "if not for my sake, then for your wife's sake," etc. And perhaps Moses hesitated because Jethro was a pagan priest. God, therefore, tells Moses he should receive this true convert:

> R. Eleazar says: This was said to Moses by God: Verily it was I who said the word by which the world came into being, I am One who welcomes, not One who repels. As it is said, "Behold I am a God who brings near, saith the Lord, and not a God who repels" (Jer 23:23). I am He that brought Jethro near, not keeping him at a distance. So also thou, when a man comes to you wishing to convert, as long as he comes in the name of God, for the sake of Heaven, do thou, likewise, befriend him and do not repel him.[36]

This midrash further reports that every mark of respect was shown

to Jethro: not only Moses, but Aaron and his sons and the elders
of Israel also went out to greet him, and "Some say the Shekinah
went with them."[37] The lesson of this tradition is plain: Israel
is to welcome and honor the sincere proselyte. The mention of the
Shekinah is particularly significant here, because "to be taken
under the wings of the Shekinah" is a traditional term for conversion. According to *Targum Pseudo-Jonathan* Moses accepted
Jethro as a convert immediately after greeting him.[38]

According to Exodus 18:9, "Jethro rejoiced (ויחד) over all
the good that the Lord had done Israel." The Sages differ over
how to understand the verb form ויחד ("and he rejoiced"). The
Mekiltas take it literally, and enumerate the various blessings
which prompted Jethro's joy. Elsewhere, however, other more homiletical interpretations based on word-plays appear. One finds,
for example, "And he became a Jew," (יהוד, reading the verb as
ויהד); and "He declared the unity of God (from אחד, "one"); Rab
(fl. 220-250 CE) says he passed a sharp (חד) knife over his flesh,
that is, he fulfilled the requirements of a proselyte by becoming
circumcised; while Samuel says he was covered with "gooseflesh"
(חידודים) out of horror over Pharaoh's end, report of which
prompted him to convert.[39]

Of Jethro's declaration, "Blessed be the Lord" (Exod
18:10), R. Pappias (fl. 80-110 CE) said: "This passage expresses
a reproach to the Israelites. For, behold there were six hundred
thousand people, and not one of them rose to bless God until
Jethro came and blessed God, as it is said, 'And Jethro said,
Blessed be the Lord.'"[40]

In Exodus 18:11, Jethro confesses the greatness of
Israel's God, saying, "Now I know that the Lord is greater than
all gods." The Rabbis were not wholly pleased, however, with a
comparative, rather than a monotheistic statement of faith, and
they compare Jethro unfavorably with Na'aman (2 Kgs 5), and Rahab
(Josh 2). These biblical proselytes knew better than Jethro, for
they denied the existence of any deity other than the one God.[41]

On the basis of his faulty statement of faith, in fact,
the Rabbis maintain that Jethro had a lurid past before he became
a convert to Judaism. They recount that there was not an idol on
earth he had not worshipped.[42] Together with Balaam and Job (or
in some accounts Balaam and Amalek), Jethro was consulted by
Pharaoh on such problems as the increasing number of Israelites
and a cure for leprosy. Another interpretation of Exodus 18:1,
"Now Jethro heard," is a typical instance of this tradition:

It is written, "When thou smitest a scorner, the simple will
become prudent" (Prov 19:25), and also, "When the scorner is
punished, the thoughtless is made wise" (Prov 21:11). Amalek
and Jethro were of the advisors of Pharaoh; but when Jethro
beheld that God had utterly wiped out Amalek both from this
world and the next he felt remorse and repented, for first it
says, "For I will utterly blot out the remembrance of Amalek
from under Heaven" (Exod 17:14), and then it says, "And now
Jethro heard" (Exod 18:1). Said he: the only thing to do is
join the God of Israel. (*Exod. Rab*. 27:6)

Noting the juxtaposition of the two chapters, the Rabbis
concluded that Jethro converted to Judaism in Exodus 18, only
after he heard what happened to Amalek in chapter 17. The midrash
continues:

Similarly of the wicked Balaam it says, "And he saw Amalek"
(Num 24:20), that is, that he did not retract from his evil
way; but when he saw that Jethro had repented, what is said?
"And he looked on the Kenite, and took up his parable, and
said: Firm be thy dwelling place and thy nest be set in the
rock" (Num 24:21) . . . Thus, "When the scorner is punished,"
refers to Amalek, and "the thoughtless is made wise," to
Jethro.[43]

Other Sages, however, took the more charitable view that
Jethro converted to the worship of the one God on his own, long
before his meeting with Moses, or the destruction of Amalek:

Jethro was an idolatrous priest at first, but when he realized
that there was nothing to idolatry, he rejected it and considered turning to God even before Moses came. So he summoned
his townsmen and said to them, "All along I have been your
priest; now I am old, choose a new priest for yourselves." He
moved all the trappings of idolatry out of his house and
handed them over to them. Thereupon they ostracized him, forbidding anyone to work for him or tend his flock. So when he
asked shepherds to work in his flock and they refused, he had
to put his own daughters to work. (*Exod. Rab*. 1:32).

This notion of Jethro's spontaneous abnegation of idolatry explained to pious readers how Moses could consent to stay with him.
It also explains the shepherds' churlish behavior to Jethro's
daughters. Along these lines legends also exist testifying that
Zipporah too had converted long before her meeting with Moses.[44]

Two conflicting purposes are at work in these traditions
of Jethro's misdeeds on the one hand, and piety on the other. The
Rabbis liked to stress the scandalous pasts of well-known converts
to emphasize the redemption awaiting even the most hardened sinner
who laid aside his evil ways and became an observant Jew. Much of
Jethro's importance in Jewish tradition, however, stemmed from his
alliance by marriage to Moses. A number of midrashic comments
make this clear. Jethro, for example, is described several times
in Exodus 18 as the "father-in-law of Moses." Upholding the

exegetical principle that every word of the Torah is significant,
the Rabbis felt this extra descriptive phrase had special meaning.
Thus, on "Jethro, father-in-law of Moses" (Exod 18:1), the *Mekilta*
comments:

> Formerly Moses would give the honor to his father-in-law, as
> it is said, "And Moses went and returned to Jethro, his
> father-in-law" (Exod 4:18). Now, however, his father-in-law
> would give the honor to him. If they asked him, "What is your
> distinction?," he would say to them, "I am the father-in-law
> of Moses."[45]

The *Sipre on Numbers* 78, makes a similar comment on "father-in-law
of Moses": "This was the greatest compliment of all, to be called
the father-in-law of a king." *Exod. Rab*. 27:3 also rhapsodizes on
the advantages of an alliance with Moses:

> Another interpretation of "Now Jethro heard." See how many
> benefits and blessings came to Jethro from the moment he al-
> lied himself in marriage to Moses! For what does it say?
> "And Aaron came, and all the elders of Israel, to eat bread
> with Moses' father-in-law before God" (Exod 18:12).

All of these remarks testify to the importance Jethro received
because of his relationship to Moses. But, to many Sages, Moses'
status as God's prophet without equal demanded that all associated
with him be of high repute. This accounts for traditions of
Jethro's conversion even before Moses came on the scene: he did
not become a proselyte out of fear or through propinquity with
Moses, but out of sincere conviction, and was therefore worthy of
a family connection with Israel's leader.

In the same way, Jethro's vocation as priest of Midian was
also a stumbling block to the Rabbis since some found it disturbing that the father-in-law of Moses, the man who received such
prominence in the life of Israel by instituting the judicial system, should have ever been a foreign priest. Accordingly, a controversy raged among certain Sages over Jethro's true profession.
According to R. Joshua, he was a "priest of idolatry, as when it
says, 'And Jonathan, the son of Gershom, the son of Manasseh, he
and his sons were priests (כהנים)' (Judg 18:30)."But R. Eleazar of
Modi'im said, "He was a chief, just as when it says, 'And David's
sons were chiefs (כהנים)' (2 Sam 8:18)."[46] This interpretation,
based on a reading in I Chronicles 18:17, which changes David's
sons from כהנים "priests," to ראשים "chiefs," removes from Jethro
any taint of foreign religion.

Following Jethro's presentation of a burnt offering and
sacrifices to God, and his participation in a festal meal with
Aaron and the elders of Israel before God,[47] Exodus 18 tells of

Jethro's advice to Moses regarding the establishment of a more
practical system of justice (vv. 13-16). In Deuteronomy 1, however, this same reform is presented as a direct command from God.
Beyond this inconsistency, an even more serious difficulty for the
commentator was the suggestion that any part of the Jewish legal
system should have issued from a human being, and a non-Israelite
at that. Perhaps this provided part of the impetus to turn Jethro
into a convert to Judaism. In any case, the contradiction is har-
monized in the *Sipre on Numbers*, 78:

> But surely all that Moses did was commanded from heaven, as
> Jethro says: "If thou shalt do this thing, and God command
> thee so" (Exod 18:23). Did Moses forget [that he had been
> commanded to reorganize the system of justice by God in Deut
> 1, when he gave the credit to Jethro in Exod 18]? [No, it was
> by the principle of] bringing about merit to the meritorious
> that he gave the credit to Jethro.

Thus, when Moses was writing the Pentateuch, he gave the credit
for re-organizing Israel's judicial system to Jethro, even though
the changes had been divinely ordained, and he did this because he
believed Jethro the convert was worthy of the great merit which
would attach to him and his descendants were he credited with such
a contribution.

A slightly different point of view is expressed by the
Mishnat R. Eliezer:

> Dear is Jethro to whom the Holy One gave a section [of the
> law] to make his own. Which is that? [The section concern-
> ing] the appointment of the judges, as it is said: "And thou
> shalt provide out of the people able men," etc. Now was not
> the appointment of the judges a proper thing in the sight of
> the Holy One? Why did he not command it to Moses in the first
> place? In order to give Jethro greatness in the eyes of Moses
> and all Israel; that they might say: Great is Jethro, with
> whose words the Holy One agreed. Moreover, Jethro said this
> only on the condition that the Holy One agree with him, as it
> is said, "If thou shalt do this thing, and God shall command
> thee so."[48]

Here then, it was God who desired to ensure that merit and respect
would belong to his convert, Jethro, and therefore, allowed him to
suggest the judicial reform. The *Mekilta* reinforces this view of
divine approval for Jethro's advice: "R. Joshua says: 'So Moses
hearkened to the voice of his father-in-law, and did all that *he*
said' (Exod 18:24) is to be taken literally as referring to
Jethro." But, R. Eleazar, seizing on the repetition in the verse,
"Moses hearkened to the voice of his father-in-law," followed by
"and did all that he said," interpreted as follows: "And did all
that *He* said,' that is, what God said."[49] In following Jethro's
advice, therefore, Moses was also following a divine ordinance

which had been delivered through Jethro. In this way, Jethro's
contribution is undercut, and it remains the case that all of
Israel's ordinances are divine in origin.

Exodus 18 concludes with the simple statement that Moses
let his father-in-law depart to his own land. This verse, however, appears to contradict the parting scene in Numbers 10, where
Jethro/Hobab is entreated by Moses to remain with the Israelites:[50]

> "And Moses let his father-in-law depart" (Exod 18:27). R.
> Joshua says: He sent him off with all the honors in the
> world. R. Eleazar says: He gave him many gifts. From the
> answer which he gave Moses you can learn all this. It is
> said, "Leave us not, I pray thee" (Num 10:31). Moses said to
> him: You have given us good advice, fair advice. And God
> agreed with your words, "Leave us not I pray thee." But
> Jethro said to him: Is a lamp of any use except in a dark
> place? Of what use could a lamp be with the sun and the moon?
> No! I shall go to my land and tell everybody and convert all
> the people of my country, leading them to the study of the
> Torah and bringing them under the wings of the Shekinah. One
> might think that he merely went back and did nothing, but
> Scripture says, "And the children of the Kenite, Moses'
> father-in-law, went up out of the city of palm trees with the
> children of Judah" (Judg 1:16).[51]

With this prophetic imagery of Jethro the converted gentile a
light unto the nations, the Rabbis tie together his story. Yes,
he did leave Moses, but he left as a convert, and the success of
his efforts is corroborated by such verses as Judges 1:16 which
describe how his descendants came to dwell among the children of
Israel.

In Numbers 10:29-32, Moses entreats Hobab several times to
remain with the Israelites, promising that he will benefit with
them, "That what good soever the Lord shall do unto us, the same
will we do unto thee" (Num 10:32). The Rabbis were somewhat surprised at the vehemence of these entreaties, and attempt to justify Moses' language:

> "And he said: Please do not leave us" (Num 10:31). נא
> "please," is to be understood as meaning a request, but if my
> entreaty means nothing to you, then I will decree that you do
> not leave [Moses' words were an imperative softened by the
> נא to a request; however if Hobab continues to be obstinate,
> the request will be hardened to a command], for if you do
> leave, Israel will say that Jethro did not convert from love
> of God but because he thought there was a part for proselytes
> in the land of Israel. Now that he sees there is no portion
> for them he has departed.[52]

Another interpretation reads, "And if this is not enough for you
[to benefit as Israel benefits], you will sit in the Sanhedrin
with us and be a teacher of the words of Torah."[53] These remarks

take the approach that Hobab did remain with the Israelites. According to the Torah, however, there was no portion for the proselyte in the land of Israel. Thus, the Rabbis had difficulty interpreting Moses' promise to Hobab that if he accompanied Israel to the Promised Land, he would benefit as Israel benefited. According to one account, this contradiction was worked out as follows:

> After the capture of Palestine, the tribes, by mutual consent agreed that the fertile strip of land at Jericho should fall to the share of the tribe on whose land the Temple was erected. But when its erection was postponed for a long time, they agreed to allot this piece of land to Jethro's sons, because they, being proselytes, had no possession in the Holy Land. Four hundred and eighty years did the descendants of Jethro dwell in Jericho, when upon the erection of the Temple at Jerusalem, they relinquished it to the tribe of Judah who claimed it as indemnity for the site of the Temple.[54]

Jethro's descendants were compensated for the loss of the land they had occupied by becoming great scholars and teachers, and eventually acceding to the highest of Israel's honors, seats in the Sanhedrin. Thus, they were benefited indeed.

Among other reasons, Moses tried to persuade Hobab to accompany the Israelites because he was familiar with the wilderness. The *Sipre on Numbers* gives Moses' request, "And you will be for us as eyes" (Num 10:31), several homiletical interpretations:

> In everything that is hidden from our eyes, you shall enlighten us, as in the case of the judicial reforms. And surely Moses already knew these rulings [from Sinai], as it is said, "And God command thee so" (Exod 18:23), and why did Moses forget that the law was from God? In order to give merit to the meritorious, that is, to give the credit to Jethro.[55]

As the "eyes" of Israel, Jethro will bring to light things that have been neglected or forgotten. In this one might hear as well a homily on the value of the convert to Judaism: he will see things through fresh eyes and perhaps pass on valuable old truths and new perceptions to his co-religionists. Another interpretation of this verse considers the value of eyes as an analogy to the worth of the proselyte, and to the way the newcomer to Israel should be treated. The presence of proselytes, in fact, permits Israel to fulfill those precepts which ordain mercifulness, and thus, takes on an additional value:

> "And you will be as dear to us as our own eyeballs," as it says, "Love the convert" (Deut 10:19), and "Do not oppress the convert "(Exod 32:9), and "A convert thou shalt not wrong, neither shall thou oppress him, for ye were strangers in the land of Egypt" (Exod 22:20).[56]

Again, Jethro becomes the exemplar of converts in general.

In contrast to these many favorable comments about Jethro,
there are other rabbinic remarks which present a different point
of view. For example, it is said that Jethro not only visited the
Israelite camp prior to the giving of the Torah, but was dismissed
by Moses before the revelation, because God did not wish him to be
present. Since Jethro had been living in comfort and peace while
Israel was enduring slavery and suffering, it was not fitting that
he share in their joy.[57] This comment is not an independent expression of hostility against Jethro, however, for it is clearly
also an attempt to explain why, if Jethro visited Moses so shortly
before the giving of the Torah at Mount Sinai, he did not stay to
witness that event. A different response to this problem, given
by R. Joshua b. Levi (fl. 220-250 CE), suggests that it was Jethro
who precipitated the giving of the Torah: after Jethro had introduced the judicial system, God feared that Israel might suppose
that Jethro was the real source of religious law. He therefore
gave them the Torah in its fullness, that they might recognize
that it came only from His hand.[58]

Two other comments ignore entirely the traditions that
Jethro became a convert to Judaism, and maintain that Moses sent
him away because he was an alien. In a comment based on "The
heart knoweth its own bitterness, and with its joy no stranger can
intermeddle" (Prov 14:10), *Pesiqta de-Rab Kahana* 12:9, suggests
Jethro as an example of the verse's meaning:

> "The heart"--Israel's--"Knoweth the bitterness" [in a heath-
> en's] soul. Hence, with [the heart's] "joy, no stranger"--
> such as Jethro--"can intermeddle." "Then Moses sent his
> father-in-law away: And he went back to his own land" (Exod
> 18:27). And what follows directly? "In the third month"
> (Exod 19:1) [the giving of the law].

A similar midrash, *Pesiqta de-Rab Kahana* 12:16, inquires:

> What reasoning led Moses to send Jethro away? Drawing an
> inference a fortiori, Moses reasoned: If, when only one com-
> mandment was involved at the time the Holy One was about to
> give the commandment concerning the Passover lamb, he decreed
> that "No alien shall eat thereof" (Exod 12:43), now that he is
> about to give the entire Torah to Israel, shall Jethro, an
> alien, be present and watch us? Therefore, "Moses sent his
> father-in-law away" (Exod 18:27), and after that, "In the
> third month" (Exod 19:1), [the Torah was given to Israel].

In asking why Jethro left the camp of the Israelites before the giving of the law, these comments echo some of the hostility towards gentiles found in the rabbinic exegesis of Job.
Although Judaism never turned away the sincere proselyte, the
great zeal for bringing gentiles under the wings of the Shekinah

shown in earlier ages eventually passed, as did the eagerness of
outsiders to join Israel's ranks. The misfortunes of the Jews had
much to do with this, as did the rise and successes of the compet-
ing religions, Christianity and Islam.[59] These late midrashim,
with their insistence, almost unique in rabbinic literature, that
Jethro did not become a convert to Judaism, reflect this diminu-
tion of enthusiasm towards proselytism. On the whole, however,
disapproving remarks about Jethro are rare. In general, the
Rabbis presented Jethro extremely positively, taking pains to
transform all his possible debilities to credits: the rabbinic
Jethro is a light unto Israel as well as to the nations.

     This favorable portrayal has several motivations. Primary
among them was the wish to show that Jethro was a beloved convert
to Judaism. The prominence accorded Jethro in both tannaitic and
later rabbinic sources is clear evidence of the importance of proselytism and proselytes in the first centuries of the Common Era.
In Jethro the Rabbis found a perfect homiletical model of the sincere convert. As a powerful foreign priest who became a humble
worshipper of Israel's God, he could be used to remind Israel of
its obligations to the proselyte, and of God's love for the convert. As a former idolater of great scope, his acceptance by
Judaism showed that all sincere converts, regardless of their
pasts, were welcome. Furthermore, as an outsider who contributed
to Israel's judicial system, and whose progeny sat in the Sanhedrin, Jethro exemplified the benefits that accrued to all converts
to Judaism. He proved to the nations that Israel held the convert
high in honor. And finally, the homilists drew from Jethro's
story comfort for Israel: If God so loved one who drew himself
near the Divine Presence by converting, how much more would God
love the children of Israel, whom He Himself had drawn near, when
they observed His Torah.[60]

     Jethro represents the ideal Jewish solution to the exis-
tence of gentiles in God's creation. By conversion and absorption
he became one with the people of Israel, as will all nations in
the days to come when the mountain of God's house will be established and beckon all peoples to walk in the ways of the Lord.

                              iii

     Jethro is not mentioned in any of the extant apocryphal or
pseudepigraphical books, nor in any of the documents from Qumran,
but he does appear in the writings of Philo Judaeus (d. ca. 40

CE), and Flavius Josephus (ca. 38-after 100 CE). Neither writer,
however, portrays him as a convert to Judaism.

In great contrast to the Rabbis, Philo views Jethro unfavorably. Where the Palestinian Sages saw Jethro as a wise man
and a proselyte to Judaism, Philo regards him as "the man of
puffed-up conceit,"[61] who will not renounce idolatry, and who
declines to follow Moses to salvation. Philo's negative view has
three biblical bases. First is Jethro's Midianite origin: Philo
remembers the evil doings of the Midianites at the rites of Baal
Peor in Numbers 25. Secondly, Philo does not understand Jethro's
blessing of God in Exodus 18:11 as a statement of true belief in
the one deity, but views it as indicative of Jethro's ignorance
and superficiality. And finally, Philo sees Jethro/Hobab's refusal to follow Moses and the children of Israel in Numbers 10 as a
rejection of the possibility of salvation.[62] In addition,
Jethro's name is interpreted against him. Philo consulted com-
pendia of Hebrew names and their meanings to gain insight into
biblical characters.[63] According to these wordlists, 'Jethro," or
"Jethor," meant "superfluous," or "uneven."[64] Thus, Jethro exemplified to Philo the unstable personality who saves appearances
and yet is incapable of true being. He is the man who seems wise
but in reality is empty.

Philo, as the Rabbis, was struck by Jethro's several appellations. In his treatise *On the Change of Names*,[65] which discusses the significance of various name changes encountered in the
Pentateuch, Philo considers Moses' father-in-law, who is sometimes
called Jethro and sometimes Reuel. For Philo each difference in
name implied a difference in state, and he found his clue to these
differing states in the meanings of the names. Since Jethro is
translated as "superfluous," Moses' father-in-law is called Jethro
when his vanity is flourishing, for "vanity is to the verities of
life a superfluity deriding as it does equalities and the mere
necessities of life, and glorifying surplusage and inequality."[66]
Thus, Jethro values the human over the divine, custom above laws,
the profane above the sacred, and seeming above being. In a cur-
ious portrayal of Jethro's encounter with Moses in Exodus 18,
Philo maintains that Jethro is the kind of person who ventures to
come self-bidden and then takes the position of an advisor, as
when he boldly suggests that Moses abandon God's ordinances and
laws for a human suggestion. But Jethro can undergo a change of
heart, for occasionally he is called Reuel, which Philo understands to mean "shepherding of God":[67]

Often this wiseacre changes round and leaves the flock which had him in his blindness for their leader: he seeks the herd of God and becomes therein a member without reproach, so much does he admire the nature of its Herdsman and reverence the skill in governing which He shows in the charge of His flock.[68]

It is along the lines of this extended allegory that Philo explains Moses' encounter with Jethro's seven daughters in Exodus 2:16-18. In this passage Jethro is called Reuel, and for Philo he symbolizes the reasoning faculties of the mind. The seven daughters stand as symbols of the mind's seven unreasoning elements: reproductive power, speech and the five senses. These daughters keep the sheep of their father, that is, through these seven faculties come perceptions from which the mind forms its impressions and thoughts. The bad shepherds who drive the daughters from the well are the passions who attempt to disrupt the reasoning powers of the mind and give it over to purely sensual phenomena:

And in this way they will persist until the mind which loves virtue and is inspired by God, called Moses, shall arise from his former seeming quietude, protect and save the maidens from their subjugators, and nourish the flock of the father with words and thoughts, sweet as water to drink."[69]

The daughters, being preserved from the mind's enemies, the unruly shepherds, return not to Jethro but to Reuel: "For they have discarded their kinship with vanity and become affiliated to the guidance and rule of law, and have resolved to become a part of the holy herd which is led by God's word as its name shows, for Reuel means 'the shepherding of God.'"[70]

According to Philo's elaborate allegory, Moses rushes in and protects the senses, Jethro's daughters, from the attack of evil impulses, with the result that the mind, Jethro/Reuel is now able to regulate the lower life. As E. Goodenough points out, Philo shows here that the mind that is able to rule its own flock is one that has come under the guidance of the supreme shepherd and king, the mind mentioned by Scripture in the words, "the Lord is my Shepherd." This allegory applies not only to Jethro but to every soul seeking salvation.[71]

It is in his treatise, On Drunkenness, that Philo examines Moses' meeting with Jethro in Exodus 18, and puts forth his harshest criticism of the priest of Midian. Here, Philo discusses the four offspring of the marriage of "right reason," or philosophy to custom, convention and secular education. Of these four children there are two, each of whom obeys one parent and not the other; one who obeys both parents; and one who obeys neither. For Philo, Jethro is typical of those who disregard the father, "right

reason," and love the mother, secular convention. Philo compares
Jethro to the Egyptian Proteus, "whose true form remained a matter
of uncertainty through his power to become everything in the universe."[72] Jethro, as Proteus, is an exemplar of instability: he
seems to be many things, but his true being is never known.
"Jethro," Philo writes, "is a compound of vanity, closely corres-
ponding to a city or commonwealth peopled by a promiscuous horde,
who swing to and fro as their idle opinions carry them."[73]

In *On Drunkenness*, Philo details all of Jethro's
misdemeanors, including his arrogant attempt to give advice to
Moses, and his refusal to follow Moses to the promised land. Of
this second offense Philo writes, commenting on Numbers 10:29,
"Come with us and we will do thee good":

> But even to words of such charm as these Jethro will pay no
> heed, nor even follow knowledge in any way but will hasten to
> return to the empty vanity which is indeed his own. For we
> read that he said to Moses, "I will not go; but I will depart
> to mine own land, and to my kindred" (Num 10:30), that is, to
> the unfaith of false opinion which is his kinsman, since he
> has not learnt the true faith, so dear to real men.[74]

It is Jethro's behavior in Exodus 18, however, that raises
Philo's fullest wrath. His anger is stirred on two main points of
Jethro's confession of faith in Exodus 18:11, "Now I know that the
Lord is greater than all gods." First of all, Jethro's use of the
word "now," symbolizes to Philo Jethro's flightiness, and the
transitory nature of his opinions. He believes in God's greatness
now, but what about previously, and what about later? Secondly,
Philo objects to Jethro's use of the comparative "greater," for
this shows that Jethro does not completely perceive the oneness of
the divine, for he still thinks there are other deities as well:

> For when he wishes to make a shew of piety and says: "Now I
> know that the Lord is greater than all gods," he does not but
> charge himself with impiety in the eyes of men who know how to
> judge. They will say to him, "Blasphemer! It is now that you
> know this, and have you never till now understood the great-
> ness of the ruler of all? Did your past experience shew you
> anything more ancient or venerable than God? Are not the
> excellences of the parents known to the children before those
> of any others? Is not the Maker and Father of the Universe He
> who presided at the beginning? So if you say that you now
> know, not even now have you true knowledge, since it does not
> date from the beginning of your existence. And you stand no
> less convicted of mere feigning when you compare two incompar-
> ables, and say that you know that the greatness of the Exist-
> ent is beyond all gods. For if you had true knowledge of that
> which is, you would not have supposed that any other god had
> power of his own."[75]

Philo concludes that the same false creed is followed by all those
who reject the things of the soul and set their admiration on

things of the body, whose many shapes and colors deceive the readily seduced senses.

    This, then, is Philo's Jethro; a figure far from the bib-
lical priest of Midian or the rabbinic proselyte. It is only in
Jethro's briefly assumed secondary guise as Reuel, that the arro-
gance is for a moment humbled by divine shepherding, and the wan-
dering thoughts restored to the paths of right reason. However,
this metamorphosis is short-lived, for like the ancient Proteus,
Jethro remains incapable of true being; in Philo's view he was
condemned to remain an eternal symbol of vanity and vacillation,
spurning the way of wisdom that leads to God.

    Philo and rabbinic tradition are far apart on Jethro's
character. Accounting for this interpretive expanse are two very
different ways of reading Scripture. The Rabbis looked at the
Bible as one whole, recounting God's saving role in the history of
Israel. Thus, they shaped their interpretation of Jethro in the
knowledge that his descendants had settled and become great men in
Israel.[76] They were impressed that he was the one man, beyond
Moses, to have contributed to Israel's governance, and many accepted his declaration of faith in Exodus 18:11 as a wholehearted
conversion to Judaism. Their reading of the texts in which he
appears was both historical, in that it recognized Jethro's past
conversion and his contributions to Israel, and homiletical, realizing his value as a model convert. Philo takes no such long
view. His concern is with the allegorical interpretation as it
applies to the individual soul's striving for the Divine. "For
Philo," writes Lewy, "each personality recorded in Scripture is
regarded (mostly by reference to the Hebrew significance of his
name) as the type of a peculiar moral quality or the embodiment of
a certain way of life."[77] Philo's Jethro, then, as a personification of superfluity and superficiality, has no continuing part in
the eternal relationship between Israel and the Almighty. He represents a false turning in the soul's search for God.

    Philo's Jethro remained unknown to mainstream Jewish tra-
dition, as was apparently the case with all Philo's writings; it
was Cyril, a Father of the Church writing in Alexandria, who would
rediscover and recast this Jethro in a Christian mold.

    Flavius Josephus (ca. 38--after 100 CE) recounts the meet-
ing of Jethro and Moses in Exodus 18 in his *Jewish Antiquities*
III, 61-66. Here Josephus describes Moses' and Zipporah's warm
reception of Jethro (here called Raguel according to the Septuagint rendering of Reuel). According to Josephus, Jethro appeared
at the camp of the Israelites alone: there is no mention of the

biblical tradition of Moses' and Zipporah's separation, nor of
Jethro's role in reuniting them. In Josephus' account it is
Moses, not Jethro, who offers the sacrifice to God, and it is
Moses who convenes the festal meal at which all praise God "as the
author and dispenser of their salvation and liberty."[78] There is
no implication that Jethro had become a convert to Judaism. At
this feast the company renders praise as well to Moses, who is
described as "their general, to whose merit it was due that all
had befallen to their hearts' content."[79]

Josephus maintains this military tone in his consideration
of the second part of Exodus 18, where Jethro suggests that Moses
lighten his load of duties by appointing judges from among the
people. Here Jethro's advice is transformed to a proposal leading
to a better organization of the army, with judging of the people
only a secondary concern:

> Follow but my advice on mundane matters, and thou wilt review
> thy army diligently and divide it into groups of ten thousand
> men, over whom thou wilt appoint selected chiefs, then into
> thousands, next thou wilt proceed to divide these into groups
> of five hundred, and these again into hundreds and fifties.
> Let each group have its own chief taking his title from the
> number of men under his command; let them be appointed by the
> whole multitude as upright and just persons, who are to sit in
> judgement on their differences, and in graver cases are to
> refer the decisions to the higher officials. Then, if these
> too are baffled by the difficulty of the case, they shall send
> it up to thee. This will secure two things: the Hebrews will
> obtain justice, and thou, by assiduous attendance upon God,
> wilt belike render Him more propitious to the army.[80]

This reorganization of Moses' forces is strikingly close to the
formation of Roman troops, where each officer took his title from
the number of men he commanded. No doubt Josephus' wish for his
military-minded Roman readers to appreciate the importance of
Jethro's innovations accounts for these alterations in the biblical text.

Josephus concludes his rendition of Exodus 18 by recording
that Moses accepted and acted on Jethro's advice, "neither con-
cealing the origin of the practice nor claiming it as his own, but
openly avowing the inventor to the multitude."[81] Josephus takes
this as evidence of Moses' integrity, for, "in the books too he
recorded the name of Raguel, as inventor of the aforesaid system,
deeming it meet to bear faithful witness to merit, whatever glory
might be won by taking more credit for the inventions of
others."[82] Josephus does not note Jethro's proviso, that Moses
adopt this new system only if it seems fitting to God, nor does he
make any mention of divine approbation of this re-organization.

iii

Jethro is rarely mentioned in the exegetical writings of the Church Fathers. The remarks of Origen, Augustine, Bede, Cyril of Alexandria, and the Syrian Father, Aphraates, examined below, comprise the greater part of commentary on Jethro in patristic texts. Jethro, so important to both the Rabbis and Philo, apparently failed to catch the imagination of Christian commentators. For one thing, Jethro is not mentioned among such New Testament models of pagan virtue as Melchizedek, Rahab or Job, and thus he never took a place among these revered righteous gentiles in patristic exegesis. Much of the reason for Jethro's slighting, moreover, lies in the very nature and aims of patristic exegesis: early Christian readers of Scripture sought out biblical prophecies which they believed had been fulfilled through the life and teachings of Christ. Through typology they discovered events and characters of Christological significance in the past history of Israel; and through allegory, these exegetes drew spiritual and moral lessons from diverse scriptural passages. Among a few interpreters, there was, as well, an incipient interest in the Old Testament's literal import.[83] Aside from the last, none of these interpretive concerns was easily applied to the biblical narratives concerned with Jethro. Here were no messianic prophecies, nor any clear reflections of Christ or his sacraments. At the most, some writers saw in Jethro's counsel to Moses an indication that through the gentile nations the old law would be fulfilled, but even here there were doubts.[84] Even Philo's elaborately allegorical account of Jethro aroused the interest of few Christian commentators.[85] Only those exegetes who were interested in textual problems on a literal level had much to say about Jethro. Apparently Moses' father-in-law was not particularly appealing to Christian expositors who had before them a Holy Scriptures full of exegetical possibilities. There is no indication that patristic writers were aware of Jewish comments on Jethro, or knew of his role as a model proselyte in rabbinic traditions. Certainly no Jewish-Christian polemic had Jethro as its focus. Jerome (d. 420), among many other expositors of Exodus, simply ignores Jethro's presence, and as for Hobab of Numbers 10, no Christian writer follows the rabbinic lead in identifying him with Jethro.[86]

Origen (ca. 184-254) discusses Jethro in his *Homilies on Exodus*. Origen, who was instrumental in increasing Christianity's appreciation of Scripture's literal import, begins his exegesis of Exodus 18 by responding to problems in the literal understanding

of the text. The placement of chapter 18 in Exodus is still a
matter of discussion. Many scholars feel its correct place is
after, rather than before, the giving of the law at Sinai.[87] Some
ancient commentators were perplexed by the chapter's placement as
well, and when precisely Jethro arrived at the camp of the Israelites was much discussed by Jewish expositors of the Bible. The
Tannaim considered three possibilities: that Jethro came to the
camp of Israel after the Red Sea had been crossed; that he came
after the defeat of Amalek; and that he came after the revelation
at Sinai; without deciding on any one.[88] Origen was also aware of
this textual difficulty, and he resolved it by placing Jethro's
arrival after the giving of the law. Thus, he delays his consideration of Exodus 18 until after he has discussed the revelation
at Sinai, and the implications of God's law.

Origen's first inquiry concerning Exodus 18 is also
prompted by the literal sense. He asks why Zipporah and her sons
had been sent away by Moses, a point on which Scripture itself is
unclear. He further inquires why Moses brought Jethro to his tent
and not to the mountain of God. Both questions are answered at
once.

> For the priest of Midian could not climb the mountain of God,
> just as he could not go down into Egypt, neither he nor Moses'
> wife. Only now did he arrive with Moses' sons. He could not
> go down into Egypt because he was not a proven "athlete," as
> he of whom the apostle speaks, "Every athlete exercises self-
> control in all things, they do it to receive a perishable
> wreath, but we are imperishable. As for me I run, but not
> towards an uncertain end: I fight, but not as one who beats
> the air with words (I Cor 9:25-26). Moses, then, who was a
> great and powerful athlete,[89] went down into Egypt for battle
> and the exertion of virtue.

Origen's comment on Jethro's lack of fitness, either to
have been redeemed from Egypt or to have been present at the mountain of God, is reminiscent of certain rabbinic comments which
maintain that Jethro could not have been present at the giving of
the law because he had not suffered in Egypt.[90] Such negative
remarks about Jethro are rare in rabbinic literature, but patristic comments on him are characterized by an ambivalent or even
negative tone, prompted in part, no doubt, by Jethro's absence
from the New Testament. Thus, Origen makes no other remark on
Jethro's character, but concentrates instead on Moses' response to
his father-in-law's counsel:

> In effect, when I consider that Moses, a full prophet of God,
> to whom God spoke face to face, took the advice of Jethro,
> priest of Midian, I am full of admiration so great it sends me
> into a stupor. Scripture says that "Moses heard the voice of

his father-in-law and did all that he had advised" (Exod 18:24). He did not object in the least, saying: "God converses with me and heavenly words dictate my conduct, how should I receive the advice of a man, who even more is a pagan, a stranger to the people of God?" But he listened and did all that Jethro said to him, considering not who spoke, but what he said. We, similarly, if we encounter by chance words of wisdom pronounced by pagans, we must not immediately reject them because of their author; it is necessary that we not, under the pretext that we have received the word of God, fill ourselves with pride and disdain the words of wise men, but as the apostle says, "Examine all and retain what is good" (I Thess 5:21).[91]

In this segment and the one that follows it, Origen emphasize two main themes. The first is the humility of Moses, who in spite of his intimate knowledge of God, did not reject a suggestion acceptable to God because it came from a surprising source. Origen wonders how many leaders of men and the Church in his own times would deign to receive the advice even of a priest of lower degree, not to speak of a layman or pagan. Moses, then, through Jethro's offices, becomes a tropological figure of the virtue of humility. The second theme Origen expounds here, that one may benefit from the knowledge or advice of a pagan, was an important one in the thinking of the early Church.[92]

Origen ends his discourse on Jethro's visit with an allegory, suggesting that Moses received the advice of an alien to give an example of humility to the leaders of the nations, and to prefigure the image of a mystery to come:

> Moses knew in advance that a day would come when the pagan nations would bring good counsel to Moses, when they would give God's Law its true and spiritual sense: he knew in advance that the Law would listen to them, and would do all that they had said. For the Law could not do what the Jews say, because it is weakened by the flesh, that is to say, if followed according to the letter, for "The law made nothing perfect" (Heb 7:19). But, according to the counsel which we bring to the Law all can be accomplished spiritually, the sacrifices which could not be offered to the flesh may be offered according to the spirit . . . And thus, according to our thoughts, and the feeling and the counsels which we give [as the gentile nations] the Law can do all; but according to the letter it can accomplish but little."[93]

Thus, Origen repeats the Christian victory over the constricting letter of the law, and the Christian understanding of its true spiritual import, at the same time as he emphasizes the contributions of the gentile nations to the true Church.

Yet in all of Origen's commentary on this chapter, there is but little mention of Jethro. We learn that he was not worthy of redemption from Egypt; through him Moses' humility is demonstrated; he seems to symbolize the nations of the world who are

the true Israel; but to Origen's mind Jethro himself is obviously
of secondary concern. Crucial to the rabbinic view of Jethro as a
proselyte is the link-up of Jethro and Hobab, and the Rechabite
descendants of Hobab who became wise men in Israel. Origen knew
the Hebrew Bible well, and he was not loath to consult contemporary learned Jews when he encountered problems in the Hebrew
Scriptures. In the case of Jethro, however, it is clear that no
such inquiries were made. Jethro's exclusion from tabulations of
righteous gentiles in the New Testament is certainly a major reason for Origen's lack of interest. Perhaps too, Jethro was so
well-known as a Jewish paradigm of conversion that the Church preferred to concentrate its exegetical attentions on other worthy
biblical gentiles whose identifications with Judaism were not so
strong. It was necessary to stress that the nations could come to
Christ without an intermediary conversion to Judaism. In any
case, Origen's Jethro is but a minor figure playing a small role
in the divine schema.

     Augustine's (d.430) comments on Jethro are also indicative
of patristic ambivalence over this figure. In his *Questions on
the Heptateuch*, Augustine is not overly concerned that Jethro, an
alien priest, offered good advice to Moses, for "in this Scripture
admonishes us that a true plan is not to be condemned no matter
what man suggests it."[94] He continues that it is fitting that
Jethro suggest that Moses choose men far from pride to be judges,
just as Moses has shown his lack of pride in accepting Jethro's
advice. This idea is reiterated in *On Christian Doctrine*, again
with Jethro as an example:

> Did not God speak to Moses? And yet did not Moses accept
> counsel concerning the government and administration of a
> great nation from his father-in-law, although he was a strang-
> er, in a most provident and humble way? For Moses knew that,
> from whatever mind true counsel might proceed, it should not
> be attributed to that mind but to Him who is the truth, immu-
> table God.[95]

     What does give Augustine pause, however, is the question
of Jethro's merit. Jethro is not listed in the New Testament or
any other Christian writing among the worthies of the nations who
anticipated the coming of Christ by sacrificing to God, yet by his
acts in Exodus 18 he would seem to deserve such inclusion. The
question for Augustine was, why was Jethro left out? Part of
Augustine's solution arises from his Latin version of Exodus 18:12
where his text reads, "And Jethro, the father-in-law of Moses took
(*sumpsit*) burnt offerings and sacrifices to God.'[96] In the Vulgate, Jerome, according to the apparent intent of the Hebrew,

wrote *obtulit*, "sacrificed," instead of *sumpsit*, "took." But Augustine's text had *sumpsit*, and this became the basis for his exegesis:

> "Took" signifies "offered"; but perhaps it is the sense which
> demands "took" and it is not just a figure of speech [for of-
> fered]. Perhaps the text wishes to give the understanding
> that Jethro handed over the sacrifices to Moses so that he
> [Moses] would offer them to God.

(that is, Jethro took up the things to be sacrificed to God and
gave them to Moses who then proceeded to actually sacrifice them).
But Augustine also considers the other side of the question:

> On the other hand, however, one had not read formerly in
> Scripture that Moses offered any sacrifice, or Aaron, or any
> of the Hebrews who had come out of Egypt. It is only said
> previously that Moses built an altar and called it "God is my
> refuge" (Exod 17). So it would be astonishing if Moses began
> to sacrifice at Jethro's arrival, rather than Jethro himself
> who was a priest [and presumably knew how to go about it].[97]

The question here is whether Jethro is among those men who worshipped the true God outside the bounds of Israel, and if, therefore, he was worthy of offering a sacrifice to Him. Augustine
takes up the question again in his *Questions on the Heptateuch*:

> "One wonders here rightly if this Jethro himself, who was not
> an Israelite, ought to be included among those religious and
> wise men who honor the true God, as Job did, although he was
> not one of the people of God. For Scripture is ambiguous, and
> does not permit us to distinguish whether Jethro offered a
> sacrifice to the true God in the midst of the people, when he
> saw his son-in-law, or if Moses himself [did it] to honor
> Jethro. It seems rather a witness of honor rendered to
> Jethro, as one sees that the patriarchs had the custom of hon-
> oring certain men respectfully; it is thus written of Abraham
> himself that he honored the children of Chet [Gen 23:7].[98]

Augustine finally seems to be saying that Jethro did not offer a
sacrifice, but was instead honored by Moses. This explains his
absence from the company of worthy gentiles who showed their devotion to the true God by sacrificing to Him.

With this dismissive conclusion, Augustine finishes his
discussion of Jethro. Further comments on Jethro are rare in the
Western Church, but a typological view of Jethro as a symbol of
the gentile apprehension of Christ was expressed by the Venerable
Bede (d. 735):

> From Jethro, that is from a man of the nations [Moses] accep-
> ted a plan, and did all that he had said, for he gave the
> example to the leader of humility, and indicated a figure of
> future sacraments [*sacramentum futuri*]. The future, indeed,
> was when through the people of the nations, that congregation
> in which the law was lacking, the law would be fulfilled, as
> the diminuation of the laws suggested by the Evangelist would

be fulfilled. Moreover, Jethro brought Zipporah and her sons to Moses, which signifies the preachers of the Church from outside the people of Israel by whose interpretation the divine law is established.[99]

In the Eastern Church, as in the Western, Jethro excited small concern. However, one writer, Cyril of Alexandria (d. 444), developed his story in a way far different from any of his Western co-religionists.[100] Cyril made over Philo's comments on Jethro,[101] and gave them a Christian application. Thus, he describes Jethro as a pagan priest who did not worship the true God, but preferred creatures of the Creator, or that which was made from stone or wood. Furthermore, he strayed from this world and worshipped demons, not God. Cyril repeats Philo's etymology of Jethro as "superfluous," and takes this to mean he was a man who cared only for worldliness, ignoring necessary concerns for vain, drunken thoughts and useless voluptuousness.[102]

Cyril also allegorized Moses' arrival in Midian. Moses now foreshadows the life and death of Christ, going from Egypt to Midian, as Christ went from Judea into Galilee; "Christ, therefore, left that according to which he was born in the flesh, the Synagogue, and turned away to the flocks of many nations, who were affected adversely by the injuries of the evil shepherds, that is the leaders of this world." These nations of the world, Jethro's daughters, are thus preserved and defended by Moses/Christ:

> Jethro, therefore, appears to us as a person of the world who overflows and streams over us with vanity and superfluity. Moreover, his seven daughters we say to be the people of the nations, so that through one of the daughters a multitude is symbolized. They are threatened by devils but saved by Christ. The girls, moreover, having avoided the injuries of the impious shepherds, return home to their father, Reuel, that is, Jethro.[103]

According to Philo the change of name from Jethro to Reuel was very significant, and symbolized a character change in Jethro for the better. Cyril adapts this allegory as well. He explains that before Moses rescued the daughters Jethro was the superfluous one, but that afterwards, under the influence of Moses/Christ, Jethro became Reuel, "shepherding of God." He writes:

> We say, therefore, that he who served as a man of the world, whose occupation was superfluous and inane, is reversed. Truly, this is the sense of the group of girls who were assisted by Christ. For after they were liberated from tyranny, and freed from the impiety of the bad shepherds, then, it says, the name of Jethro was changed to Reuel, which is "the flock of God," or "the shepherding of God." He submitted, indeed, to the hand of him who is the chief of all shepherds,

that is Jesus Christ through whom and with whom is God, and the Father of Glory with the Holy Spirit for ever and ever, amen.[104]

Here is one of the few comments on Jethro the man in patristic exegesis, and he appears as Philo's Reuel, a reformed character, transformed by the divine power of the Logos/Christ.

One patristic writer who did elevate Jethro to the rank of righteous gentile without reservation was the Syrian Father, Aphraates (ca. 300-350 CE). In 337, while serving as Bishop at Mar Mattai, north of Ninevah, Aphraates wrote a series of *Demonstrations* on various issues of concern to Mesopotamian Christians. Among these *Demonstrations* are ten which respond wholly or in part to Jewish criticisms of Christianity.[105] One major theme of Aphraates' defense of Christianity is his conviction that Israel has been supplanted by the nations. He maintained as well that "The vocation of the peoples was prior to that of the people of Israel, and from of old; whoever from among the peoples was pleasing to God was more justified than Israel."[106] Among the gentiles Aphraates cites as proof of his claim are Jethro, the Gibeonites, Rahab, Ebedmelech the Ethiopian, and Uriah the Hittite. Of Jethro he writes:

> Even from of old, whoever from among the peoples was pleasing to God was more greatly justified than Israel. Jethro the priest, who was of the peoples, and his seed were blessed: "Enduring is his dwelling place, and his nest is set on a rock" (Num 24:21).[107]

That Aphraates seems to stand alone in patristic tradition in his unstinting praise of Jethro may be explained by his remoteness from the main centers of Christian life and thought, and from his highly independent method of scriptural commentary and argumentation. His approach to the Bible is almost entirely historical and without allegorization. As Jacob Neusner notes, Aphraates' "exegeses of Scriptures are reasonable and rational, for the most part not based on a tradition held by the church and not by the synagogue, but rather on the plain sense of Scripture as he thinks everyone must understand it."[108] It is significant, as well, that although Aphraates quotes widely from the Hebrew Scriptures, he cites the New Testament rarely.[109] In fact, Aphraates' view of Jethro, although brief, is more in accord with the plain meaning of the biblical text than that of most other exegetes considered in this chapter. Its simplicity and inevitability underscores again the mystery of Jethro's absence from the New Testament and the ongoing patristic tradition.

Aphraates has been cited in the past for his apparent awareness of and even dependence upon rabbinic traditions.[110] While it might be held that the prominence Aphraates accords Jethro is a response to knowledge of his glorification in rabbinic literature as a proselyte, this seems to me unlikely. With the exception of Rahab, who is also cited in rabbinic writings as a convert, the other gentiles Aphraates mentions are not of any importance as proselytes in rabbinic tradition. Thus, any intended polemic would have little meaning. I don't think there is any Jewish influence here. Rather in the agreement of Aphraates and the Rabbis on the merits of Jethro and Rahab, we see the results of independent readings of a shared text.[111]

Aside from Aphraates, then, and the unique case of Cyril of Alexandria, Jethro remains a virtual nonentity in Christian exegesis, and moreover, there was little, if any, contact between rabbinic and patristic commentators concerning his character or actions. The fundamental rabbinic convictions of Jethro's identification with Hobab, of Jethro/Hobab's conversion to Judaism, and of the merits of his descendants as great men in Israel, were apparently unknown, or at least uninteresting to Christian exegetes. Jethro is not numbered among the righteous pagans listed in various parts of the New Testament, and was therefore regarded with suspicion by most Fathers who considered him at all. The biblical chapter, Exodus 18, in which Jethro mainly appears, attracted interest primarily on the literal level. In the case of Jethro, unlike those of Job and Balaam, we see a biblical character of major importance to Jewish exegesis who goes virtually unmentioned in Christian commentary. It would seem that Jewish-Christian contacts occurred only when a biblical figure or event was interesting to both religious communities.

CHAPTER THREE

BALAAM: THE PROPHET OF THE NATIONS

i

The biblical Balaam is a complex figure, combining apparent prophetic power with manifestly evil intention. His story
begins in Numbers 22, when he is summoned by Balak, king of Moab,
to curse the invading Israelites. At first Balaam is forbidden by
God to fulfill Balak's request, for the people of Israel are not
cursed but blessed. At night, however, God speaks to Balaam and
gives him permission to set out on the journey to Moab. In the
ensuing passage, however, a seeming contradiction occurs in the
text; God appears to have reconsidered his decision, and becomes
angry at Balaam for leaving home.

To express his displeasure, God sent an angel to block
Balaam's path; at first the angel was visible only to Balaam's ass
who moved off the path to avoid it. Balaam vociferously re-
proached the ass, and only when the beast suddenly answered did
Balaam see the angel. At once Balaam fell on his face before the
divine messenger, and offered to return to his home. The angel,
however, allowed Balaam to continue on his way, again with the
proviso, "Go with the men; but only the word that I shall speak
unto thee, that thou shalt speak" (Num 22:35).

When Balaam arrived in Moab he immediately advised Balak
that he had no power to speak anything but God's word. Still, the
next morning Balaam and Balak began the process of divination.
Three times Balaam moved to a bare height and received God's word,
and three times Balaam opened his mouth and blessed the children
of Israel. At last, faced with Balak's wrath, Balaam reminded him
that he could only speak what the Lord spoke to him (Num 24:12-
13). As if to emphasize the point, in his fourth blessing of
Israel, Balaam detailed the destruction Israel would wreak among
Moab and the other nations in the end of days. At this point the
narrative concludes, and Balaam and Balak return to their separate
lands.

Balaam's actions in this pericope seem harmless enough; he
professes his inability to speak other than as God wills; in fact,
he blesses Israel and his blessings are seen as efficacious.
Later references, however, expand and color his story, and these
additional associations provide the fuel for later animus against
him. Two passages, credited to the Deuteronomic writer,[1] diminish

Balaam's part in blessing Israel. Deuteronomy 23:5-6 implies not
only that Balaam was motivated by gain in wishing to curse Israel,
but also that he persevered in his intention to anathematize:
"Nevertheless, the Lord thy God would not hearken unto Balaam, but
the Lord thy God turned the curse into a blessing unto thee,
because the Lord thy God loved thee." Similarly, Joshua 24:9-10
emphasizes divine agency in rescuing Israel from Balaam's evil
designs: "Then Balak the son of Zippor, king of Moab, arose and
fought against Israel; and he sent and invited Balaam the son of
Beor to curse you, / but I would not listen to Balaam; therefore
he blessed you; so I delivered you out of his hand." Alexander
Rofe has suggested that these verses reflect a reappraisal of
Balaam, from prophet to sorcerer, which has its roots in the
Deuteronomic vision of prophecy. Thus, God becomes the author of
the blessings Balaam pronounces, and God delivers Israel from the
wicked Balaam's hand.[2] This effort to strip Balaam of any elements of prophecy is particularly evident in the Septuagint's
rendering of Joshua 24:9-10: "And Balak, son of Zippor, King of
Moab, rose up and fought against Israel, and sending, he summoned
Balaam to curse you, / and the Lord your God did not wish to destroy you and He blessed you and He took you out of their hands and
handed them over." Here all blessings are of divine origin, and
not only is Israel preserved, but Balaam's and Balak's fates are
sealed.

It is in some verses attributed to the Priestly writer
that Balaam's evil character is most thoroughly revealed and his
end described.[3] Thus, Numbers 31:8 records, "And they slew the
kings of Midian with the rest of their slain . . . Balaam, also,
the son of Beor, they slew with the sword." (This event is also
chronicled in Josh 13:22, where Balaam is additionally described
as a soothsayer). Numbers 31:6 justifies this ignominious end by
associating Balaam with the episode at Baal Peor in which Israelite men were seduced into idolatry by the immorality of foreign
women: "Behold, these caused the children of Israel, through the
counsels of Balaam to revolt so as to break faith with the Lord in
the matter of Peor, and so the plague was among the congregation
of the Lord."

These accusations of immorality and idolatry, as well as
the belief that Balaam served as adviser to Israel's adversaries,
provide the bases for most later Jewish comment. As Baal Peor
became a symbol of the evils of gentiles in rabbinic literature,
so its originator, Balaam, came to exemplify all that was worst in
the nations of the world. Balaam's predictive abilities are not

denied, however; rather, by the misuse of his prophetic powers, he
stands for the enemy who knew the way but chose not to follow it.
Balaam provides a resounding rabbinic answer to the mystery of
Israel's uniquely privileged relationship with the Almighty:
given all the advantages of Israel, the nations have squandered
their potential for righteousness and have no grounds for complaint.

Balaam is also of enormous interest to Christian exegetes,
for his prophecy, "A star shall rise out of Jacob" (Num 24:17),
was read as predicting the Incarnation of Christ. Christian readers, however, could not discount the biblical evidence of
Balaam's wrongdoings, and had to face the dilemmas raised by an
unworthy prophet. Thus, while the Rabbis could afford the luxury
of damning Balaam outright, Christian commentators had the more
difficult task of separating the man from his predictions.

Comments about Balaam are also found in the writings of
Philo and Josephus, and in the *Biblical Antiquities* of Pseudo-
Philo. Philo, who was a major influence on patristic exegesis, is
especially concerned with the implications of an apparently
unworthy prophet. Josephus and Pseudo-Philo, whose works reflect
some facets of early rabbinic traditions, both have distinctive
views of Balaam which also find their way into the commentary of
various Church Fathers.

ii

The Sages of Israel had little reason to look kindly on
the nations of the world. Past catastrophe and present circumstances combined to foster Israel's view of itself as a belea-
guered island in a hostile sea. The Rabbis' general wariness of
the gentile is, therefore, hardly surprising; rather it's their
insistence that righteous non-Jews do exist, and that the sincere
proselyte be warmly welcomed, which seems extraordinary. The
usual exemplar of the nations, however, would naturally take a
more sinister form, and the rabbinic Balaam possesses most of the
requisite characteristics. As a subtle villain, endlessly plot-
ting the destruction of Israel, he comes to symbolize a variety of
rabbinic perceptions of Israel's enemies.

The imputation of idolatrous and immoral practices to the
gentiles was the traditional cause of Jewish antipathy towards
them. From biblical times avoidance of the nations was predicated
on these grounds, which were commonly linked. Thus, Exodus 23:33
proclaims of the foreign inhabitants of Canaan, "They shall not

dwell in the land--lest they make thee sin against Me, for thou
wilt serve their gods--for they will be a snare unto thee," and
Deuteronomy 20:18 warns against contact with the Canaanites, "that
they teach you not to do after all their abominations, which they
have done unto their gods, and so ye sin against the Lord your
God." Sacred prostitution, a common practice in the ancient Near
East, encouraged the association of idolatry with immoral behavior
in the biblical mind, as did narrative accounts of various gentiles whom the people of Israel encountered. As Greenberg notes,
"The dissolute character of the pagans is exemplified in the
patriarchal contacts with them (Gen 19:5-9/Sodomites; Gen 39/
Potiphar's wife); by the vicious Phoenician queen Jezebel (I Kgs
21/Naboth's vineyard); and by the corruption of Israelites who
apostasized (e.g., Ahaz/2 Kgs 16:3; Manasseh/2 Kgs 21:16). To
give sufferance to such persons was to risk learning from them."[4]

By rabbinic times, idolatry and immorality were included
with murder among the three things for which a man should prefer
death to sin (B. Sanh. 74a), and a popular rabbinic saying proclaimed, "Whoever acknowledges idolatry disavows the whole Torah,
and whoever disavows idolatry acknowledges the whole Torah."[5] Nor
did idolatry consist only in the worship of idols. Any denial of
God's unique power as understood by Judaism, whether by Gnostics,
Christians, or others, fell into the same category.[6]

The Rabbis associated not only the worship of false
deities and the disavowal of God's special attributes with idolatry, but, as Urbach says, the sorcerer and his sorcery as well:

> Magical acts were a concomitant of the nature of idolatry.
> Idolatry in all its forms believed in the existence of a
> source of power apart from the godhead, for it did not recog-
> nize a god who transcended the existential system that con-
> trolled everything and whose will was absolute. Magic flows
> from the desire to utilize these forces and idolatry associ-
> ates man with the deity in the need for magic.[7]

Accordingly, past enemies of Israel, such as Pharaoh and Amalek
become sorcerers in rabbinic literature, as did more present
adversaries. Thus, in B. Sanhedrin 107b, a master teaches that
"Jesus practiced magic and enticed and led Israel astray,"[8] and
elsewhere the books of the Minim, by whom either Christian or
Gnostic sects are probably meant, are called diviner's books, that
is works on witchcraft.[9] In effect, what rabbinic Judaism opposed, or saw as a threat to proper belief and practice, was said
to represent either magic or blasphemy.

The Rabbis found the biblical soothsayer Balaam an ideal
symbol of the perceived gentile evils of immorality, idolatry and

_sorcery. Throughout rabbinic writings Balaam appears as a typical
example of the evil man. He is rarely referred to without an
added epithet such as "wicked," "evil," or "that villain." Evi-
dences of his malevolence were found in the very meanings of his
name. One proposed etymology, "he corrupted a people" (בלה עם),[10]
was an obvious reference to Balaam's part in leading the Israelites into immorality; a second, "he devoured a people" (בלע עם),
evokes the results of his evildoing--the deaths of twenty-four
thousand Israelites (Num 25:9).[11] Sometimes Balaam serves as a
general example of wickedness and its punishment, with no particular attention paid to his gentile origin. Thus, he is included
with six Israelites in a mishnaic discussion of the seven men who
have no place in the world to come.[12] Besides Balaam, the other
scriptural outcasts are Doeg, Ahitophel and Gehazi (all com-
moners), and Jeroboam, Ahab and Manasseh (three kings). All are
barred from future redemption on account of their evil actions.[13]
More often, however, Balaam is identified with Israel's gentile
enemies, not with the wicked within her midst, and a distinction
between Balaam and those Israelites who lost the world to come was
clearly stated by the Amora, Mar, the son of Rabina (fl. 320-350
CE), who said of him:

> In the case of all [those mentioned as having no portion in
> the future world] you should not take [the biblical passages
> dealing with them] to expound them to their discredit, ex-
> cepting in the case of the wicked Balaam: whatever you find
> [written] about him, lecture upon [it to his disadvantage].[14]

In several instances, Balaam is said to have been other,
specific opponents of Israel. Some rabbinic comments, for example, presuppose the identification of Balaam with Laban, Jacob's
wily father-in-law.[15] Balaam is elsewhere said to be identical to
Job's contemporary Elihu, who was seen in a negative light by some
of the Sages.[16] It seems likely that polemical concerns also
contributed to the determination with which rabbinic literature
blackens Balaam's character, and some scholars have suggested that
various remarks about Balaam may be veiled references to Jesus, or
are at least aimed at early Christianity. These hypotheses are
discussed below.[17]

A study of rabbinic literature makes clear that Mar's
advice was followed. There is little positive about Balaam in
either the close exegesis of those biblical passages in which he
appears extensively, or in the many references to him elsewhere in
midrashic and talmudic texts. The biblical accounts of Balaam had
already spelled out his nefarious involvement at Baal Peor, and no

pretexts were needed for the condemnations he evoked. The basic
themes are already present in tannaitic texts, as is evident in a
comparison of the qualities of his disciples with those of Abraham
in M. 'Abot 5:19[18]:

> Whoever possesses these three things, he is of the disciples
> of Abraham, our father, and whoever possesses three other
> things, he is of the disciples of Balaam the wicked. The dis-
> ciples of Abraham our father possess a generous eye, a humble
> spirit, and a lowly soul. The disciples of Balaam the wicked
> possess an evil eye, a haughty spirit and enormous greed.
> What is the difference between the disciples of Abraham our
> father and the disciples of Balaam the wicked? The disciples
> of Abraham our father enjoy their share in this world, and
> inherit the world to come, as it is said, "That I may cause
> those who love me to inherit substance and that I may fill
> their treasuries" (Prov 8:21) [inheriting substance refers to
> this world and filling their treasuries is a reference to the
> world to come]. But the disciples of Balaam the wicked in-
> herit Gehenna, and descend into the nethermost pit, as it is
> said, "But Thou, oh God, wilt bring them down to the nether-
> most pit, men of blood and deceit shall not live out half
> their days, but as for me, I will trust in Thee" (Ps 55:24).

Here, Balaam is called "the wicked," and his loss of eternal life
confirmed. His evil eye was his desire for wealth, which led him
to follow Balak's emissaries to Moab, even though he knew it was
against God's wishes. His haughty spirit is evident in his claim
to know the knowledge of the most High (Num 24:16), and his greed
was revealed in his treatment of Balak, and in his attempts to
outwit God in hope of reward. The prooftext from Psalm 55 is particularly apt, because by his deceit and evil counsel Balaam had
brought about the deaths of many Israelites, and precipitated his
own end by the sword. He is, indeed, a man of "blood and deceit."

        However, scriptural testimony also made clear that Balaam
possessed oracular powers. He was able to receive and deliver
God's word, and this aspect of his persona could not be ignored.
In fact, his prophetic powers are universally acknowledged in rabbinic literature, and in a tannaitic text, the Sipre on Deuteronomy, Balaam's prophetic powers are favorably compared with those
of Moses:

> "And there has not arisen a prophet since in Israel like
> Moses" (Deut 34:10). "In Israel" there has not arisen one
> like him, but among the nations of the world one arose. And
> who was this? This was Balaam, the son of Beor. There was a
> difference, however, between the prophecy of Moses and the
> prophecy of Balaam. Moses did not know who was speaking with
> him, but Balaam knew who was speaking with him, as it says,
> "The oracle of him who hears the word of God" (Num 24:16).
> Moses did not know when He would speak with him until He spoke
> with him, but Balaam knew when He would speak with him, as it
> says, "And knows the knowledge of the Most High" (Num 24:16).
> Moses did not speak with Him except when he was standing, as

it says, "But you, stand here with me" (Deut 5:28). But
Balaam spoke with Him when he was prostrate, as it says, "Who
sees the vision of the Almighty, / Falling down, but having
his eyes uncovered" (Num 24:4). [Here is] a parable to which
this thing is similar: [It is] like a cook who knows how
large the expenses are for the royal table.[19]

Balaam, then, appears to have abilities that Moses lacked, yet as
the final parable makes clear, his relationship to God is quite
different in nature from that of Moses. Balaam is a menial whose
menial tasks give him special knowledge; only Moses knew God face
to face, uniquely, in a reciprocal relationship.

The belief that Balaam was an advisor to the nations of
the world is also a feature of tannaitic exegesis. The *Mekilta*
recounts that at the time of the giving of the law, the nations
were frightened that another flood was about to occur and appealed
to Balaam for enlightenment. He reassured them, and explained
that the Lord was giving his Torah to Israel.[20]

Although the Tannaim apparently found no difficulty in
accepting Balaam's prophetic gifts, and the relationship with the
Almighty these implied, amoraic commentators were not so much at
ease. In fact, in the amoraic and post-amoraic analyses of the
passages in which Balaam appears, or which suggest Balaam, there
is an intensification of animus towards him which goes far beyond
any tannaitic comment. Such sustained midrash collections as *Numbers Rabbah* and *Midrash Tanḥuma* painstakingly analyze each phrase
of the text to uncover Balaam's most nefarious motives. Drawing
on similar expositions, talmudic commentators and legalists made
use of Balaam in other contexts, variously as the failed gentile
prophet, a counsellor to Israel's enemies, and the quintessential
gentile soothsayer who corrupts by immorality and the arts of
sorcery. Some possible reasons for this flow of malice are discussed below.

As the talented man who rejects the opportunity for good,
Balaam plays an important role in rabbinic literature. Tradition-
ally Balaam was the last of the gentile prophets. In him the
nations had the possibility of greatness, but he scorned his
divinely given powers for sorcerer's illusions and monetary gain.
He is proof that the nations of the world were given all the advantages of Israel, but forfeited Israel's reward by their evil
behavior. The following midrash from *Numbers Rabbah* 14:20 makes
this point. It is also a very interesting elaboration of the
earlier text in *Sipre* which compares Balaam with Moses:

It was taught [of Moses], "And there hath not arisen a prophet
since in Israel" (Deut 34:10). "In Israel" there had not

arisen one like him, but there had arisen one like him among
the nations of the world. This was in order that the nations
of the world might have no excuse for saying, "Had we possessed a prophet like Moses we should have worshipped the Holy
One, blessed be he." What prophet had they that was like
Moses? Balaam the son of Beor. There was a difference, however, between the prophecy of Moses and that of Balaam. There
were three features possessed by the prophecy of Moses which
were absent from that of Balaam. When He spoke with Moses the
latter stood on his feet, as it says, "But as for thee, stand
thou here by me, and I will speak unto thee" (Deut 5:28).
With Balaam, however, He only spoke while the latter lay prone
on the ground, as it says, "Fallen down, and his eyes are
opened" (Num 24:4). With Moses He spoke mouth to mouth, as it
says, "With him do I speak mouth to mouth" (Num 12:8), while
of Balaam it says, "The saying of him who hears the word of
God" (Num 24:4), which teaches that He did not speak with him
mouth to mouth. With Moses He spoke face to face, as it says,
"And the Lord spoke to Moses face to face" (Exod 33:11), but
with Balaam he spoke only in parables, as it says, "And he
took up his parable, and said" (Num 23:7). There were three
features possessed by the prophecy of Balaam that were absent
from that of Moses. Moses did not know who was speaking with
him while Balaam knew who was speaking with him, as it says.
"The saying of him who heareth the words of God, and seeth the
vision of the Almighty" (Num 24:16). Moses did not know when
the Holy One, blessed be He, would speak with him, while
Balaam knew, as it says, "And knoweth the knowledge of the
Most High" (Num 24:16). In illustration of this Balaam has
been compared to a king's cook who knows what fare the king
will have on his table and how much is spent by the king on
his board. It was in the same way that Balaam knew what the
Holy One, blessed be He, would speak to him about. Balaam
spoke with Him whenever he pleased; for it says, "Fallen down,
and his eyes are opened," which signifies that he used to
prostrate himself on his face and straightaway his eyes were
opened to anything that he inquired about. Moses, however,
did not speak with Him whenever he wished. R. Simeon [fl.
135-170 CE] says that Moses also received communications from
Him whenever he pleased; for it says, "And when Moses went
into the tent of meeting, that he might speak with Him, then
[immediately] he heard the voice speaking unto him" (Num
7:89).

This midrash from *Numbers Rabbah* is far more elaborate than the
passage it would appear to have been based upon in *Sipre*. It also
has some different concerns. Unlike the *Sipre* text, this midrash
is anxious to explain why the gentiles should have had any prophet
at all. Having established the reasons for Balaam's existence, it
then makes further attempts to downgrade his abilities. Thus,
before he is compared rather favorably with Moses, as in *Sipre*,
three features which made Moses' words prophecy of a special and
elevated sort are described. Only then are Balaam's prophetic
powers, also three to balance Moses' abilities, enlarged upon.
The parable of the royal cook is repeated, but this time its derogatory implications are more clearly spelled out. And finally,
a minority opinion from R. Simeon is added, that suggests that

Moses was not outdone by Balaam but could also elicit divine communication at will. The authors of this midrash appear to have
been far more uncomfortable with the idea of a genuine and efficacious gentile prophet than earlier Sages; they certainly do not
want to sanction the idea that anyone could have competed with
Moses, whose intercourse with God had perforce to have been of a
unique and superior kind.[21]

The Amoraim could not deny that Balaam was a prophet, but
his very abilities and powers raised considerable difficulties in
rabbinic discussions of Israel's unique place in God's affections.
This was especially the case in those early centuries of the Common Era when Judaism found its privileged relationship with the
Almighty challenged by sectarians who considered themselves, in
the words of Paul "sons of the promise," and "sons of the free
woman" (Gal 4:22, 31), and who sought not only to compare the
nations to Israel, but also to demonstrate their superiority to
the descendants of Jacob.[22] Some Sages responded by insisting the
election of Israel was evidence of divine preference and had been
ordained from the beginning. In rabbinic passages addressing
these issues, Balaam's name appears again and again. Thus, *B.
Sanhedrin* 39a-39b records the following tradition, apparently part
of a contemporary polemic:

> A *min* [sectarian] once said to R. Abina [fl. 290-320 CE]: It
> is written, "And what one nation in the world is like Thy peo-
> ple, Israel" (2 Sam 7:23). Wherein lies their superiority?
> Ye too are combined with us, as it is written, "All the na-
> tions are as nothing before Him" (Isa 40:17). He answered:
> One of yourselves [Balaam] has already testified for us, as it
> is written, "And he [Israel] shall not be reckoned among the
> nations" (Num 23:9).

Similarly, in *Numbers Rabbah* 20:18, Balaam asks God if He would
not prefer to be worshipped by seventy nations rather than one.
"The Holy Spirit answered him: 'Better is a dry morsel and quiet-
ness therewith' (Prov 17:1); better that is to say, is 'A meal-
offering, mingled with oil, or dry' (Lev 7:10), 'Than a house full
of feasting with strife' (Prov 17:1)."[23]

Other Rabbis, however, declared that it was the nations
themselves who had forfeited divine approbation by ultimately
proving unworthy. These Sages maintained that God gave prophets
to the nations of the world as well as to Israel. Indeed, to deny
this would have been to ignore copious biblical evidence that gentiles such as Enoch, Noah, Melchizedek and Job, as well as Balaam,
has been privileged to communicate directly with God.
Still, the question remained, if Israel was God's chosen nation,

and the treachery of the nations was long established, why did God
give prophets to the gentiles at all? *Numbers Rabbah* 20:1 responds as follows:

> The Holy One, blessed be He, did not afford the idolators an
> opportunity of saying in the time to come: "It is Thou that
> has estranged us!" What did the Holy One, blessed be He, do?
> In the same way as He raised up kings, sages and prophets for
> Israel, so he raised them up for the idolators.

Thus, even though the nations showed themselves undeserving of
such special attentions, they could not claim that they had lacked
any of Israel's special privileges.

The differences between the prophets of Israel and those
of the nations, both in terms of God's attitude towards them, as
well as in their own behavior, were great. Catalogues of these
variations appear in rabbinic sources. It is said, for example,
that God reveals Himself to the heathen nations incompletely,
while to Israel His revelation is complete. This is the meaning
of "The Lord is far from the wicked / But he heareth the prayer of
the righteous" (Prov 15:29). The first line alludes to the heathen prophets, whereas "the righteous" are the prophets of Israel.
God is said to hold Himself remote from the heathen prophet; He
appears to him like one who comes from a far country.[24] In *Leviticus Rabbah* 1:13, R. Hanina b. Papa (fl. 290-320 CE) offered the
following parable to explain the distinction:

> This may be compared to a king who was together with his
> friend in a hall, with a curtain between them. When he con-
> versed with his friend he folded back the curtain so that he
> saw him face to face; but with others he did not do so, but
> conversed with them while the separating curtain was drawn
> across, and they were unable to see him.

Similarly, it is commonly said that God communes with the gentile
prophets only at night. Thus, *Numbers Rabbah* comments on "And God
came unto Balaam at night" (Num 22:20) as follows:

> Why did He reveal Himself to Balaam at night? Because he was
> not worthy of receiving the Holy Spirit (except at night), for
> with all the prophets of the nations He speaks at night.[25]

The contradiction between this passage and another midrash in *Numbers Rabbah*, quoted above, that Balaam was able to speak with God
whenever he pleased,[26] is a glaring one. It seems likely that
earlier tradition, as seen in the original midrash in *Sipre*,
granted Balaam the power to speak with God at any time. Efforts
at limitation tie in with other amoraic efforts to denigrate and
downgrade Balaam's abilities.

The trend which stressed Balaam's special abilities persisted, however, but these unique powers usually take forms which are easily frustrated. Balaam, or at least the evil forces he symbolizes, is thereby rendered far less threatening. Along these lines, there is a tradition that Balaam had an advantage over Moses in that he knew the exact moment of God's wrath, and this is what rendered his curses so efficacious. This was said to be the meaning of "knowing the mind of the Most High" (Num 24:16). *B. Sanhedrin* 105b recounts that normally God is angry every day; this could have had grave consequences for Israel during the days of Balaam, had not God, out of His special love for Israel, suspended the natural order:

> The Holy One, blessed be He, said to Israel: Know now how many acts of charity I performed for you in that I did not become angry all that time, in the days of Balaam the Wicked, for had I waxed angry during that time none would have remained or been spared of [Israel].[27] And thus Balaam said to Balak, "How shall I curse, whom God hath not cursed? or how shall I rage, when the Lord hath not raged?" (Num 23:8). This teaches that for the whole of that time the Lord had not been wroth.

According to rabbinic literature, prophecy among the gentiles was a limited phenomenon. Since there is no clear biblical reference to any gentile prophet after the time of Balaam, and given the tenor of their times, rabbinic exegetes were understandably insistent that all of God's friendly dealings with gentile seers took place before or during the time of the Exodus. As we have seen, those Rabbis who believed Job to be a gentile were therefore careful to date his death no later than the Israelite spies' entry into Canaan.[28] As one might expect, this loss of the prophetic gift was blamed on the nations themselves. One tradition declares that prophecy disappeared from the nations at the moment the Torah was given to Israel. By not accepting it, the gentiles forfeited forever their right to divine indulgence.[29] The second version of the *'Abot de Rabbi Nathan* § 45, in fact, attributes Balaam's hatred for Israel to the divine revelation:

> As long as the Israelites were in Egypt, Balaam was considered the wisest of all men, and all nations came to him for advice; but after the Exodus [and the giving of the Torah] a Jewish bondwoman possessed more wisdom than Balaam. He therefore hated the Israelites out of envy.

Leviticus Rabbah 1:12, on the other hand, maintains that the establishment of the Tabernacle heralded the end of the nations' prophetic powers:

R. Isaac [fl. 135-170 CE] said: Before the Tabernacle was set up prophecy was current among the heathen nations of the world; after the Tabernacle was erected it departed from them, as it is said, "I held him [the gentile nations held through the power of prophecy] and would not let him go until I had brought him [Israel] into the chamber of her that conceived me [elsewhere expounded as referring to the Tabernacle]" (Cant 3:4).

Leviticus Rabbah 1:13, however, blames the greatest of the gentile prophets, Balaam himself, for the nations' loss:

See what a difference there is between the prophets of Israel and those of the idolaters! The prophets of Israel caution Israel against transgressions, as it is said, "Son of man, I have appointed thee a watchman unto the house of Israel--and thou shalt give them warning" (Ezek 3:17). The prophet who rose from the nations, however, made a breach in the moral order [a reference to the immorality recorded in Num 25: 1ff. attributed to Balaam]. Nay, more: All the prophets of Israel retained a compassionate attitude towards both Israel and the idolaters. Thus Jeremiah says, "My heart moaneth for Moab like pipes" (Jer 48:36); and it was the same for Ezekiel, "Son of man, take up a lamentation for Tyre" (Ezek 27:2). But this cruel man [Balaam] rose to uproot a whole nation for no crime! The reason, then, why the section dealing with Balaam was recorded is to make known why the Holy One, blessed be He, removed the Holy Spirit from the idolaters, for this man arose from their midst and see what he did.

Balaam, then, was, perforce, the last of the gentile prophets. The affront inherent in his very appearance in the Torah is explained as an object lesson for Israel and an answer to the nations. And according to at least one sage, Balaam was given the privilege of prophecy so late in Israel's history only because of the blessings he was to pronounce on Israel.[30]

Some Rabbis, were disturbed, however, that divine blessings should emanate from such an evil source. One solution to this apparent paradox was offered by *Deuteronomy Rabbah* 1:4:

R. Aḥa b. Ḥanina [fl. 290-320 CE] said: It would have been more fitting for rebukes to have been uttered by Balaam and blessings by Moses. But had Balaam uttered the rebukes, then Israel would say, "It is an enemy who rebukes us," and had Moses uttered the blessings, then the other nations would say, "It is their friend who blesses them." Therefore, the Holy One, blessed be He, commanded, "Let their friend Moses reprove them, and their foe Balaam bless them, so that the genuineness of the blessings and the rebukes of Israel may be clear beyond question."

In this manner, Balaam's evil intentions lend a sense of authenticity to his praise. Other commentators, however, deny entirely that Balaam himself ever blessed Israel. Numbers 23:5 recounts, "And the Lord put a word in Balaam's mouth," "word" here referring to the blessings of Israel. This "word" (דבר), may also be understood as "thing," and in an ingenious attempt to eradicate

Balaam's part in wishing Israel well, this word becomes many
things to many sages. R. Eleazar (fl. 135-170 CE) understood the
"thing" that the Lord put in Balaam's mouth as an angel, who
delivered the blessings in Balaam's place, while for R. Jonathan
(fl. 135-170 CE) it was "a hook."[31] Enlarging on this, *Numbers
Rabbah* 20:20 teaches:

> And the Lord met Balaam and put a דבר in his mouth" (Num
> 23:16). As a man puts a bit in the mouth of a beast and makes
> it go in any direction he pleases, so the Holy One, blessed be
> He, perforated his mouth. When He said to him, "'Return to
> Balak' (Num 23:16) and bless them," he answered, "Why should I
> go to him and break his heart?" He wanted to go away, so the
> Holy One, blessed be He, bridled him, saying, "Return unto
> Balak, and thus shall you speak" (Num 23:16).

Although Balaam's fitness to bless Israel was questioned,
his worthiness even to be a prophet was not the major issue for
rabbinic exegetes that it would be for Philo and Christian commentators. First of all, there was the irrefutable biblical evidence
that God spoke with Balaam. In addition, many Rabbis believed the
nations so nefarious that Balaam was the only kind of prophet they
could have produced. Moreover, the conviction that the already
evil nations were given prophets only to prevent their complaining
of injustice itself accounts for a general lack of concern with
Balaam's fitness to transmit God's word beyond the question of his
blessings of Israel.

Certainly Balaam's wickedness did not go unpunished.
According to the Rabbis, Balaam lost his prophetic powers as a
result of his attempt to harm Israel. One sage writes, "He was
first an interpreter of dreams, then merited the Holy Spirit, only
to become a sorcerer again."[32] *Numbers Rabbah* 20:19 recounts
Balaam's fall in more detail:

> "And he took up his parable and said: From Aram Balak bring-
> eth me [ינחני]" (Num 23:7). He began his oration by saying:
> "I was among the high (רמים) and Balak brought me (ינחני) down
> to the nethermost pit." ינחני is to be understood in the
> sense of the verse, "Wail [נהה] for the multitude of Egypt,
> and cast them down . . . with them that go down into the pit"
> (Ezek 32:18). Another exposition is that the expression "From
> Aram" (מן-אָרם) signifies "with the All high" (עם רם), and that
> he implied: "I have been high up and Balak has brought me
> down from my glory." It is like the case of a man who was
> walking with a king when he saw a robber, and forsaking the
> king he walked with the robber. When he returned to the king
> the latter said to him, "Go with the person with whom you have
> been walking, for you cannot possibly walk with me." It was
> the same with Balaam. He had been attached to the Holy Spirit
> and had returned to be a diviner as at first, a fact that can
> be inferred from the text, "Balaam also the son of Beor, the
> soothsayer" (Josh 13:22). Consequently, he cried, "I was high
> [רם] and Balak brought me low."

Through these word plays and analogies to other scriptural verses,
the point is strongly made that through his efforts to hurt Israel
Balaam forfeited his status as prophet. A remark in B. *Sanhedrin*
106a teaches a similar lesson, also commenting on the description
of Balaam as a soothsayer: "A soothsayer? But he was a prophet!
R. Joḥanan [fl. 250-290 CE] said: At first he was a prophet, but
subsequently a soothsayer. R. Papa [fl. 350-375 CE] observed:
This is what men say: She who was a descendant of princes and
governors, played the harlot with carpenters."[33]

Balaam plays a further role in rabbinic literature as an
advisor to Israel's enemies. The Rabbis had considerable respect
for Balaam's trouble-causing abilities, and thus sought to find
scriptural evidence that he was present during other occasions
when Israel was distressed, even if he was not specifically mentioned. The notion of one ubiquitous malefactor was evidently
more acceptable than the possibility of numerous effective adversaries. One may also note here the midrashic tendency to turn a
biblical figure's sporadic act into an identifying characteristic.
The complex biblical Balaam is reduced to a few stereotypical
traits, and among them is the advisor to Israel's enemies. From
here the tradition arose that Balaam put his undeniable powers at
Pharaoh's disposal as one of his counsellors. The connection was
not difficult to establish. Exodus 7:11 recounts that Pharaoh
consulted his wise men concerning the enslaved Israelites. The
Rabbis asked which wise gentiles were supposed to have been con-
temporaneous with Pharaoh. The choice of Balaam, who had already
appeared in another biblical context as the wise advisor to
another king, Balak, was obvious.[34] Indeed, Balaam becomes counsellor to others of Israel's adversaries as well. These nations
turned to him whenever they wanted an explanation of God's special
relationship with Israel. When the law was given on Sinai and the
kings of the world trembled in their palaces, they asked Balaam if
another flood had been loosed upon the world. It was he who explained that, rather, the Lord was giving His Torah to His people.[35] On another occasion the nations of the world asked, "Why
did God command Israel, and not us, to bring sacrifices?" Balaam
answered, the purpose of sacrifices is to establish peace; but
peace without the Torah is impossible. The Israelites accepted
the Torah; they were therefore commanded to bring sacrifices, but
ye who rejected it are not to bring sacrifices, as it is written,
'The sacrifice of the wicked is an abomination' (Prov 21:27)."[36]

Among Balaam's most nefarious schemes was the seduction of
Israelite men by foreign women at Baal Peor, which as Numbers 25:9

relates, led to the deaths of twenty-four thousand Israelites.
Balaam's part in the Baal Peor disaster is chronicled with considerable imagination in *B. Sanhedrin* 106a. In order to ensnare
Israel, Balaam first advised Balak, king of Moab, to erect stalls
and sell linen garments to the Israelite men. Old women outside
the stalls were to offer the linen at its current value, but young
women within would sell it for less. After this happened two or
three times, the woman would say to the Israelite:

> "Thou art now like one of the family: sit down and choose for
> thyself." Gourds of Ammonite wine lay near her, and at that
> time Ammonite and heathen wine had not yet been forbidden.
> Said she to him, "Wouldst thou like to drink a glass of wine?"
> Having drunk, [his passion] was inflamed, and he exclaimed to
> her, "Yield to me!" Thereupon she brought forth an idol from
> her bosom and said to him, "Worship this!" "But I am a Jew,"
> he protested. "What does that concern thee?" she rejoined,
> "nothing is required but that thou should uncover thyself"--
> whilst he did not know that such was its worship. "Nay," said
> she, "I will not leave thee ere thou hast denied the Torah of
> Moses thy teacher," as it is written, "They went in to Baal
> Peor, and separated themselves unto shame, and their abomina-
> tions were according as they loved" (Hos 9:10).

Balaam so exercised the Rabbis, they lost no chance to
vilify him. Several times Balaam is accused of committing bestiality with his ass,[37] and of practicing enchantment by means of
his *membrum*.[38] Indeed, for the Rabbis, as Jonathan Slater has
pointed out, Balaam's sexual depravity was as dangerous as his
ability to curse. Balaam knew that the God of Israel hates lewd-
ness; "to introduce prostitution and idolatry into Israel, through
his advice to Balak and its execution was to attack the covenant."[39] It was, as Slater says, a direct attack on the social
fabric of the Israelite community.[40]

Balaam's sexual deviance and his abilities as a sorcerer,
therefore, are complementary aspects of his perversity. Both
place him outside a properly functioning, healthy society, Israel,
and emphasize his essential differentness as paradigmatic gentile.
Nor do the Rabbis doubt the efficacy of Balaam's magical powers.
Many traditions attest to his skills,[41] and those built around the
account of his death in Numbers 31:8 are particularly revealing.
Here it is recorded that Balaam was killed along with the five
kings of Midian by the avenging Israelites. According to rabbinic
traditions, Balaam was present when the kings were slain only
because he had gone to receive his reward for having destroyed
twenty-four thousand Israelites. Of this, Mar Zutra b. Tobiah
(fl. 250-290 CE) remarked in Rab's (fl. 220-250 CE) name, "When

the camel went to demand horns, they cut off the ears he had."[42]
So Balaam, demanding a reward, lost his life.

Numbers Rabbah 22:5 describes Balaam's end in more detail:

> Another explanation of the text, "Avenge the children of
> Israel of the Midianites" (Num 31:2). This bears on what
> Scripture says, "He withholdeth not from the righteous His
> eyes; but with kings upon the throne / He setteth them for-
> ever" (Job 36:7). What is the meaning of the expression, "He
> withholdeth not from the righteous his eyes?" The Holy One,
> blessed be He, does not withhold from the righteous man what
> he desires to see with his eyes. This serves to teach you
> that Moses longed to witness the vengeance upon the Midianites
> before he died and begged the Holy One, blessed be He, that he
> might behold it with his own eyes. Of Moses it says, "The
> righteous shall rejoice when He seeth the vengeance" (Ps
> 58:11), namely, the vengeance upon the Midianites. "He shall
> wash his feet in the blood of the wicked" (Ps 58:11), namely,
> of Balaam. Moses said to Phinehas and to the men of war: "I
> know that the wicked Balaam is there, for the purpose of re-
> ceiving his reward. Before the wolf comes to the flock spread
> a net for him. If you see that wicked man practicing witch-
> craft and flying in the air, show him the plate upon which is
> inscribed the phrase, "Holy to the Lord" (Exod 28:36), and he
> will fall down and you will kill him. "And they slew the
> kings of Midian *upon* the rest of their slain" (Num 31:8), for
> they were practicing witchcraft together with Balaam and fly-
> ing, but when they beheld the plate they fell "*upon* the rest
> of their slain."[43]

The belief that sorcerers could fly is a popular folklore motif.[44]
In this case, the Rabbis find proof from the biblical text itself
that Balaam and the kings of Midian flew above the battlefield.
In Numbers 31:8 the preposition על is used with the sense of "in
addition to," or "with," but it can also mean "upon." Balaam and
the kings of Midian would, therefore, have flown through the air
until their magic was destroyed, falling then "upon" the rest of
the slain. The plate which undid Balaam's powers and caused him
to descend was said to be the high priest's plate of pure gold
upon which the ineffable name was engraved,[45] an appropriate symbol for divine power which destroys magic underfoot.

Numbers 31:8, "Balaam also the son of Beor they slew with
the sword," gave rise to one final superstition, the belief that s
specific weapon is necessary to kill a sorcerer. Later traditions
insist that "*the* sword" of Numbers 31:8 referred to a specific
sword, and legends evolved around its history and peculiar
efficacy.[46]

Even after his death, when he was consigned to suffering
in Gehenna, Balaam remained unrepentant for his attempts to harm
Israel. His state is revealed in a rather bizarre tale related in
B. Giṭṭin 56b-57a about a certain Onqelos who was considering conversion to Judaism. This prospective proselyte raised by magical

arts Titus, who had burnt the Temple, and inquired who was held in
the greatest repute in the other world. The reply was Israel. He
then asked Titus what his punishment was, and Titus replied, "What
I decreed for myself: Every day my ashes are collected and sentence is passed over me and I am burnt and my ashes are scattered
in the seven seas." Onqelos then went and raised Balaam by incan-
tations and asked the same questions. Balaam too answered that
Israel was held in the highest repute. "What then about joining
them?" Onqelos inquired. Balaam replied, "Thou shalt not seek
their peace nor their prosperity all thy days forever" (Deut
23:7). He then asked what Balaam's punishment was. Balaam replied, "With hot boiling semen," because he had enticed Israel to
pursue the daughters of Moab. The passage concludes with Onqelos
raising Jesus. His punishment is to be immersed in boiling excre-
ment, for "Everyone who mocks at the words of the wise is sen-
tenced to boiling filth." Nevertheless, Jesus, unlike Titus and
Balaam, recommends that Onqelos join Israel, saying, "Seek their
good and seek not their harm; everyone who injures them, it is as
if he injured the apple of his eye." The passage concludes, "Come
and see what there is between the transgressors of Israel and the
prophets of the people of the world."

Two main points stand out in this passage. One is that
punishment in Gehenna fits the crime. The second is that Balaam
and Titus, gentile malefactors, remain unrepentant, and despite
their punishments still wish to harm Israel. Jesus, however, is
perceived as a sinner of Israel; he has learned his lesson and now
seeks Israel's peace. A polemic against Christian universalism
probably lies behind this story; significantly, it is Israel's
uniqueness that Jesus defends.

So unfavorable is the rabbinic portrait of Balaam that a
number of scholars have suggested that something more lies behind
this obloquy then the mere castigation of a biblical villain. It
seems likely that some polemical purpose fueled the rabbinic fires
against Balaam. A proposal which found considerable support in
the nineteenth century suggested that rabbinic criticisms of
Balaam were often meant to refer to Jesus.[47] More recent scholars, however, have disagreed. Ginzberg, for instance, says that
"the entire Talmudic-Midrashic literature does not know of any
nickname for Jesus or his disciples . . . Jesus is never named in
old sources otherwise than Yehoshua, Yeshu, Yeshua or Jesus the
son of Pantera."[48] Morris Goldstein has examined in detail all
the tannaitic and amoraic comments about Balaam which have been
said to refer to Jesus. Although certain elements in these

rabbinic remarks seem to encourage the identification, Goldstein
ultimately rejects it.[49] The differences are more important:
"Unlike Balaam, Jesus was not recognized as a prophet or soothsayer. He was not lame. He was not slain by Pinhas the
robber."[50] Most telling, however, is the fact that Jesus and
Balaam are mentioned as separate persons in certain unfavorable
remarks--the *Giṭṭin* tradition quoted above is a case in point.
Ephraim Urbach concurs with Goldstein's conclusions.[51] He points
out that the homiletic method of the Rabbis did not involve the
identification of personalities to the extent that their names
were turned into epithets and symbols; there is no precedent which
would allow us to think the name Balaam served as a by-word for
Jesus. Urbach believes rather that Balaam reflects the Rabbis'
opinions of "foreign prophets, both pagan and Christian, who were
known in the Hellenistic world."[52]

Urbach's remarks are important. To reject a strict identification of Balaam with Jesus does not mean that the intent of
some rabbinic commentary on Balaam was neither polemical nor
anti-Christian. As with the evolution of the figure of Job in
rabbinic commentary,[53] many comments on Balaam were doubtless
influenced by a knowledge of Christian claims and exegetical
teachings. Balaam was given particular importance in Christian
teachings because one of his oracles, "A star shall come forth out
of Jacob, / And a scepter shall rise out of Israel" (Num 24:17),
was interpreted as a prophecy of Christ.[54] It is not surprising
that Palestinian Amoraim of the third and fourth centuries,
acquainted with Christian argument, and in no mood for fairminded-
ness, imbued Balaam with qualities similar to those they associated with gentile religious spokesmen of their own time.[55]
These Rabbis' exegeses of Balaam and his oracles would naturally
contain hints and supporting proofs directed against those who
also cited them, and in particular against those christological
homilies of the Church Fathers which represented Balaam as a
prophet of Christ. Balaam, as a gentile, could not easily represent the Jewish Jesus, but he could certainly stand for those who
attempted to appropriate Scripture while preaching the Incarnation, the abrogation of Mosaic law, and the victory of the "New
Israel."

Several rabbinic comments lend credence to this view. R.
Abahu (fl. 290-320 CE), for example, who lived in Caesarea (where,
it should be noted, Origen lived from 232 on), and who disputed
frequently with sectarians, explained the words of Balaam, "God is
not a man, that he should lie, neither the son of man, that he

should repent" (Num 23:19), in such a way as to leave no doubt for
whom his words were intended:

> If a man says to you, "I am God"--he is lying: [If he says]
> "I am the son of Man"--he will regret this in the end; [if he
> says] "I shall go up to Heaven"--[of him it is said] "He it
> was who said [it] . . . and will not make it good" (Num
> 23:19).[56]

Similarly, Resh Lakish (fl. 250-290 CE), a contemporary of Origen,
expounded another of Balaam's oracles, "Alas who shall live after
God hath appointed him" (Num 24:24), as "Woe unto him who brings
life to himself with the name 'God.'"[57]

Balaam, then, is made the reprover of the nations, warning
them against being caught up in the net of the new belief.[58] The
irony of the prophet of the gentiles, refuting the claims of the
Messiah he is said to have prophesied, must have seemed particularly appropriate. It is equally likely that Balaam was discred-
ited, at least in part, to discredit those whose interpretations
of his oracles were not acceptable to rabbinic circles. The
initial evidence of Balaam's unworthiness was biblical, and this
provided the bases for the tannaitic attack on the talented if
ultimately unworthy gentile prophet, and his transformation into a
symbol of the evil man. The Amoraim and later exegetes, combining
these traditions with Balaam's recent elevation to a prophet of
Christ, found ample justification for their unswervingly severe
representation of Balaam as an immoral and idolatrous soothsayer
and counsellor to Israel's enemies.

iii

Philo (d. ca. 40 CE) was far more concerned than the
Rabbis with the implications of Balaam's role as a prophet. In
his *Life of Moses*,[59] he questions whether this foreign seer could
indeed have served as a spokesman for God. Rabbinic exegetes
accepted the biblical evidence that God had spoken with and
through Balaam; his wicked character was not seen as a major draw-
back to such communication. Philo's theory of prophecy, however,
was far more stringent in the instances of true prophecy it
allowed.[60]

Philo's view of prophecy had its origins in Greek speculation. Following Platonic doctrine he believed that man is placed
by nature midway between the remote deity, the essence and source
of pure intellect, and the material substance, the domain of car-
nal desires. Man is linked with the world of intellect by reason,
the higher portion of his soul, and the physical world by the

lower portion of his soul, and by his body. The first seeks to
elevate man towards his heavenly origin, the second drags him down
into earthly passions. Man's task is to abandon his lower existence and raise himself to God; the way to such perfection is wisdom.[61] In Philo's system, however, sensible perception and logi-
cal reasoning are of no help in actually apprehending the existence of the deity. Such knowledge is intuitive and comes to the
mind spontaneously. The individual's share is limited to preparing himself as far as possible for the reception of the divine
ray; its actual appearance is an act of grace. Prophecy itself is
an inspired frenzy:

> No pronouncement of a prophet is ever his own; he is an inter-
> preter prompted by Another in all his utterances, when knowing
> not what he does, he is filled with inspiration, as the reason
> withdraws and surrenders the citadel of the soul to a new visi-
> tor and tenant, the Divine Spirit, which plays upon the vocal
> organism and raises sounds from it which clearly express its
> prophetic message.[62]

    This representation of prophecy is derived from Plato. In
the *Timaeus*, Plato writes that a man is incapable of inspired or
true prophecy when in his right mind. Prophecy is a power of the
irrational mind; it comes only when the power of understanding is
inhibited by sleep or when a man is in an abnormal condition owing
to disease or divine inspiration.[63] Thus, prophetic pronounce-
ments must be interpreted by someone other than their speaker:

> Hence the custom of setting up spokesmen to pronounce judge-
> ment of inspired prophecies; they are sometimes called
> prophets by those who are ignorant that they are in fact not
> prophets, but expounders of riddling oracles and visions, and
> so most exactly called spokesmen of those who prophesy.[64]

Applying Plato's formulations to his own experience, Philo concludes that he himself has experienced such divine possession:

> On other occasions, I have approached my work empty and sud-
> denly become full, the ideas falling in a shower from above
> and being sown invisibly, so that under the influence of the
> Divine possession I have been filled with corybantic frenzy
> and been unconscious of anything, place, persons present,
> myself, words spoken, lines written.[65]

The genuineness of Balaam's experience, however, is another
matter. For Philo, prophecy is a privilege; it is another step
towards comprehension of the divine. Prophetic possession must be
prepared for by diligent study and the acquisition of wisdom, but
it can only be achieved by divine grace. How, then, could someone
like Balaam, whom Scripture shows to have had evil intentions and
base desires be considered a prophet? According to Philo, such an

exalted title for Balaam is impossible. Balaam, who could never
have enjoyed God's confidence, could not have been a prophet. He
is only pretending, out of his immense vanity to be one. Rather,
Balaam is a great soothsayer, renowned for his proficiency in
augury:

> To some he had foretold rainstorms in summer, to others
> drought and great heat in mid-winter, to some barrenness to
> follow fertility, or again plenty to follow dearth, to some
> rivers full or empty, ways of dealing with pestilences, and
> other things without number.[66]

It was in such matters that Balaam possessed ability, not in
receiving the word of God. Philo maintains, in fact, that the
visions described in Numbers 22:9-22 never took place, but were
invented by Balaam, and show us another instance of his deceit and
greed:

> Enticed by those offers present and prospective [from the
> princes of Moab] and in deference to the dignity of the ambas-
> sadors, he gave way, again dishonestly alleging a divine com-
> mand. And so on the morrow he made preparations for the jour-
> ney, and talked of dreams in which he said he had been beset
> by visions so clear that they compelled him to stay no longer
> but follow the envoys.[67]

It was only on the road to Moab that a true vision occurred, the appearance of the angel of God, and in this instance
Balaam was bested by his ass: "For the unreasoning animal showed
a superior power of sight to him who claimed to see not only the
world but the world's Maker."[68] Like the Rabbis, Philo believed
that Balaam was permitted to continue on his fatal journey only
because his desire to do so was so great:

> Yet even then, when he should have returned, he asked of the
> apparition whether he should retrace his steps homewards. But
> the angel perceived his dissimulation, for why should he ask
> about a matter so evident, which in itself provided its own
> demonstration and needed no confirmation by word, as though
> ears could be more truthful than eyes, or speech than facts?
> And so in displeasure he answered: "Pursue your journey."[69]

When Balaam arrived in Moab and attempted to curse Israel,
once again he pretended to inquire of God what to say, but this
time he *was* invaded by the divine Spirit:

> He advanced outside, and straightaway became possessed, and
> there fell upon him the truly prophetic spirit which banished
> utterly from his soul his art of wizardry. For the craft of
> the sorcerer and the inspiration of the Holiest might not live
> together. Then he returned, and seeing the sacrifices and
> altars flaming, he spake these oracles as one repeating words
> which another had put into his mouth.[70]

After he had delivered the blessings which came from outside himself, Balaam attempted to find other ways in which to harm
Israel. Thus, he offered some suggestions of his own design so
that the Israelites might be ensnared through wantonness and
licentiousness. It was as if, Philo comments, Balaam believed
that his own personal counsels were more powerful than the divine
utterances.[71] With this final impiety, Balaam vanishes from
Philo's *Life of Moses*.

For Philo, Balaam is a villain, with the additional conviction of false claims to prophecy. God speaks through Balaam,
but only that He might protect Israel. Balaam was not worthy, and
therefore in no way benefited from the divine visitation. In
fact, in his attempt to curse Israel, he lost whatever special
powers he had possessed.[72] In *On the Cherubim*,[73] Philo writes
that Balaam, whose name he takes to mean "foolish people,"[74] is
symbolic of the man unpurified in his vanity; he is the man who
devotes his life to mercenary gain, and lays the blame for his
misfortunes, not on his folly, but on wholly guiltless objects.
Thus, the ass, which in Philo's account does not speak, signifies
the unreasoning rule of life which is ridden by every fool.[75]

Philo, like the Rabbis, portrays Balaam as a scoundrel.
His dislike, however, lacks the vitriol of the rabbinic accounts,
primarily because his concerns and purposes were quite different.
The predominant rabbinic view of Balaam is based not only on the
biblical figure, but on the role he was being made to play in the
polemics of the time. For Philo, Balaam is just another biblical
character whose traits and foibles can be shown to mirror some
greater pattern and truth.

Josephus' (ca. 38-after 100 CE) account of Balaam in the
Jewish Antiquities[76] offers a similar contrast to rabbinic concerns. As with Philo, there is no apparent extra-biblical refer-
rant or target, and the portrait of Balaam which emerges is again
relatively mild in comparison to the rabbinic depiction.

Josephus begins his rendition of Numbers 22-24 with a few
editorial comments on the peaceful intentions of the Israelites.
So anxious was Balak to harm this ever-increasing people that he
did not even bother to learn that "the Hebrews were not for inter-
fering with other countries, God having forbidden them to do so,
upon their conquest of the land of Canaan."[77] (Josephus ignores
the presumption that the events of Numbers 22-24 took place before
the conquest). With these apologetic remarks for the benefit of
his gentile readers, Josephus moves on to Balaam, whom he
describes as "hailing from the Euphrates and the best diviner of

the day."[78] Josephus does not doubt that Balaam consulted with
God about Balak's invitation, nor that God refused Balaam permission to proceed to Moab. But when the second group of messengers
arrived, Balaam was hesitant to again refuse their request. Thus,
Balaam

> fain to give these men some gratification, consulted God anew;
> whereat God, indignant that he should even tempt His thus,
> bade him in no wise to gainsay the envoys. So he, not dream-
> ing that it was to delude him that God had given this order,
> set off with the envoys.[79]

Josephus' familiarity with some midrashic traditions is evident in
this comment which reflects the rabbinic belief that God, seeing
Balaam's eagerness to harm Israel, deluded him and set him on the
path to his own destruction.[80] Unlike other commentators, however, Josephus believed that Balaam's terror before the angel who
reproaches him on the road to Moab is real:

> Terrified, Balaam was prepared to turn back; God, however,
> exhorted him to pursue his intended way, while enjoining him
> to announce just whatsoever He Himself should put into his
> heart.[81]

Charged with these behests from God, Balaam arrived in
Moab, and made preparations for sacrifice and for prophecy. When
he began to speak, however, the words were not his own. "Such,"
Josephus writes, "was the inspired utterance of one who was no
longer his own master but was overruled by the divine spirit to
deliver it."[82] Balaam himself describes this prophetic possession
when he responds to Balak's reproaches:

> "Balak," said he, "hast thou reflected on the whole matter and
> thinkest thou that it rests with us at all to be silent or to
> speak on such themes as these, when we are possessed by the
> spirit of God? For that spirit gives utterance to such lan-
> guage and words as it will whereof we are all unconscious
> . . . For nothing within us, once He has gained prior entry,
> is any more our own. Thus, for my part, I neither intended to
> extol this army nor to recount the blessings for which God has
> designed their race; it is He who, in His gracious favor to
> them and His zeal to confer on them a life of felicity and
> everlasting renown, has put it into my heart to pronounce such
> words as these."[83]

This description of ecstatic possession is far more reminiscent of
Philo's Platonic view of divine inspiration than of the biblical
and rabbinic understanding of the transmission of God's word.
Writing for a hellenized audience, Josephus is describing Balaam's
delivery of God's intended blessings of Israel in terms his
readers will understand.

Twice more Balaam attempted to give voice to curses but
each time he was overwhelmed and gave forth prophecies of Israel's

greatness. At last, acknowledging his inability to cause permanent harm to Israel, Balaam suggested to Balak a way in which he
might cause Israel at least some small misfortune and difficulty.
In words reminiscent of the rabbinic account of the events of Numbers 25, Josephus describes Balaam's plan. The Midianites were to
send their most comely young women into the camp of the Israelites
to entice the young men:

> Then, when they shall see these youths overmastered by their
> passions, let them quit them, and, on their entreating them to
> stay, let them not consent until they have induced their
> lovers to renounce the laws of their fathers and the God to
> whom they owe them, and to worship the gods of the Midianites
> and the Moabites. For thus will God be moved to indignation
> against them.[84]

Having proposed this scheme, Balaam went on his way.

Like Philo, Josephus does not record Balam's death at the
hands of an Israelite army, but he does comment on Moses' integrity in recording Balaam's prophecies in Scripture and in attributing them to their correct author, despite Balaam's evil doings:

> This was the man to whom Moses did the high honor of recording
> his prophecies; and though it was open to him to appropriate
> and take the credit for himself, as there would have been no
> witness to convict him, he has given Balaam this testimony and
> deigned to perpetuate his memory.[85]

This final comment recalls Josephus' closing remarks on Jethro:
again Moses is eulogized for his probity in preserving with due
credit the contributions of a non-Israelite to Israel's heritage.

Josephus' account of Balaam is totally without the animus
that characterizes the rabbinic traditions. Certainly Balaam
caused harm to Israel, and was deluded by God about the purpose of
his journey to Moab; the implication, however, is not that God
deluded Balaam in order to destroy him, but rather that he might
be brought to Moab and deliver blessings which would benefit
Israel. Balaam is sincere in his fear of God, and his belief in
His powers; his major fault seems to be his anxiety not to disap-
point his employer Balak. Yet even when he advises Balak on how
to harm Israel, he counsels as well:

> Doubtless this race of Hebrews will never be overwhelmed by
> utter destruction, neither through war, nor through pestilence
> and dearth of the fruits of the earth, neither shall any other
> unlooked for cause exterminate it. For God is watching over
> them to preserve them from all ill and to suffer no such
> calamity to come upon them as would destroy them all.[86]

An even more favorable view of Balaam is found in the
pseudepigraphical *Biblical Antiquities*.[87] This book, which was
long attributed to Philo, may date from the first century CE. It

now survives only in a Latin translation. In a number of cases
this work appears to preserve motifs and legends that are found in
no other extant source.[88] Certainly the portrait of Balaam it
presents is quite different from that found in most rabbinic
texts.

This Balaam, for example, knows at once that Balak's request to curse Israel may be displeasing to God, and replies:
"Lo, this is good in the sight of Balak, but he knoweth not that
the counsel of God is not as man's counsel. And he knoweth not
that the spirit which is given to us is given for a time, and our
ways are not guided except by God's will."[89] Thus, Balaam makes
clear both his consciousness that his powers come only from God,
and that he possesses them only as long as God wills. Balaam's
further knowledge of and obedience to God is expressed in their
nightly consultation. When God asks, "What men are these with
thee" (Num 22:20), Balaam responds, not as the Bible records, but
as follows:

> Wherefore, Lord, dost thou tempt the race of man? They there-
> fore cannot sustain it, for thou knowest more than they, all
> that was in the world, before thou foundest it. And now en-
> lighten thy servant if it be right that I go with them.[90]

This is the very answer various midrashic texts chastise Balaam
for not making. In this work, Scripture has been altered to
Balaam's benefit.

When Balak's messengers return, God is angry not only with
Balaam, but with Balak as well. Thus, He commands: "Go with them
and thy journey shall be an offense, and Balak himself shall go
unto destruction."[91] Again, the rabbinic traditions are reversed;
it is Balak not Balaam who is destined for destruction. Similarly, Balaam is not accused of venality; rather Balak is de-
nounced for seeking to buy God's favor. This is the import of one
of Balaam's prophecies:

> And Balak himself hath not known it, because his mind is
> puffed up, to the intent his destruction may come swiftly
> . . . for Balak desired to persuade the Most Mighty with gifts
> and to purchase decision with money."[92]

According to the *Biblical Antiquities*, none of Balaam's
oracles were inspired by the Spirit of God. From the moment he
entered Moab, "the spirit of God abode not in him."[93] In fact,
the *Biblical Antiquities* records almost none of the biblical
Balaam's oracles, but concentrates instead on Balaam's realization
of his misfortune. Thus, Balaam laments:

I am restrained in the speech of my voice, and I cannot express that which I see with mine eyes, for but a little is
left to me of the holy spirit which abideth in me, since I
know that in that I was persuaded of Balak I have lost the
days of my life.[94]

It is only now, when Balaam sees his mistake in coming to
Moab, that he becomes sympathetic to Balak's cause and delivers
his evil counsel as follows:

Come and let us advise what thou shalt do to them. Choose out
of the most comely women that are among you and that are in
Midian and set them before them naked, and adorned with gold
and jewels, and it shall be when they shall see them and lie
with them, they will sin against their Lord and fall into your
hands, for otherwise thou canst not subdue them.[95] And so saying Balaam turned away and returned to his place.

Geza Vermes has described the Balaam of the *Biblical Antiquities* as a tragic hero, a figure far different from the Balaam
represented in other Palestinian writings. His downfall, according to Vermes, was that he pitied Balak whose cause he knew to be
hopeless. In going to Moab, however, he brought about not only
Balak's destruction but his own. Vermes writes:

Finally, realizing that there would be no return to his former
familiarity with the Lord, he decided, in his despair, to com-
mit spiritual suicide by giving evil advice to the king. In
short, having made his initial mistake, Balaam felt himself
caught, as it were, in the claws of Fate, and instead of de-
parting in joy, went off hopeless, towards his inescapable
end.[96]

Vermes has maintained that the rather sympathetic portrait
of Balaam in the *Biblical Antiquities* is unique. Yet several elements in Pseudo-Philo's account are reminiscent of certain midrashic traditions. In *Numbers Rabbah* 20:19, Balaam is compared to
a man who was walking with a king, but forsakes his noble companion to walk with a robber. When he attempts to rejoin the king he
is rebuffed, for after such behavior there is no return.[97] Similarly, other *midrashim* tell of Balaam's realization that he has
sacrificed all his former glory by his journey to Moab and his
attempts to curse Israel. Thus, he loses the Spirit of God and
returns to the level of a mere soothsayer.[98] The *Biblical Antiquities* presents a sympathetic view of Balaam and his misfortunes,
but this moderate approach is also a minor theme in the body of
midrash about this pagan seer. It seems likely that the *Biblical
Antiquities*, and Josephus' *Jewish Antiquities* as well, reflect
early, milder rabbinic teachings which were all but overwhelmed by
the development of Jewish-Christian polemics and the far more
severe and hostile views of the gentile soothsayer these
engendered.[99]

iv

Christian tradition saw in Balaam both villain and prophet. His prediction of the star which would rise from Jacob in Numbers 24:17, widely read as foretelling the Incarnation, secured him a place among the gentile prophets of Christ, and established him as founder of the Magi. His biblically recorded misdeeds, however, raised serious questions about the legitimacy of his prophecy. An unusually large number of borrowings from Philo and rabbinic tradition in patristic commentary on Balaam also bear witness to the difficulties many Church Fathers encountered in their attempts to understand and elucidate the significance of this contradictory gentile seer.

The New Testament parallels rabbinic literature in its wholly negative estimation of Balaam. Revelations 2:4, for instance, recounts Balaam's part in leading the Israelites to idolatry and debauchery:

> But I have a few things against you: You have some there who
> hold the teaching of Balaam, who taught Balak to put a stum-
> bling block before the sons of Israel, that they might eat
> food sacrificed to idols and practice immorality.

The belief that Balaam had been tempted by the promise of riches is a motif in the two other New Testament references to him, Jude 1:11, "Woe to them! For they walk in the way of Cain, and abandon themselves for the sake of gain to Balaam's error, and perish in Korah's rebellion"; and 2 Peter 2:15-16, describing the ungodly, "Forsaking the right way they have gone astray: They have followed the way of Balaam, the son of Beor,[100] who loved gain from wrongdoing but was rebuked for his transgression; a dumb ass spoke with human voice and restrained the prophet's madness."[101]

But Balaam played a more important part in early Christian thought as a predictor of Christ, and thus Christianity was required to see in him not only a villain but a divinely inspired prophet. The discovery in the Hebrew Bible of various proof texts which could show that the prophecies of Scripture had been fulfilled in Jesus Christ was a popular method of interpretation in the early Church.[102] Among those verses frequently cited was Numbers 24:17, Balaam's prediction that a star would rise from Jacob.[103] Early Christian apologists, such as Justin (d. 165) and Clement of Alexandria, (d. ca. 215) anxious to establish the antiquity of the Christian tradition, used such messianic texts eagerly to lend their arguments against pagan and Jewish opponents greater authority. As the words of a foreign prophet, who was said to have made Christ known to the gentile peoples, Balaam's prophecy must have seemed particularly apt.

Thus, in his *Apology*, Justin used this verse as a proof of Old Testament verification of Christ's coming. It is illustrative of patristic disquiet with Balaam, however, that he amalgamates the star prophecy of Balaam with the root of Jesse prophecy of Isaiah, and attributes the whole to Isaiah.[104] Justin also refers to Balaam's prophecy in his *Dialogue with Trypho*, this time placing it correctly in the books of Moses, but again he does not attribute it to Balaam.[105] A similar effort to separate the man from his prophecy is found in an oration of Athanasius. In the *Incarnation of the Word*, the fourth century Father quotes the prophecy of Balaam under the name of Moses.[106] And when Augustine (d.430) writes in the *City of God* that we should not be surprised to hear of foreigners, not of the people of Israel, who have prophesied something about Christ, it seems likely that he too has Balaam in mind:

> It is not incongruous to belief that even in other nations there may have been men to whom this mystery was revealed, and who were also impelled to proclaim it, whether they were partakers of the same grace or had no experience of it, but were taught by bad angels, who, as we know, even confessed the present Christ, whom the Jews did not acknowledge.[107]

In this passage, where Augustine endorses any true prophecy of Christ, regardless of its origin, he might well be supporting the authenticity of Balaam's predictions, without in any way sanctioning either his character or his standing as a prophet.[108] This might explain the reference to "bad angels," as well, if they are meant as the source of Balaam's knowledge.

In rabbinic tradition Balaam was a gentile prophet, ultimately unworthy, but a prophet nonetheless. But many Christian thinkers maintained, as Philo had done, that a prophet must possess special spiritual qualities.[109] That a prophet appointed to make Christ known to the gentiles might be villainous was disturbing. Some patristic exegetes, as we have seen, simply separated the man from the prediction. But the contradictions apparent in Balaam's character forced others to question the godly nature of both the prophet and the prophecy. What they decided had much to do with their thinking on the nature of prophecy itself. Athenagoras (2nd century) thought, with Philo, that the prophets "spoke out what they were in travail with, their own reasoning falling into abeyance and the Spirit making use of them as a flutist might play upon his flute."[110] Justin, too, supported the Philonic doctrine,[111] writing in his *Apology*: "When you hear read passages of the Scriptures supposed to have been uttered by various characters do not imagine that they are said by the inspired people themselves, but by the divine Word who prompted them."[112] Clement of Alexandria called the prophets "organs of the divine voice," but distinguished between the ecstasy of false prophets and the inspiration of authentic prophets.[113] Following this line of reasoning it was quite simple to relegate the wicked Balaam to the category of false prophet, as Philo had done, and attribute his messianic prophecy to the divine voice which overpowers the chosen speaker.

Other fathers, such as Irenaeus (d. 202), allow Balaam the designation of prophet for the occasion, but insist no inner transformation took place.[114] But some writers maintain, on the other hand, that it was through Balaam that God made his love known to the nations, and he is sometimes allegorically seen as the representative of the gentile Christian.[115] The depth of the controversy is evident in his other allegorical designations: he is the type of the Pharisee; the Jewish people who would not accept Christ, and the adversary of God.[116] Origen (d. ca. 253) sees in Balaam's father, Beor, the type of the heretic,[117] and Ambrose (d. 397) projects back on Balaam the heresy of Manichaeism.[118] Indeed, Ambrose writes in one of his epistles that Balaam was only allowed to prophesy so that through an adversary's word the proof of God would be raised even higher.[119]

The perplexities raised by Balaam were further complicated by Balaam's relationship with the Magi. He was thought by many to be the founder of this order of magicians and seers, whose representatives came to worship the infant Jesus. Whether such an equation is implied in Matthew 2:2, the account of the adoration of the Magi, is impossible to say, but certainly by the time of Origen this connection was presented as fact.[120] J. Bidez and F. Cumont write:

> L'apocalyptique mazdéene ayant fortement influencé le messianisme d'Israël, peut-être l'équation Balaam-Zoroastre est-elle antérieure a notre ère. Mais, plus probablement elle fut imaginée quand on s'avisa de faire de Zoroastre le révélateur de la naissance de Jésus. L'exégèse chrétienne affirma que l'institution des Mages en Orient remontait à Balaam, et que ceux-ci, descendent de lui, avaient ainsi conservé le texte de ses prédictions, qu'ils virent se réaliser lorsqu'ils aperçurent l'astre announcé par lui.[121]

These descendants were not viewed as disciples of Balaam the villain, but students of the seer who pronounced blessings on Israel, and foretold the coming of the Messiah. This identification of the Magi as Balaam's progeny constitutes a further facet of the many-sided Balaam who emerges from Christian tradition.[122]

A number of these aspects of Balaam come together in the writings of Origen, who devoted a good deal of attention to understanding this perplexing figure. Not only did Origen write a series of homilies about Balaam in his commentary on Numbers, but he takes other opportunities to refer to him as well. Clearly, the integration of the two disparate accounts of the biblical Balaam presented a special challenge this exegete chose to meet.

Origen's views on prophecy were more complicated than those of many Church Fathers. While a few passages in his writings suggest that he occasionally adopted the "ecstatic" view of how the Holy Spirit inspired its agents, on the whole he believes that inspiration does not remove or paralyze the prophet's control of his rational faculties.[123] When the prophets spoke under the influence of the Holy Spirit, he explicitly declares, they were not in ecstasy: "voluntarily and consciously they collaborated with the word that came to them."[124] Indeed, prophets could refuse to speak if they chose, and Origen finds instances of such deliberate refusals in I Corinthians 14:30, Numbers 22:35, and Jonah 1.[125] Hanson attributes this rejection of ecstasy to Origen's intense rationalism: he did not like any theory which tended to put reason into the background in an account of the relation between man and God. Instead, he maintained that a prophet's individual character and consciousness are preserved, even when he is inspired.[126] Consistent with this admission, Origen holds that each prophecy has an immediate reference as well as a future one. At one point, he specifies three ways in which prophecy may be interpreted: things the prophet spoke to his contemporaries, predictions to those who lived later, and most of all, oracles of a certain Savior who was to come and live among mankind. Among the prooftexts Origen provides as examples of this last type of prophecy is Numbers 24:17.[127]

Given his belief that true prophets participate in their prophecy, as well as his acceptance of Balaam's oracle as messianic, Origen had to establish the natures of both Balaam and his prophetic utterance. In his *Homilies on Numbers*, Origen examines Balaam's claims, and attempts to account not only for the meanings of Balaam's prophecies, but, consistent with his own theory of prophecy, to establish whether or not Balaam was a prophet.

Origen was concerned with the literal meaning of the biblical text, and not surprisingly, many of his comments on the basically straightforward story of Balaam are literal rather than

allegorical. For Origen, however, the whole of Scriptures also
had a deeper meaning which could be revealed through allegory, and
much of his exegesis of the Balaam story unfolds on the allegorical level. Since Origen believed that in its literal sense the
Bible was too little concerned with the spirits and cosmic forces
which regulate the universe, he expressed through allegory his own
speculative opinions about the primeval causes of disorder in the
cosmos, and the processes by which harmony was being reestab-
lished.[128] Since Origen sees Balaam first and foremost as a sorcerer and soothsayer, a diviner in touch with evil spirits, he
portrays the battle between Israel and Balaam as a microcosm of
the larger universal struggle between good and evil. Thus, he
draws a parallel between the contrasting uses of words as weapons
by each side:

> ["And Moab said to the elders of Midian] 'This horde will now
> lick up all that is round about us, as the ox licks up the
> grass of the field'" Num. 22:4). He uses this example, for
> just as a bull licks up the field with his mouth, so the holy
> people fight with their lips: they have their defenses in
> their mouths through prayers. Thus, since Balak knew that in
> previous wars this obviously had happened, he too wished to
> enter a fight with the force of lips and he called upon Balaam
> who had the arms of the contrary power in his lips, namely his
> curses.[129] The holy angels come to the aid of the just to do
> good works of salvation; devils come to the support of the
> evil to do evil works which endanger the salvation of men.
> The holy, of course, fight by words of prayer, the impious and
> sinners by magic incantations.[130]

Origen's Balaam, then, is presented as a warrior with
words, who fights for the darker forces against the righteous.
His goal, and that of his shadowy mentors, is to deceive the God-
fearing. God wished to hinder Balaam on his journey, Origen maintains, not because he feared Balaam's curses, but in order to
prevent the greater misfortunes which would befall Israel as a
result of Balaam's demonic counsel.[131] Indeed, Origen emphasizes
Balaam's magic abilities and his intercourse with evil forces:

> This Balaam was most famous in the magic arts and foremost in
> harmful incantations. He did not truly have power to bless
> but rather to curse. Demons, indeed, were invoked for curs-
> ing, not for blessing. And therefore he was well known in
> such things according to all who were in the East.[132]

Such occult abilities, of course, are not conducive with godli-
ness, but God saw in Balaam's mastery of them a way to bring many
people to true worship; according to Origen, in fact, it was
Balaam's skill at divination which made him an appropriate vehicle
for God's word.

Origen holds that Balaam was chosen to prophesy, even if
only momentarily, that he might turn the peoples of the world from
the invocation of demons to worship of God. It was because God
saw Balaam's wide renown that He perceived his usefulness as a
divine spokesman to the nations, and came uncalled to turn him,
and with him the gentile nations, from necromancy to sacred pro-
nouncement:

> Balaam was accustomed by these sacrifices to invoke demons.
> Indeed, in this way sacrifices are offered in the demon world.
> Thus, God instituted from the first the offering of sacrifices
> for the people, so that they, in offering to God, would cease
> offering to demons.[133]

Origen goes on to say that, here, "Balaam is the symbol of the
people of the nations who follow auguries, but seeing that God
does not fulfill these, cease."[134]

Origen offers several allegorical interpretations of
Balaam along these lines. In his *Selecta on Numbers*, he suggests
that Balaam is the adversary who has enchained his ass, the gentile peoples, in false worship.[135] Only when Christ sends his
disciples is the ass freed, and, clothed in vestments, that is the
evangelical virtues, able to enter the holy city. Elsewhere,
Origen offers Balaam as a type of the scribes and Pharisees of the
Jewish people,[136] who oppress and bind the ordinary people, the
ass upon which they ride:

> Moreover they were the scribes and Pharisees who were sitting
> on that ass and were keeping it bound. The angel therefore
> grew angry at these, and if it weren't with regard to the
> future, he would have certainly killed them. He instead saved
> the ass which saw and revered him who came into the vineyard
> and stood among the vines. He [the ass] pressed moreover the
> foot of the one who was sitting on him against the wall, and
> perhaps for this reason this former rider was not able to
> walk, nor to come to Him who said, "Come to me, all who labor
> and are heavy laden, [and I will give you rest]" (Matt 11:28).
> The ass, however, came, led by the disciples, and where pre-
> viously sat Balaam, desirous of wealth, now sits Jesus.[137]

Origen makes similar comparisons elsewhere in his homilies as
well, hailing the ass as the Church, which first carried false
belief, but now carries Christ.[138] By having Balaam represent
both false pagan beliefs and the hypocrisy of the Pharisees,
Origen turns him into a metaphor for the spiritual enslavement
which he believes kept all mankind in thrall until the advent of
Christianity. Similarly, Balaam's messianic message is directed
to the nations and the Jews alike, that all may share in the glor-
ious knowledge.[139]

Balaam, then, is an ambiguous figure, for despite his obvious malevolence he was privileged to deliver a divine prophecy. As Origen remarks, it is very difficult to define Balaam's character.[140] On the one hand, he appears to be blameworthy in many ways, as when, "forbidden by God to go to the king, he persists in his intention to go."[141] "He is culpable when he builds altars, and sets out sacrifices to demons, demanding divine counsel by means of magic,"[142] and "he is guilty when he gives lewd counsel, so that the people are beguiled by the Midianite women and the cult of idols."[143] Yet Balaam also has a praiseworthy side as well, for,

> When the word of God is placed in his mouth, then the Spirit of God overcomes him, then he prophesies of Christ, then he makes known to the Jews and to the nations the future mystery of the coming of Christ, then in place of curses he bestows blessings on the people, and extols the name of Israel for great glory with mystical utterances.[144]

As Origen notes, Balaam himself appears to express inner confusion when, despite his evil intentions, and evil activities yet to come, he asks that he might die the death of the righteous (Num 23:10).[145]

The great question for Origen, however, is whether or not Balaam should be numbered among the prophets, and in the end he is clear that, however inspired Balaam may have been, his oracles were both unwilling and shortlived, and he was therefore not a true prophet. In his *Commentary on John*, he writes of Balaam: " . . . the fact that he was not a prophet is evident; indeed it is written that he was a soothsayer. And truly, if someone is a prophet, he prophesies genuinely; but if indeed someone prophesies, he is not by consequence also a prophet."[146] Along these lines Origen remarks elsewhere that no one should be surprised that Balaam, or any other miscreant, was granted momentary prophecy, nor should one feel that he is therefore totally praiseworthy:

> No one should be extolled because he prophesies, even if his foreknowledge is wondrous, for as Scripture says, "[Love never ends,] as for prophecies they will pass away, as for tongues they will cease, as for knowledge it will pass away. [For knowledge is imperfect, and our prophecy is imperfect"] (I Cor 13:8).[147]

Balaam's prophecy is flawed for the word of God was not truly in him. His prophetic utterances were neither collaborative nor ecstatic. Rather his divination and avarice fitted him only for momentary use as a divine vessel. "If Balaam," Origen writes, "had been worthy, the word of God would have been not in his mouth

but in his heart. Since, however his heart was filled with greed
for wealth and money, God's word could be placed only in his
mouth."[148]   Thus, Origen cautions that it is the prophetic message, not the messenger which is important:

> He was propelled by miracles and with a great charge, since
> the words of the prophets, which were contained within the
> confines of Israel, could not reach the nations. It would be
> through Balaam, in whom all nations had faith, that the secret
> mystery of Christ might become known, and the great treasure
> be offered to the people, even though carried, not through the
> heart and senses, but through the mouth and by discussion.[149]

Through their trusted soothsayer, then, the nations would have
their ears opened, and move beyond him, to more worthy beliefs.

Origen's view of prophecy is clear. The true prophet col-
laborates in the delivery of the divine message; he speaks with
his heart, and is perforce a righteous man. Yet, to bring all
people to righteousness, unworthy men may occasionally serve as
vessels for the divine message, though they will always speak with
their mouths, not with their hearts. Yet to be in some ways
unworthy is inherent in the human condition, and even the unworthy
may find redemption. Origen believed that as a result of the
prophecy Balaam delivered and through its fulfillment, Balaam
found a measure of salvation.

This redemption was achieved through Balaam's descendants,
the Magi, the first representatives of the nations to recognize
and worship the infant Jesus. Origen reveals the key to Balaam's
future in his exegesis of Balaam's plea, "Let me die the death of
righteous, let my seed be like his" (Num 23:10).[150]

> From the fact that Balaam says "Let my seed be as the seed of
> the righteous," we can discern that these Magi who came from
> the East to be the first to adore Jesus are seen to be from
> his seed, whether through the succession of his seed, or
> through the disciples of his tradition. It is evident from
> the fact that these recognized the star which Balaam foretold
> would rise in Israel, and that they came and adored the king
> who was born in Israel . . . Nor are we speaking only of
> these, that their seed would be like the seed of the right-
> eous, but all of those of the nations who believed in Christ
> are saved. From which it is clear, as the Apostle said, "For
> in Christ Jesus neither circumcision nor uncircumcision is of
> any avail, but faith working through love" (Gal 5:6).[151]

Through the Magi Balaam finds forgiveness for his excesses, and
when he prays, "Let my seed be like his," he provides proof that
all gentile believers will be saved.

Origen's Balaam, then, is no longer contradictory. As a
miscreant who summoned up demons and harmed others through incan-
tations, he certainly warranted condemnation. Yet in Origen's

eyes Balaam becomes worthy of redemption, both because he was
chosen, however involuntarily, to deliver a prophecy of Christ
which could bring the nations to true worship, and because of the
merit of his descendants. In this transformation both biblical
Balaams are accounted for, and a lesson in redemption and gentile
salvation imparted.

Origen's picture of Balaam influenced his immediate successors in varying degrees, and became a major source for later
exegetes, although few adopted his theory of transformation and
redemption. Only Jerome shares Origen's conviction of Balaam's
repentance and salvation.[152]

Another Alexandrian who also had an effect on patristic
views of Balaam was Philo. His influence is particularly evident
in one of Ambrose's epistles, which comments extensively on the
Balaam story.[153] In this letter Ambrose asks if it is possible to
deceive God. Was God mistaken in Balaam's character when he chose
him as the messenger of His blessings of Israel? Ambrose responds
in the negative. Balaam was corrupted by his own avarice, and God
was not deceived. Like Philo, Ambrose recounts that at first
Balaam sent away the messengers as God had commanded. But when
they returned, Balaam was won over by their promises of reward,
and accompanied them, "as if thinking," writes Ambrose, "that
God's will might be changed by money or reward.[154] Because Balaam
responded as an avaricious man, not as one who sought the truth,
God was willing that he accompany the Moabites, and "be deluded,
rather than informed."[155]

Echoing Philo again, Ambrose reports that Balaam's response to the angel he encountered on the road was insincere and
ambiguous. In fact, Ambrose is not convinced that Balaam truly
apprehended the angel at all, so blinded were his eyes by avarice.
It was for this reason that the angel said, "Go with the men; but
only the word that I shall speak unto thee, that thou shalt speak"
(Num 22:35). In going to Moab, Balaam had lost his power of
vision, and was capable only of transmitting God's words.[156]

Even after delivering God's blessings, Balaam still desired reward, and thus he gave Balak advice on how to corrupt the
Israelites. To Ambrose, as Philo, Balaam lacks any redeeming
qualities, and so he concludes:

> Therefore God is not unjust, nor changeable in His wisdom. He
> found out Balaam's mind and the secret of his heart, and
> therefore treated him as a diviner, not as a chosen prophet.
> And indeed He kept back from him the gift of His greatest ora-
> cles and most sublime revelations. The soul full of wicked-
> ness brought forth full-bodied speech, but he did not confer

faith. Avaricious, he weakened by plots what he had announced
of the future. And because he was not able to prophesy falsely, he offered a false plan, by which the people of the Jews
would be tempted, although they would not be destroyed.[157]

Another negative view of Balaam is found in the writings
of Augustine. Augustine expresses his views on prophecy in *De
Diversis Quaestionibus ad Simplicianum*.[158] He holds that the
Spirit of God influences different prophets in different ways, so
that some are imbued with the gift of prophecy permanently while
others are affected only for short periods of time. Only a true
prophet, however, possesses *caritas*. Thus, Augustine distinguishes between true and false prophets:

> There is as great a distance between the prophecy of prophets
> such as Isaiah and Jeremiah and that transitory passing proph-
> ecy as appeared in Saul, as the distance when humans speak and
> speech as it appeared in Balaam's ass. And that instance only
> occurred because God found it necessary to demonstrate his
> will to Balaam; it was not an indication that the beast was
> permanently to be able to speak with men. If God can make an
> ass speak, he can certainly make an ungodly man submit to the
> spirit of prophecy for a short time.[159]

Accordingly, Augustine advises that the evil man who appears to
have been granted the gift of prophecy is not to be esteemed, for
even an evil man could have foretold the coming of Christ.[160]
Similarly, no one should suppose, because he has momentarily
prophesied, that he will be enumerated among the prophets.[161]

In his *Quaestionum in Heptateuchum*,[162] Augustine deems
Balaam totally evil and unworthy. Yet he must account for
Balaam's reception of the divine presence. Augustine explains
that this communication was not direct, but took place while
Balaam was asleep. He cites, "And Balaam arose in the morning"
(Num 22:13), as proof that Balaam had received the divine communication in his sleep, a sign of his unworthiness: "Lest anyone
glory in the fact that God has spoken to him in this way, know
that all such references refer to evildoers."[163]

As for Balaam's blessings, Augustine stresses that he was
not allowed to say what he wished, but what the Spirit produced.
Balaam himself remained evil throughout, as evidenced by 2 Peter
2:15. He was, in fact, chosen to deliver divine prophecy only
that he might provide an example of the hypocrite, who affects
piety in false hopes of benefiting from Christ's saving powers:

> It is impossible to be a prophet and lack charity. But how
> are we to understand the evil man who appears to have been
> granted a prophecy? For Balaam appears evil, and Scripture
> does not forebear to say that he is damned by divine justice,
> yet nevertheless he had prophecy. But we must remember that
> he lacked charity and was only inspired to bless by prophecy

when he was unwilling to bless on his own. Thus, he must be understood as one of those who are meant in Matthew 7:22-23, "On that day many will say to me 'Lord, Lord, did we not prophesy in your name and cast out demons in your name, and do many mighty works in your name,' and then I will declare to them, 'I never knew you: Depart from me, you evildoers.'" He is like those who say, if they are evil or unfaithful, "in your name we prophesied," but they are not able to say, "Your desire as you commanded we have maintained." For if they should say it they will *not* receive this answer: "By this all men will know that you are my disciples" (John 13:35).[164]

Augustine echoes Origen and Ambrose: Balaam was granted prophecy of the mouth only, not of the heart. Indeed, for Augustine, Balaam was at best God's unwilling mouthpiece.

Augustine so condemns Balaam that he refuses to connect him with the Magi. Origen had felt no hesitation in calling these stargazers direct descendants of Balaam; nor did Gregory of Nyssa (d. 394) who wrote in a Christmas sermon, "Behold how the Magi, who stem from Balaam, observed, according to his prophecy, the newly appointed star."[165] Yet, while Augustine praises the Magi in various of his Christmas orations for their recognition of the star heralding Christ's birth, he never characterizes Balaam as either an ancestor and teacher of the Magi, or a prophet of Christ to the nations. In several sermons, however, he does connect the Magi with the nations, and hence with the large body of Christians who came from the gentile peoples. This indicates his familiarity with the tradition, and further underscores his refusal to allow Balaam any positive features. In one Epiphany address he writes: "The Magi came from the East at the time of the birth of Christ to adore the Virgin. These were the first fruits of the nations, as we are the people of the nations. To us, through the Magi, the tongue of the apostle announced the star."[166] In another sermon he praises the Magi for their perspicacity, and the consequent shaming of the Jews:

> It is truly the righteous who see, as when the three Magi were the first from the nations to recognize Christ, and they were influenced, not by a sermon, but by the star itself, and so they appeared before the infant. So it was granted to the first fruits of the nations to recognize Christ and to acknowledge him with gifts. This is that humility which was more in these who were from the nations than in the Jews.[167]

By contrast with Augustine, and more in line with Origen, the Church Father Jerome (d. 420) stressed Balaam's positive aspects as a prophet to the nations and founder of the Magi. He believed that no prophet had prophesied the future coming of Christ so clearly.[168] In accord with the *Biblical Antiquities*, Jerome saw Balaam as a tragic figure who lost his powers through

giving into temptation: "First he was a holy man, and a prophet
of God, afterwards through his disobedience and desire for reward,
he wanted to curse Israel, and then he was taken over by divine
words, as it says, "Then was kindled the wrath of Elihu the son of
Barachel the Buzite"[169] (Job 32:3).

Jerome believes that Balaam ultimately repented his misdeeds. In his commentary on Ezekiel he comments as follows:

> "May my soul die the death of the righteous" (Num 23:10).
> This has the meaning that Balaam desired to die for his sins
> of previous times, and also to live as the righteous do, as
> the life of Christ is, and so it is foretold in Matthew 22:32,
> "I am the God of Abraham, Isaac and Jacob. He is not the God
> of the dead but the living." And if Balaam, whose name means
> "vain people,"[170] perceived that formerly he had been a vain
> member of the nations, now he wished to be joined with the
> souls of the just, Abraham, Isaac and Jacob, who are called
> upright and righteous. Thus prophesies John, "Truly, truly, I
> say to you, he who hears my word and believes Him who sent me,
> has eternal life: He does not come into judgement, but has
> passed from death to life" (John 5:24).[171]

Perhaps part of Balaam's appeal to Jerome is his connection with the Magi, and their indirect refutation of the Jews. On
Matthew 2:1-2, which recounts the coming of the wise men from the
East to view the infant Christ, Jerome writes: "The star rose in
the East as Balaam prophesied to his successors who recognized it
by prophetic means, in order to confuse the Jews so that they
would learn of the birth of Christ from the gentiles."[172] As we
have seen in Augustine, this was a popular theme; in a Christmas
hymn, the Father Ephraem (d. 373), for example, emphasized the sin
of the Jews, evidenced by the fact that a foreigner had known of
the rising of the star and they had not.[173]

The contrast between the wholly evil Balaam of Ambrose and
Augustine, and the repentant prophet of Origen and Jerome is
striking. One explanation lies in the different sources these
Fathers used. Ambrose followed the negative line laid down by
Philo, and his pupil Augustine appears to have followed suit. In
the writings of Origen and Jerome, however, there are borrowings
from other Jewish sources, rabbinic and otherwise.

Both Origen and Jerome are known to have consulted contemporary Jewish sages for help in resolving difficulties in the biblical text, and both occasionally incorporated rabbinic solutions
in their translations and exegeses. In Origen's comments on
Balaam, rabbinic influence is evident in several direct comments.
Origen's exegesis of Numbers 22:4, "This horde will now lick up
all that is round about us, as the ox licks up the grass of the
field," quoted above, seems to reflect a rabbinic tradition found

in such sources as *Numbers Rabbah* and *Tanhuma*.[174] Origen repeats
the rabbinic idea that the people of God "fight not with their
hands and arms but with the voice and tongue" elsewhere as
well.[175] Similarly, Origen's condemnations of Balaam's involvement in magic and sorcery echo rabbinic opprobrium. As for
Jerome, he identifies Balaam with Elihu, "according to the
Hebrews," in his *Questions on Genesis*,[176] and his comments, as
Origen's, on "May my soul die the death of the righteous," seem to
parallel rabbinic traditions now recorded in *Numbers Rabbah*.[177]
Finally, it seems likely that Jerome was also acquainted with the
Biblical Antiquities to whose repentant Balaam his own bears a
strong resemblance.

It seems likely that Christian commentators only approached their Jewish counterparts when they encountered particular exegetical difficulties. The frequent incidence of apparently
parallel remarks in the case of Balaam bears eloquent testimony to
the consternation this pagan seer excited. As Jay Braverman
points out, "The parallel traditions in rabbinic and patristic
literature concerning the character, personality and identification of Balaam are indeed striking."[178]

Such consultations, however, were ultimately of little aid
in solving the puzzle of Balaam. The dual persona remained. The
conviction that the star of the Magi was predicted by Balaam was
represented almost unanimously by the Fathers from the second to
the fifth century, and side by side with this, although to a lesser degree, the belief in the providential appointment of Balaam
as a prophet to the pagan world. Thus, Balaam was linked in early
Christian tradition with the Epiphany star and the Christmas celebration. Concurrent with this positive valuation, however, ran
the view of Balaam as villain and false prophet. It would seem
that neither image ever wholly superseded the other; they continued to exist side by side into the medieval period. In the popular mind, as evidenced in medieval art and drama, Balaam remained
a prophet of Christ and the forebear of the Magi; in theological
writings he was always the archetypal villain, momentarily inspired, through no merit of his own, with the Holy Spirit.[179]

CONCLUSION

In rabbinic interpretation, Job, Jethro and Balaam came to
assume typical roles, ultimately separate from their biblical contexts. As Pharaoh's counsellors, each became a model of one kind
of gentile the Rabbis encountered or postulated: Job epitomized
the righteous gentile, Jethro the proselyte to Judaism, and Balaam
the villain and failed prophet. Rabbinic exegesis of these symbolic figures, therefore, goes beyond an elucidation of the passages in which they appear to a general revelation of views about
gentiles. Although these opinions were never wholly static, varying with time and circumstances, certain distinct and encompassing
trends emerge.

Generally, rabbinic attitudes towards gentiles are negative; at best, the prevailing stance is one of ambivalence, tem-
pered with suspicion. This posture is evident in the discussions
of Job, where we have seen the efforts to prove this model of
righteousness an Israelite; in the instance of Jethro, whose
praises are sung because the Rabbis believed he converted to Jewish belief and practice; and especially in the case of Balaam, who
becomes a symbol of every imagined evil of gentile society.

This jaundiced appraisal of the nations of the world is
found throughout rabbinic literature. Various reasons for this
mistrust have been discussed above; certainly, uneasiness in
regard to non-Jews is not surprising in light of Jewish experience
and history. Nevertheless, since God's universality was as essential an element of biblical religion and rabbinic theology as
Israel's particularity, rabbinic tradition was compelled to admit
the theoretical possibility of gentile righteousness. Although
rabbinic opinion was divided,[1] the Talmud states, as a majority
view, that gentile salvation is in fact possible.[2] This acknowledgement of virtue and redemption outside the Jewish fold is a
central and remarkable tenet of rabbinic Judaism. It is a consideration that colors the exegeses of Job, Jethro and Balaam.

Jethro escaped the criticism levelled against most gentiles, since the Rabbis believed he was a convert to Judaism.
Indeed, the enthusiasm with which Jethro is hailed in many
sources, and the favorable responses he elicited, are eloquent
testimony to the welcome accorded sincere proselytes. The elevation of Jethro, formerly a priest among his own people, to progenitor of illustrious Israelites, became an exegetical example,

particularly in times of intensive Jewish proselyte activity, of
the full honor bestowed upon the convert to Israel.[3] Remarks hostile to Jethro may reflect some residual rabbinic hostility to
gentiles regardless of their beliefs, but generally they stem from
particular historic periods and circumstances in which the Jewish
community had experienced hardship because of insincere proselytes.[4]

Comments on Balaam reflect rabbinic attitudes towards the
majority of gentiles. As a paradigmatic villain and personification of rabbinic perceptions of gentile idolatry and immorality,
he is also identified with other historical enemies of Israel.[5]
More than Jethro or Job, Balaam's role in rabbinic literature has
a certain immediacy. While it is doubtful that Balaam represents
Jesus in rabbinic writings, it seems likely that he does stand for
those who claim to have predicted the new religion, or to speak
for it. The denigration of this pagan seer has a special
urgency.[6]

Balaam also finds a place in rabbinic literature as one of
the gentile prophets. Biblical evidence makes clear that the
nations of the world were granted divinely inspired prophets; certainly the Rabbis did not deny that the Almighty had given the
nations an opportunity to deserve His favor. That they did not
prove worthy of such a boon is manifest in Balaam. Endowed with
God's word, he might have changed gentile ways, but instead suc-
cumbed to wickedness and ultimately forfeited his prophetic talents.[7] Not only did he fail to elevate gentile piety, he also
urged the nations to entrap Israel into idolatry through sexual
temptation.

In rabbinic eyes, then, Jethro and Balaam represent the
two ultimate options available to gentiles. Each figure epito-
mizes the potential for good or evil inherent in the gentile as
one of God's creatures. Jethro realizes his possibilities for
good by grasping the highest truth and becoming a convert to Judaism. Balaam, on the other hand, profanes both his intrinsic gifts
and prophetic abilities when he shuns the way to God and devotes
himself to encouraging immoral and idolatrous practices.

The man in the middle is Job. As the model of the righteous gentile, Job is evidence of the Rabbis' belief that one
could, in theory, live a life pleasing to God beyond the boundaries of Israel. The basically hostile rabbinic stance towards the
nations, however, is simultaneously reflected in those comments
that compare Job unfavorably with various Israelites. Thus, Job
is contrasted to his disadvantage with Abraham;[8] he does not bear

suffering as bravely as David or Hezekiah;[9] and he is deemed an undesirable husband for Jacob's daughter Dinah.[10] Nor is Job's righteousness left unquestioned: the Rabbis could not accept the premise that Job's torments were undeserved, and went to great lengths to explain his misdeeds.[11] The Job who emerges from these revisions is a rather ambiguous figure. At best, he is a fallible man whose punishments were merited; at worst, he is a hardened sinner who receives his reward in this world so that he might be excluded from the world to come.[12] That many of those Rabbis who still found Job worthy of praise felt compelled to represent him as an Israelite demonstrates the extent to which rabbinic Judaism, although prepared to admit the theoretical existence of worthy gentiles, in practice rarely found such righteousness. True religiosity and virtue expressed themselves in conversion to Judaism's beliefs and practices.

Patristic views of gentiles are clearcut. Early Christianity approached all gentile nations as potential converts; those of the nations who could be shown to have lived in a godly way even before the Incarnation, were also reckoned among the witnesses to Christ. These onetime citizens of the earthly city of God now share in the glories of its celestial counterpart. In typological terms, such righteous gentiles are exemplars of the gentile Church, or representatives of the gentile prophets to the nations. Augustine's idea that it is not incongruous to believe that the coming of Christ was revealed to certain gentiles as well as to certain Jews was typical.[13] Nor, as he maintained, could it be denied "that there have been certain men even of other nations [than Israel] who belonged, not be earthly but heavenly fellowship to the true Israelites, the citizens of the country that is above."[14]

Job was of great importance to Christian exegesis and spiritual literature, both as a member of the true Israel that existed before the Incarnation, and as a type of the suffering Christ.[15] He was proof that the gentiles produced righteous and worthy men long before the Christian dispensation. Job's fortitude in suffering was praised as the model to be followed by all Christians,[16] just as his trials were believed to have foreshadowed those of Christ. His restoration was a clear indication to the gentiles of the salvation that Christianity could offer them, and of the honor the Church gave the righteous of the nations.[17]

Jethro is not a figure of importance in patristic exegesis. While Christian writers were eager to include in the community of the true Israel those gentiles of the Hebrew Bible

who are described as praising or offering sacrifices to the one
God, their reaction to Jethro was nevertheless highly tentative.
Since he was not mentioned with other righteous gentiles in the
New Testament, nor ever connected with Hobab or his Kenite descendants, his status remained undefined. Augustine is not sure if
Jethro truly sacrificed to God, or if instead offerings were made
in his honor by Moses.[18] Christian exegetes who considered Jethro
were reluctant to proclaim him either a convert to true religion,
or to include him among the band of saintly pagans. At best,
Jethro was praised for his advice to Moses, and was described as a
man who typified the value the Church could find in the wisdom of
the gentile nations.[19] In his case, we do not see a reflection of
Christian attitudes towards gentiles, but an apparent opportunity
to express such views that was forgone.

In Balaam's prophecy of Numbers 24:17, Christian commentators found a true prediction of the coming of Christ. They could
not, however, discount the biblical evidence of Balaam's wrongdoings, and had to face the dilemma of how to approach an unworthy
prophet. Some commentators solved the difficulty by citing the
prophecy apart from its source.[20] Others, like Origen, held that
Balaam had prophesied with his lips, but not with his heart, and
was therefore not a true prophet.[21] Jerome believed that Balaam
was a righteous prophet who had been led into sin and disgrace by
his avaricious desire for gain.[22] Yet, despite these different
appraisals of his character, Balaam's prophecy was universally
cited in early Christianity. Through the connection of his prophesied star with that followed by the Magi, Balaam was credited
with special disciples, and became a model of the gentile prophet
of Christ who guides the nations to true religion.[23] According to
Origen, in fact, through these illustrious descendants Balaam himself found a measure of redemption.[24]

The differing attitudes towards the gentiles expressed by
Jewish and Christian exegetes are a vivid reflection of the very
different outlooks and expectations of the two religions. Christian exegesis of Job, Jethro and Balaam affirms the conviction
that some gentiles were members of the true Israel long before the
Incarnation, and it reiterates as well the welcome gentile converts will always be accorded in Christianity. Such commentary
also acknowledges the wisdom of the gentile world and its contributions to Christian life and doctrine. That the gentile Job was
typified as a biblical prefiguration of the suffering Christ was a
final Christian celebration of its gentile origins and destiny.
Rabbinic literature is less sanguine about the prevalence of

gentile virtue. Only the sincere convert to Judaism is whole-
heartedly approved. Nevertheless, it is striking that it is the
Rabbis who admit the possibility of enduring gentile righteousness
outside of Judaism, while the more particularistic Church allowed
no salvation beyond the Christian sphere.

    Patristic parallels to rabbinic exegesis have long been
noted; many have been pointed out in the course of this study.[25]
They are found especially in the works of Origen and Jerome, both
of whom knew Hebrew and consulted contemporary Rabbis when they
encountered difficulties, particularly when they encountered a
textual problem, whether of Job's origin and era, or the meaning
of Balaam's prophecies.[26] While resulting rabbinic-patristic parallels are indicative of intellectual contacts between Jews and
Christians, their importance should not be exaggerated. Jewish
borrowings never played an important part in Christian exegesis
because they are not central to the Christian commentator's major
concerns. They flesh out his biblical portraits, they provide
guidance on difficult passages, but they do not affect his theme
or direction. Christian indifference to Jethro, so important in
rabbinic tradition, illustrates patristic ignorance of, or at
least lack of interest in, major rabbinic interpretive trends.

    Christian influences on rabbinic exegesis have been
pointed out far less frequently, even though they usually are more
indicative of the state of rabbinic-patristic relations. In the
rabbinic interpretations of both Job and Balaam reactions to such
non-Jewish commentary strongly influence the direction the rabbinic traditions take. In both cases the rabbinic stance is
defensive. The intensity with which some Palestinian Amoraim
insist on Job's Israelite origin, for instance, despite evidence
of earlier rabbinic praise of Job as a gentile, seems in great
part to be a reaction to Christian glorification of Job as a gentile saint and precursor of Christ.[27] Jerome, in fact, corrobor-
ates that Job was at the center of Jewish-Christian debate, when
he mentions that the Rabbi he engaged to teach him Jewish traditions about Job was insistent on Job's Israelite identity.[28]
Similarly, the vehemence with which the Rabbis attack Balaam is
comprehensible only if it is understood as a response to widespread Christian use of Balaam's prophecies as predictions fulfilled by the coming of Christ. Far worse biblical enemies of
Israel do not receive a fraction of the calumnies heaped on
Balaam.[29] Christian reactions to these attacks may in turn be
seen in the tendencies of some patristic exegetes to quote
Balaam's prophecy without attribution.[30] These two examples

indicate that in certain times and places, most especially Palestine of the third, fourth and fifth centuries of our era, some
Rabbis were aware of and combatted through their exegeses various
claims of the Christian Church which were seen as threatening to
Judaism.

Ultimately, however, the differences between rabbinic and
patristic biblical interpretations are far greater than their
points of contact. The contrasting principles and aims that
inform these two bodies of commentary account for the vast differences in the interpretations of Job, Jethro and Balaam. On the
whole, rabbinic exegetes approached biblical narratives in a
straightforward spirit of investigation. Their knowledge of all
of biblical literature was thorough, their belief in its unity
unshakeable. Drawing on this broad knowledge, and on the conviction that the Bible contained all of human history and knowledge,
they attempted to fill in any textual gaps, resolve any apparent
contradictions and discover whatever applications, legal or homiletical, were suggested by the text. Biblical characters could
become types of various qualities or characteristics; entire his-
tories were woven to explain an inconsistency or unusual phrase.
Yet while rabbinic exegesis may occasionally seem fanciful, it is
always prompted by biblical cues, and supported, at least ini-
tially, by biblical proofs. These processes are manifest in the
rabbinic portraits of Job, Jethro and Balaam.

Christian exegetes approached the Hebrew Bible more pur-
posefully. If their aim was not always to proselytise, it was at
least to buttress the beliefs of the faithful. A first desidera-
tum was to prove that the New Testament found its preparation and
prefigurement in the Old, which it in turn completed. Overall,
Christian interpretation was christologically oriented: each biblical passage was examined for what it might reveal about the life
of Jesus and his teachings, or the spiritual state most proper to
the individual Christian. Jewish exegesis was never without its
homiletical component; Christian exegesis, however, consciously
attempted to find spiritual sustenance everywhere in Scripture.
The best patristic exegetes considered the literal import of the
text as well, but their major concern was always with a passage's
typological or allegorical significance. A figure like Jethro,
therefore, who was not seen to point to anything beyond himself,
was of scant interest to the patristic commentator. Balaam found
his major place as a prophet of Christ and founder of the Magi.
And Job, as a type of the suffering Christ, provided especially
fertile ground for the flowering of Christian allegory.

Rabbinic and patristic exegetes shared a common text, the Hebrew Scriptures, and frequently reached similar assessments of biblical characters and situations. Yet an exegete cannot but bring his own beliefs and preconceptions, and those of his society, to the biblical text he hopes to elucidate. It would be difficult indeed to understand any biblical commentary if one were ignorant of the interpreter's special convictions and concerns. This work, therefore, has studied the Jewish and Christian exegesis of Job, Jethro and Balaam in the context of rabbinic and patristic attitudes towards gentiles, and has found an eloquent guide not only to the letter and spirit of the Hebrew Bible itself, but to the minds, beliefs and differences of some of its most devoted expositors.

ABBREVIATIONS

AB	*The Anchor Bible*
'Abod. Zar.	*'Aboda Zara*
ANF	*The Ante-Nicene Fathers*
Apoc. Paul	*Apocalypse of Paul*
'Abot R. Nat.	*'Abot de Rabbi Nathan*
B.	*Babylonian Talmud*
BA	*Biblical Archaeologist*
B. Bat.	*Baba Batra*
B. Qam.	*Baba Qamma*
Ber.	*Berakot*
Bib. Ant.	*Biblical Antiquities of Pseudo-Philo*
Bik.	*Bikkurim*
CBQ	*Catholic Biblical Quarterly*
CBQMS	*Catholic Biblical Quarterly Monograph Series*
CC	*Corpus Christianorum.* Series latina.
CCAR Yearbook	*Central Conference of American Rabbis Yearbook*
CHB	*Cambridge History of the Bible*
Deut. Rab.	*Deuteronomy Rabbah*
Eccl. Rab.	*Ecclesiastes Rabbah*
'Ed.	*'Eduyyot*
EJ	*Encyclopedia Judaica*
Exod. Rab.	*Exodus Rabbah*
F of Ch	*A Library of Fathers of the Holy Catholic Church*
Gen. Rab.	*Genesis Rabbah*
Giṭ.	*Giṭṭin*
HTR	*Harvard Theological Review*
HUCA	*Hebrew Union College Annual*
Ḥag.	*Ḥagiga*
IDB	*Interpreter's Dictionary of the Bible*
J.	*Jerusalem Talmud*
JAOS	*Journal of the American Oriental Society*
JBL	*Journal of Biblical Literature*
JE	*Jewish Encyclopedia*
JNES	*Journal of Near Eastern Studies*
JPS	*Jewish Publication Society*
JQR	*Jewish Quarterly Review*
JR	*Journal of Religion*
J. Ant.	*Jewish Antiquities of Flavius Josephus*

Ker.	*Keritot*
LCL	*Loeb Classical Library*
Lev. Rab.	*Leviticus Rabbah*
M.	*Mishnah*
Meg.	*Megilla*
Mek.	*Mekilta de-Rabbi Ishmael*
Mek. RS	*Mekilta de-Rabbi Simeon*
Midr. Teh.	*Midrash Tehillim*
Mish. R. El.	*Mishnat Rabbi Eliezer*
NovTSup	*Novum Testamentum Supplements*
NPNF	*A Select Library of the Nicene and Post-Nicene Fathers*
Ned.	*Nedarim*
Nid.	*Niddah*
Num. Rab.	*Numbers Rabbah*
PG	*Patrologia Graeca*
PL	*Patrologia Latina*
Pesaḥ.	*Pesaḥim*
Pesiq. Rab Kah.	*Pesiqta deRab Kahana*
Pesiq. R.	*Pesiqta Rabbati*
Pirqe R. El.	*Pirqe Rabbi Eliezer*
Praep. Evang.	*Praeparatio Evangelica*
4QTestim	*Testimonia Text* from Qumran Cave 4
RB	*Revue Biblique*
RHPR	*Revue d'histoire et de philosophie religieuses*
RHR	*Revue de l'histoire des religions*
RQ	*Römische Quartalschrift für christliche Alter-tumskunde und Kirchengeschichte*
RSV	Revised Standard Version
SBLMS	*Society for Biblical Literature Monograph Series*
SC	*Sources chrétiennes*
S. 'Olam Rab.	*Seder 'Olam Rabbah*
Sabb.	*Sabbat*
Sanh.	*Sanhedrin*
Sem	*Semitica*
Sem.	*Semaḥot*
SH	*Studia Hierosolymitana*
Sipre Deut.	*Sipre Deuteronomy*
Sipre Num.	*Sipre Numbers*
SP	*Studia Patristica*
T.	*Tosepta*
Ta'an.	*Ta'anit*

Tanḥ.	*Tanḥuma*
Tanḥ. B.	*Tanḥuma*, ed. S. Buber
Tar	*Tarbiz*
Test. Job	*Testament of Job*
Texts T	*Society for Biblical Literature Texts and Translations*
Tg. Onq.	*Targum Onqelos*
Tg. Ps.-J.	*Targum Pseudo-Jonathan*
Tg. Yer.	*Targum Yerushalmi*
VC	*Vigiliae Christianae*
Yebam.	*Yebamot*
Zebaḥ.	*Zebaḥim*

[1]References to Job, Jethro and Balaam as Pharaoh's counsellors are found in *B. Soṭa* 11a, *B. Sanh.* 106a, and *Exod. Rab.* 1:9.

[2]See, for example, Louis Ginzberg, *Die Haggada bei den Kirchenvätern* (Amsterdam, 1899; and in numerous supplements through 1935); Gustave Bardy, "Les traditions juives dans l'oeuvre d'Origène," *RB* 34 (1925) 217-252; and Raphael Loewe, "The Jewish Midrashim and Patristic and Scholastic Exegesis of the Bible," *SP* 1 (1957) 492-512. Jay Braverman's *Jerome's 'Commentary on Daniel': A Study of Comparative Jewish and Christian Interpretations of the Hebrew Bible CBQMS* 7 (Washington, D.C., 1978), also takes a similar approach. A limited but useful bibliography of works in this area is Emilien Lamirande,"Etude bibliographique sur les pères de l'Eglise et l'aggadah" *VC* 21 (1967) 1-11. Several recent works which consider a particular Church Father's use of rabbinic sources against the wider background of Jewish-Christian cultural and intellectual contacts are N. R. M. de Lange, *Origen and the Jews. Studies in Jewish-Christian Relations in Third-Century Palestine* (Cambridge, 1976); Jacob Neusner, *Aphrahat and Judaism. The Christian-Jewish Argument in Fourth-Century Iran* (Leiden, 1971); and R. L. Wilken, *Judaism and the Early Christian Mind. A Study of Cyril of Alexandria's Exegesis and Theology* (New Haven, 1971).

[3]See, however, Marcel Simon, *Verus Israel. Etude sur les relations entre Chrétiens et Juifs dans l'Empire Romain 135-425* (Paris, 1948); and "Melchisédech dans la polémique entre juifs et chrétiens et dans la legende" *RHPR* 17 (1937) 58-93; Ephraim Urbach, "Homilies of the Rabbis on the Prophets of the Nations and the Balaam Stories," *Tar* 25 (1955-56) 272-289 [Hebrew], English summary iii-vii; and "The Homiletical Interpretations of the Sages and the Expositions of Origen on Canticles and the Jewish-Christian Disputation," *SH* 22 (1971) 247-275; and Reuven Kimelman, "Rabbi Yoḥanan and Origen on the Song of Songs: A Third Century Jewish-Christian Disputation," *HTR* 73 (1980) 567-595.

[4]Viktor Aptowitzer, *Kain und Abel in der Agadah, den Apokryphen, der hellenistischen, christlichen und muhammedanischen Literatur* (Vienna and Leipzig, 1922).

[5]Samuel Sandmel, *Philo's Place in Judaism: A Study of Conceptions of Abraham in Jewish Literature* (New York, 1956, 1971).

[6]Jack P. Lewis, *A Study of the Interpretation of Noah and the Flood in Jewish and Christian Literature* (Leiden, 1968).

[7]A.F.J. Klijn, *Seth in Jewish, Christian and Gnostic Literature. NovTSup.* 46 (Leiden, 1977); Steven D. Fraade,*Enosh and his Generation: Pre-Israelite Hero and History in Post-biblical Interpretation SBLMS* (Chico, Ca., forthcoming).

[8]Herman Ezekiel Kaufmann, *Die Anwendung das Buches Hiob in der Rabbinischen Agadah* (Frankfurt am Main, 1893).

[9]Nahum Glatzer, "The Book of Job and its Interpreters," *Biblical Motifs. Origins and Transformations* (ed. Alexander

Altmann; Cambridge, Mass., 1966) 197-220; and *The Dimensions of Job. A Study and Selected Readings* (New York, 1969).

[10]Lawrence Besserman, *The Legend of Job in the Middle Ages* (Cambridge, Mass., 1979).

[11]Günther Datz, *Die Gestalt Hiobs in der Kirchlichen Exegese und der Arme Heinrich Hartmanns von Aue* (Goppingen, 1973).

[12]Bernard Bamberger, *Proselytism in the Talmudic Period* (Cincinnati, 1939), 182-91; 182.

[13]Geza Vermes, *Scripture and Tradition in Judaism* (Leiden, 1961).

[14]E. Kirschbaum, "Der Prophet Balaam und die Anbetung der Weisen," *RQ* 49 (1954) 129-171.

[15]Jay Braverman, "Balaam in Rabbinic and Early Christian Tradition," *Joshua Finkel Festschrift* (ed. Sidney B. Hoenig and Leon D. Stitskin; New York, 1974) 41-50.

[16]Urbach, "Homilies of the Rabbis." A recent article which traces traditions about Balaam in Islam is Heinrich Schützinger, "Die arabische Bileam-Erzählung. Ihre Quellen und ihre Entwicklung," *Der Islam* 59 (1982) 195-221.

[17]See, for example, Elie Benamozegh, *Israël et Humanité: Etude sur le Problème de la Religion Universelle et sa Solution* (Paris, 1914); Alfred Bertholet, *Die Stellung der Israeliten und Juden zu den Fremden* (Freiburg and Leipzig, 1896); and Joseph Bloch, *Israel and the Nations* (Berlin-Vienna, 1927). See, also, Jacob Z. Lauterbach, "The Attitude of the Jew towards the Non-Jew," *CCAR Yearbook* 31 (1921) 186-233.

[18]Samuel Hugo Bergman, "Israel and the Oikumene," *Studies in Rationalism, Judaism and Universalism. In Memory of Leon Roth* (ed. R. Loewe; London, New York, 1966) 47-65.

[19]Moshe Greenberg, "Mankind, Israel and the Nations in the Hebraic Heritage," *No Man is Alien. Essays on the Unity of Mankind* (ed. J. Robert Nelson; Leiden, 1971) 15-40.

[20]Hans Joachim Schoeps, *The Jewish-Christian Argument. A History of Theologies in Conflict* (London, 1963).

[1]Marvin Pope, *Job. A New Translation and Commentary. AB* (New York, 1973), 3-4. Pope discusses the evidence for the location of Job's homeland and concludes that it appears impossible to reconcile the conflicting claims and opinions as to the exact location of the land of Uz.

[2]For discussions of biblical, and also rabbinic, attitudes towards gentiles, see E.J. Hamlin, "Nations," *IDB* 3. 515-523; "Gentiles," *EJ*; Introduction, notes 17-20; and below, 8-9.

[3]Hamlin, "Nations," contrasts various biblical trends, 518-520.

[4]Pope, *Job*, xxiii-xxx, notes that scholars agree that there are at least two distinct elements in the book, probably of separate origin. A prologue and epilogue, Job 1,2 and 42:7-17, differ in style and content from the main body of the text, the poetic dialogue between Job and his companions. These framing chapters would seem to be the remnants of an ancient folktale describing a righteous sufferer, Job, who maintained his faith in God throughout unwarranted torments, and who was eventually rewarded with the restitution of his health, prosperity and family. It is likely that the only other mention of Job in the Hebrew Bible, Ezek 14:14-20, refers to this ancient and doubtless well-known tale. The poetic dialogues which occupy the body of the book are a far more sophisticated and complex literary achievement. Shalom Spiegel, "Noah, Danel and Job, touching on Canaanite Relics in the Legends of the Jews," *Louis Ginzberg Jubilee Volume. English Section* (New York, 1945) 305-357, suggests, p. 333, that the author of the dialogues deliberately chose this simple and popular legend as a base from which to explore in his own way the problem of "unmerited suffering." Pope agrees, p. xxxvii, writing that "The author of the Dialogue, as well as the later editors and redactors, may have made considerable changes in the ancient folktale of Job, but have retained the chief features of a story already well-known."

[5]Robert Gordis, *The Book of Man and God* (Chicago and London, 1965) 220. Gordis goes on to note: "This fact undoubtedly explains the relative ease with which the book was accepted by all groups in Judaism. With little or no opposition it was canonized as Holy Scripture, was speedily translated into the languages spoken in Palestine and the Diaspora, and was elaborated upon in post-biblical literature." Gordis also points out, p. 221, that unlike other disputed biblical books, Job "alone contained the words of the Lord himself, speaking out of the whirlwind (Job 38:1 ff). Here was no mere human voice, prone to error, but God himself, speaking to man."

[6]*Sipra*, Kedoshim 4.12 (Weiss, 89b).

[7]These precepts can be found in *B. Sanh.* 56a, and in *Gen. Rab.* 16:16 and 34:19.

[8]Thus, commenting on "You must keep my rulings," (Lev 18:5), *Sipra*, Aḥarei Mot 13:10 (Weiss, 86a) records: "This refers to injunctions of the Torah, which had they not been written in it, by right should have been written, such as prohibition of robbery, incest, idolatry, blasphemy and homicide."

[9]Moshe Greenberg, "Mankind, Israel and the Nations in the Hebraic Heritage," *No Man is Alien. Essays on the Unity of Mankind* (ed. J. Robert Nelson; Leiden, 1971) 15-40, 33. Victor Tcherikover, "Social Conditions," *The Hellenistic Age. World History of the Jewish People* 6 (ed. A. Schalit; New Brunswick, N.J., 1972) 87-114, has written, pp. 87-89, of the changes in the makeup of the population of Palestine in the hellenistic period: "From the time of Alexander the Great, Judea was open to immigrants from Western countries; peoples of diverse origins settled or visited there. Inevitably, the native population noticed and sometimes absorbed foreign mores, as the process of the fusion of Eastern and Western elements progressed. The social and religious changes and dislocations these events wrought profoundly threatened Jewish life and institutions." And Ephraim Urbach, *The Sages. Their Concepts and Beliefs* (2 vols.; Jerusalem, 1975), writes 1.545-546, of a somewhat later period: "For about a hundred and fifty years, from after the Revolt of Bar Kokhba until Christianity became dominant in the Roman Empire, the Sages of Israel stood embattled on two fronts—one facing them and the other at the rear. They joined issue with the pagans, who proceeded to negate Israel's election with politico-territorial arguments . . . and they polemicized against the Christians, who boasted that they had inherited the election-birthright of the Jewish people and its covenant with its God, as well as the accompanying spiritual attributes, precisely because they were 'not a people' but a 'church of the peoples'."

[10]Greenberg, "Israel and the Nations," 31-33. He points out, p. 33, the rabbinic conviction that a proper aim of the Torah was to establish harmony among all men. When a situation arises in which harmony between Jew and gentile could be furthered, to do so becomes a dictate of the Torah: "Thus, even when intercommunal hostility alienated Jews from gentiles, Jewish thinkers and legists applied the grand principles of sanctification of God's name, imitation of God, and harmony among men to create unilateral obligations towards the gentiles—obligations that did not depend on reciprocity."

[11]On the two separate elements in the Book of Job, see above, 8, notes 4, 5.

[12]This study is concerned with rabbinic remarks on the figure of Job. For rabbinic commentary on the book as a whole, see Herman Ezekiel Kaufmann, *Die Anwendung das Buches Hiob in der Rabbinischen Agadah* (Frankfurt am Main, 1893); and *Majan-Gannim. Commentary on Job of Rabbi Samuel ben Nissim Masnuth* (ed. Solomon Buber; Berlin, 1889). This twelfth century commentary gathers rabbinic remarks from the Talmud and midrash on each chapter and verse of the Book of Job.

[13]Nahum Glatzer, "The Book of Job and its Interpreters," *Biblical Motifs. Origins and Transformations* (ed. Alexander Altmann; Cambridge, Mass., 1966) 197-220, writes, p. 197: "The figure of Job, more so than others in the Bible lent itself to a considerable diversity of interpretations. The reasons for this are to be sought in the variety of views reposed in the book itself, in its position in the biblical canon, and last, but not least, in the multifariousness of motifs employed in the Talmudic-Midrashic literature in its presentation of Job . . . Such latitude permitted remarkable freedom of interpretation and provoked the conception of a number of self-contained compositions in which Job appears as a symbolic representation of a particular attitude to God and the world."

[14]See dispute recorded above on 9.

[15]See below, 22-24.

[16]See below, 24-26.

[17]On Job as one of Pharaoh's counsellors, see below, 15-16.

[18]*S. 'Olam Rab*. 3; also *J. Soṭa* 20c which recounts: "R. Jose b. Ḥalafta [fl. 135-170 CE] said: Job was born at the moment of the descent into Egypt, and at the time of the return from Egypt he died."   The evidence that Israel's stay in Egypt was 210 years comes from a rabbinic consideration of God's pledge to Abraham, "Know of a surety that thy seed shall be a stranger in a land that is not theirs, and shall serve them: And they shall afflict them four hundred years" (Gen 15:13). The prevailing view was that the 400 years prophesied in Gen 15:13 referred not only to the slavery in Egypt, but to all the time that Israel spent in a land which was not their own. Thus, the 400 years began with the birth of Isaac. According to calculations based on the ages of Isaac and his descendants, the total period Israel spent in Egypt was only 210 years. Louis Ginzberg, *The Legends of the Jews* (7 vols.; Philadelphia, 1925, 1953) 5. 420, n. 126, writes: "The rabbinic literature offers many solutions of the contradiction between Genesis 15:13, and 'Now the time that the children of Israel dwelt in Egypt was four hundred and thirty years' (Exod 12:40). The prevalent view is that the slavery of Abraham's descendants began with the birth of Isaac (*Mek*. Bo 14 [Horovitz-Rabin,151]: Mek. *RS* 27; *S. 'Olam Rab*. 3; *Pirqe R. El*. 8; *Tg. Yer*. to Exod 12:40), while their stay in Egypt amounted to only two hundred and ten years (according to some, two hundred and four years), of which eighty-three (*Pirqe R. El*.) or eighty-seven (S. 'Olam Rab.) were years of suffering."

[19]*S. 'Olam Rab*. 3.

[20]*B. B. Bat*. 15a.

[21]*S. 'Olam Rab*. 21; also *B. B. Bat*. 15b.

[22]For a discussion of rabbinic views on prophecy and the role of the gentile prophet, see below, chapter 3.

[23]Rabbinic suggestions as to when Job lived are as follows:

a) the time of Abraham, see 13.

b) the time of Jacob, see 13.

c) the time of the servitude of the Israelites in Egypt, and the time of the spies, see 11-13.

d) the days of the judges: "R. Eliezer" (*B. B. Bat*. 15b), "said that Job was in the days of the judges, as it says, 'Behold all of you together have seen it: Why then are ye become altogether vain?' (Job 27:12). What generation is it that is altogether vain? You must say, the generation when there is a judging of the judges;" (that is, when the judges no longer inspire respect in the people).

e) the time of the kingdom of Sheba. R. Nathan (fl. 135-170 CE) says, in *B. B. Bat.* 15b, that Job was in the time of the kingdom of Sheba, since Job 1:15 recounts: "The Sabeans fell on them and took them away."

f) the time of the kingdom of the Chaldeans, *B. B. Bat.* 15b records the following tradition: "The sages said that he was in the time of the Chaldeans, as it is written, "The Chaldeans made three bands" (Job 1:17).

g) the time of Ahasuerus, *B. B. Bat.* 15b quotes R. Joshua b. Korḥah (fl. 135-170 CE) as saying, "Job was in the time of Ahasuerus, for it says, 'And in all the land were no women found so fair as the daughters of Job' (Job 42:15). What was the generation in which fair women were sought out? You must say this was the generation of Ahasuerus," and see 21.

h) the time of the return from the exile in Babylon, see 14.

i) Job never existed at all, but his story is told as a parable to teach the virtue of resignation. *B. B. Bat.* 15a records the following tradition: A certain rabbi was sitting before R. Samuel b. Naḥmani [fl. 250-290 CE] and in the course of his exposition remarked, "Job never was and never existed, but is only a parable." He replied: "To confute such as you the text says, 'There was a man in the land of Uz, Job was his name' (Job 1:1)." But [the first rabbi] retorted, "If that is so, what of the verse [from Nathan's parable to David] 'The poor man had nothing save one poor ewe lamb, which he had brought up and nourished,' etc. (2 Sam 12:3)." The remark that Job never existed was disturbing to most of the Rabbis, for it seemed to deny scriptural evidence. Thus, it is presented in a modified and more acceptable form in *J. Soṭa* 20d, and in *Gen. Rab.* 57:4. In these locations it is attributed to R. Simeon b. Lakish (fl. 250-290 CE), and refuted as follows: "This view of Resh Lakish is self-contradictory, for elsewhere he said in the name of Bar Kapparah [fl. 200-220 CE], 'he flourished in the days of Abraham.' Now he denies his existence!" What Resh Lakish really meant, according to these sources, is that Job did exist but all his sufferings did not take place. They are described to teach that if they had come upon him he would have been able to stand them. Thus, the descriptions of his resignation in suffering are meant to be a model to all God-fearing men.

[24]If Job did in fact live from the time of the entry of Israel into Egypt until her redemption from slavery, then the rabbinic sources would not be wholly inconsistent in claiming Job as a contemporary of both Jacob and Moses. The tradition that Job married Dinah is also preserved in the pseudepigraphical *Test. Job*, see below, 30-32.

[25]*B. B. Bat.* 15b. Responding to this inclusion of Elihu in the list of gentile prophets, one Rabbi said: "Granted as you say that Job was one of these, was not Elihu, the son of Barachel, from Israel, seeing that Scripture mentions that he was from the family of Ram? Had he not been from Israel, his genealogy would not have been given. Evidently, the reason why he is included is because he prophesied to the heathen. So too, Job is included because he prophesied to the heathen, although he himself was an Israelite. But did not all the prophets prophesy to the heathens? Their prophecies were addressed primarily to Israel, but these addressed themselves primarily to the heathen."

[26]In *J. Soṭa* 20c, R. Johanan is also quoted as declaring that Job was an Israelite and among the exiles who returned from Babylon. On R. Johanan's approach to Job, see below, 24, notes 66-69.

[27]Urbach, *The Sages*, 1.411.

[28]*Gen. Rab.* 22:1 In *Tanḥ*. B.: Lev. 9, and *Tanḥ*. B.: Num. 157, Obadiah is also listed as one of the men who were called "God-fearing." In *Deut. Rab.* 2:4, Job is called the most pious gentile who ever lived, and in *'Abot R. Nat.* B 43, he is listed among the eighteen servants of God.

[29]*'Abot R. Nat.* 2, on the statement, "And make a hedge about the Torah," (*M. 'Abot* 1:1). Compare *M. Ned.* 3:11 for the same understanding of חם . Marcel Simon, *Verus Israel. Etude sur les relations entre Chrétiens et Juifs dans l'Empire Romain 135-425* (Paris, 1948) 226, discusses the significance of being born circumcised in the context of Jewish/Christian debate. To counter the Christian argument that before Moses gave the law just and great men had lived without its observance and in particular without circumcision, the Rabbis responded that many among the righteous before Moses had been born circumcised, and that Abraham, for one, had anticipated the law and observed it in all its details. (See *Pesiq. R.* 28:1, 28.5; *Gen. Rab.* 11:46; *Num. Rab.* 14:9). Thus, the statement that Job was born circumcised takes on polemical overtones. The Rabbis who made it were, in effect, claiming Job as an Israelite against Christians who were placing him among the righteous gentile witnesses of Christ.

[30]*'Abot R. Nat.* 2: "What is the hedge which Job made about his words: Lo, it says, 'A wholehearted and an upright man, one that feareth God and shunneth evil' (Job 1:8). This teaches that Job kept himself far from things which lead to transgression, from what is hideous, and from whatever seems hideous."

[31]This tradition is also found in *B. B. Bat.* 16a. A similar passage in *B. Meg.* 28a reads: "Job was generous with his money; he used to leave with the shopkeeper a פרוטה of his change." Traditions about Job's generosity and hospitality also found their way into Christian sources; see below, p. 36 and n. 122. This trend to praise Job culminates in the pseudepigraphical *Test. Job* (see below, 30-32), as well as in a medieval addendum to *'Abot R. Nat.* (see below, n. 106).

[32]*M. 'Abot* 4:15.

[33]The belief in unswerving divine justice is a basic assumption of rabbinic theology. The *Mek.* Be-Shallaḥ 6 (Horovitz-Rabin, 112) records that the Sage Pappias (fl. 80-110 CE) once expressed views implying a certain arbitrariness on the part of God on the authority of "But He is at one with Himself, and who can turn Him? / And what His soul desireth, even that He doeth" (Job 23:13). He was severely rebuked by R. Akiba (fl. 110-135 CE), who said: "There is nothing to answer the words of Him by whose word the world was called into existence, for He judges all in truth and everything in judgement." A later Rabbi is quoted in *B. B. Qam.* 50a: "He who says the Holy One, blessed by He, is lax in dealing out justice, let his life disintegrate. He is longsuffering but collects his debt in the end."

[34]On Job as one of Pharoah's counsellors, see *B. Soṭa* 11a, *B. Sanh.* 106a, and *Exod. Rab.* 27:3.

[35]*Exod. Rab.* 21:7; *Gen. Rab.* 57:4; *J. Soṭa* 20d.

[36]*B. B. Bat.* 16a.

[37]*B. B. Bat.* 16a-16b, and *B. Nid.* 52b. A second pun accounts for the mentions of hair: "whirlwind," or "tempest," סערה, spelled differently means "hair" שׂערה .

[38]Some of the Rabbis do attempt to mitigate these harsh judgements, for as Gordis, *Book of Man*, points out, p. 222, "regardless of what Job may have said in his anger and suffering, in the end he is humbled by the display of God's omnipotence and admits his own ignorance and presumption." The Rabbis did not overlook this, which accounts for the following remarks. When Raba, in *B. B. Bat.* 16a, comments on "The earth is given into the hands of the wicked, He covereth the faces of the judges thereof: if it be not so, where and who is He?" (Job 9:24) that "Job sought to turn the dish upside down," that is, he attempted to declare all God's work worthless, Abaye (fl. 320-350 CE) responded that "Job was only referring to Satan." Raba himself admits, in *B. B. Bat.* 16a, that Job's impotent ranting teaches that a man is not held responsible for what he says in distress. Similarly, a comment in *Exod. Rab.* 14:11 teaches that Job finally came to his senses and recognized that God's greatness and power are indeed beyond human imagining. Of Elihu's remark to Job, "The Almighty, we cannot find Him, excellent in power" (Job 37:23), Judah Ha-Nasi (fl. 170-200 CE) said: We are indebted to Job, because he added to everything Elihu said. Job said to his companions, "Do you imagine that even all you said exhausts all His praise? Who can declare all the praises and the mighty deeds of the Lord? All the things you have said, why 'These are but the outskirts of his ways' (Job 26:14)."

[39]See also *Tanḥ.* B: Gen. 166, where Job is similarly compared unfavorably with various of the patriarchs. For like traditions, see below, 16-19.

[40]This teaching appears as well in *Gen. Rab.* 73:9, and *B. B. Bat.* 15b. See Ginzberg, *Legends*, 1.396.

[41]*'Abot R. Nat.* 2.

[42]*B.B. Bat.* 16a. Gordis, *Book of Man*, 224, explains this tendency as a fear that Job's righteousness might place the patriarch and other Jewish saints in the shade. Even more important, he believes, was the need to justify the suffering that God had brought upon Job. Thus, all of his faults and shortcomings were exaggerated. Marcel Simon, "Melchisédech dans la polémique entre juifs et chrétiens et dans la légende," *RHPR* 17 (1937) 58-93, shows a similar process at work in rabbinic remarks about Melchizedek. Early *midrashim* praise Melchizedek highly, and bring him into the fold of Israel by identifying him as Noah's son Shem. However, when Christian exegesis made Melchizedek into a prototype of Christ, a refuter of Jewish legalism and a symbol of the priest outside the Aaronic priesthood, the Amoraim began to diminish his virtues, especially in comparison with Abraham's. Simon comments, p. 66, on a constant rabbinic preoccupation with removing attributes and honors from Melchizedek and adding them to Abraham.
In amoraic times, in fact, Abraham came to represent the acme of human perfection. Alexander Altmann, in "*Homo Imago Dei* in Jewish and Christian Theology," *JR* 48 (1968) 235-259, has observed, p. 251, that in this period, "Abraham assumes the role which Christian theology assigned to Jesus." Reuven Kimelman,

"Rabbi Yoḥanan and Origen on the Song of Songs: A Third-Century Jewish-Christian Disputation," *HTR* 73 (1980) 567-595, 583-584, cites several rabbinic homilies which describe Abraham as "the greatest man among the giants," and hold that the world was created on his account. He notes, p. 584, that according to midrashic tradition, Abraham was the subject of Ps 110, a clear rabbinic response to the "quintessentially christological" reading of that psalm by the Church. Thus, the comparison of Abraham and Job also takes on polemical consideration if the gentile Job is seen as representing Christian claims. See below, 23-24.

[43]For the rabbinic view of Balaam, see below, ch. 3.

[44]*B. Soṭa* 31a. G.F. Moore, *Judaism in the First Centuries of the Christian Era* (2 vols.; Cambridge, Ma., 1927, 1931) 2. 98-99, writes that in the Hebrew Bible the religious attitude toward God which translates itself into a motive for doing his will is either the fear of God or the love of God: "In Deuteronomy, in particular, the two occur in exactly similar contexts, without any apparent consciousness of a difference between them, much less that they were conflicting." Such a distinction did come to be made by some of the Rabbis, however, who saw a difference between an obedience motivated by fear and one motivated by love, obedience motivated by love being superior. Thus *Sipre* on *Deut* 32 (Finkelstein, 54) declares: "The Scripture makes a difference between the man who acts from love and him who acts from fear, and the reward of the former is far greater than of the latter."

[45]Urbach, *The Sages*, 1.404.

[46]Urbach, 1.406.

[47]*Sem.* 8; *Midr. Teh.* 26:2.

[48]*M. 'Ed.* 2:10.

[49]J. *Ber.* 14b.

[50]R. Meir's statement, equating love of God with fear of God, in effect renders the dispute moot. A similar sentiment is expressed in *J. Soṭa* 20c: "In the name of R. Nathan they said: 'He also shall be my salvation, for an hypocrite shall not come before Him' (Job 13:16). A verse says, 'And thou shalt love the Lord thy God' (Deut 6:5), and another verse, the following, 'Thou shalt fear the Lord thy God and serve Him' (Deut 6:13). Thus, one should be impelled by both love and fear."

[51]Ginzberg, *Legends*, 5. 381-382, n. 3.

[52]Urbach, *The Sages*, 1.415.

[53]*J. Soṭa* 20d, and *Gen. Rab.* 57:4.

[54]*Tanḥ.* B.: Num. 132; *Gen. Rab. 20:1.*

[55]On *Test. Job*, and the *Life of Job* by Aristeas, see below, section (iii), 29-32.

[56]Marcel Simon, *Verus Israel*, and "Melchisédech dans la polémique." See also Yitzhak Baer, "Israel, the Christian Church, and the Roman Empire from the time of Septimus Severus to the Edict of Toleration," *SH* 7 (1961) 79-149; and A. Marmorstein, "Judaism and Christianity in the middle of the Third Century,"

HUCA 10 (1935) 223-263; H. J. Schoeps, *The Jewish-Christian Argument. A History of Theologies in Conflict* (London, 1963).

[57]For examples of such polemics, see A. Lukyn Williams,
*Adversus Judaeos; A Bird's Eye View of Christian Apologiae until
the Renaissance* (Cambridge, 1935).

[58]Simon, *Verus Israel*, 212, writes that Jerome was an
active participant in this learned polemic: "Son oeuvre
exégétique tout entière en porte la marque. Elle est nourrie de
traditions juives, qu'il a recueillies auprès des rabbins, ses
maîtres en exégèse et en hebreu."

[59]Simon, 222; and see his "Melchisédech."

[60]Simon, 222.

[61]See below, 32-35.

[62]See above, 12-13.

[63]John Bowker, *The Targums and Rabbinic Literature. An
Introduction to Jewish Interpretation of Scriptures* (Cambridge,
1969), 83, dates the compilation of *Song of Songs Rab.* as between
600 and 750. He notes that it primarily reflects Palestinian
traditions.

[64]Simon, *Verus Israel*, 228.

[65]On Melchizedek, see Simon, "Melchisédech"; and on Job,
see below, 23-24.

[66]Ronald Reuven Kimelman, *Rabbi Yoḥanan of Tiberias.
Aspects of the Social and Religious History of Third Century
Palestine* (unpublished Yale University dissertation, 1977), 257.
Also see Kimelman, "Rabbi Yohanan and Origen."

[67]Origen's knowledge and use of Jewish traditions is well-
known. See, most recently, N.R.M. de Lange, *Origen and the Jews:
Studies in Jewish-Christian Relations in Third-Century Palestine*
(Cambridge, 1975), and bibliography below.

[68]Kimelman, "Rabbi Yoḥanan and Origen," 569; and see
Kimelman's article, notes 1-4, for other scholarly work on this
particular subject.

[69]For some of R. Joḥanan's remarks about Job, see above,
14, n. 26; 17; and see below, 24-25. On 17 R. Joḥanan is quoted
from *Deut. Rab.* 2:4 as describing Job as the most righteous of
gentiles. This statement is so much at odds with R. Joḥanan's
comments about Job elsewhere that the attribution of the statement
must be called into question. Bowker, *Targums and Rabbinic Literature*, notes, p. 82, that *Deut. Rab.* in its present form is a late
compilation (probably tenth century), and that it does not "take
so much care as earlier works in preserving accurately the names
of authorities and sources." It seems likely that there is a mis-
attribution in this case.
      Origen discusses Job as a paragon of Christian patience
who did not sin against God despite his sufferings in his *Libellus
De Oratione* 30 (*PG* 11, col. 547).

[70]Origen, *Homilies on Ezek* 4 (*PG* 13, col. 699). In this
homily, Origen is discussing Ezek 14:14, the verse which links Job

with Noah and Daniel. Jay Braverman, *Jerome's 'Commentary on Daniel': A Study of Comparative Jewish and Christian Interpretations of the Hebrew Bible. CBQMS* 7 (Washington, D.C., 1978), 57-62, discusses several other rabbinic traditions which are prominent in this homily. See also A. Vaserstein, "A Rabbinic Midrash as a Source of Origen's Homily on Ezekiel," *Tar* 46 (1977) 317-318 [Hebrew]; English summary vi. For tannaitic citations that Job lived from the entry into Egypt until the Exodus, see above, 11-13, n. 18.

[71]Jerome, *Letter* 73 (*PL* 22, col. 677); italics are my own. For Jerome's comments on Job, see below, section iv, 38-40.

[72]See below, 38-39.

[73]For further discussion of the issue of Job's descent from Esau, see below, 29-31.
     Job continued to be a subject of Jewish-Christian debate in the Middle Ages. In Peter Abelard's *Dialogue of a Philosopher with a Jew and a Christian*, trans. Pierre J. Payer, *Medieval Sources in Translation* 20. Pontifical Institute of Medieval Studies (Toronto, 1979), the Philosopher (usually reckoned to be the spokesman for Abelard himself in the dialogue with the Jew [Payer, 11]), offers Job as an example of a man who lived and was justified by natural law, p. 42: "The pagan Job who, you do not doubt, lived after Abraham and without the Law, the Lord commanded so far as to say, 'that there is none on earth like him, blameless and upright, fearing God and avoiding evil' (Job 1:8). While demonstrating to us his own justice which we should imitate, Job makes no mention of the works of the Law, but only the works of the natural law of which natural reason itself convinces each and every one." The Jew responds, 52-53: "There are no grounds for your adducing the pagan Job as an example, since you cannot prove he was uncircumcised or that he lived after the institution of circumcision. For it is clear that just as Ishmael was circumcised by Abraham, so were Esau and Jacob, and both the outcast sons as well as the chosen were circumcised by the patriarchs according to the command of the Lord . . . We know that our people had many proselytes from the Gentiles who converted to the Law, and this surely not so much out of imitation of their parents as out of a kindred virtue. This could also have been the case with Job, who, we see, even offered sacrifices acceptable to God according to our practice for his sons as well as for his friends." It is interesting that the Jewish view on Job cited here is one that regards Job as linked in some way to the Jewish community, if not as an Israelite by birth then at least as a convert. I thank Professor Jaroslav Pelikan for bringing this reference to my attention.

[74]*B. Ber.* 17a.

[75]This homily also appears in *Pesiq. Rab Kah.* 16:6.

[76]For the *Test. Job*, see below, 30-32.

[77]On Jethro, see chapter 2.

[78]*T. Šabb.* 13:2, p. 128; quoted in Urbach, *The Sages*, 1.410, n. 60.

[79]Urbach, 1.410.

[80]Urbach, 1.411. On the Septuagint version of Job, see below, 28-30. As Urbach notes, 2.866, n. 63, "It is difficult to come to any definite conclusions regarding the character of the fragments of the Aramaic translation of Job discovered in Qumran, cave 11." Although this *Targum* is fragmentary (containing less than one-sixth of the biblical book), it clearly agrees in large part with the structure of the Hebrew text as we know it in the Masoretic version. The text has been published: J. van der Ploeg, A. van der Woude, *Le Targum de Job de la Grotte de Qumran* (Leiden, 1971). J. A. Fitzmeyer, "Some Observations on the Targum of Job from Qumran Cave 11," *CBQ* 36 (1974) 503-524, points out, p. 506, that the *Targum* bears witness to the importance of Job in the thought of the Qumran sect: "In one way or another, all three paradigms of righteousness, Noah, Daniel and Job, mentioned in Ezek 14:14, turn up as figures who fed the piety of the Qumran community."

Although the *Targum's* translation is, on the whole, a literal one, scholars such as Fitzmeyer; E. M. Tuinstra, *Hermeneutische Aspecten van de Targum van Job uit Grot XI van Qumran* (Groningen, Dissertation, 1971); A. Caquot, "Un écrit sectaire de Qumran: le 'Targum de Job'," *RHR* 185 (1974) 9-27; and Bruce Zuckerman, "The Process of Translation in *11QTGJOB*; *A Preliminary Study* (Yale University Dissertation, 1980), believe that the Job of the *Targum* seems more an innocent and humble sufferer than a complaining and questioning man broken by pain. Such a shift in emphasis would not be at variance with certain aspects of rabbinic, and as is discussed below, 29-31, non-rabbinic tradition.

[81]Gordis, *Book of Man*, 222.

[82]Pope, *Job*, xliv. He also points out, pp. xliii-xliv, that "A Coptic version of Job, published in 1899, agrees in the main with the pre-Origen text, generally omitting the passages which Origen marked with asterisks."

[83]Pope, xliv.

[84]Pope, xliii.

[85]Pope, xliv. Among those who share this view are Donald H. Gard, "The Concept of Job's Character According to the Greek Translator of the Hebrew Text," *JBL* 72 (1953) 182-186; G. Gerleman, *Book of Job. Studies in the Septuagint I* (Lund, 1946); and Urbach, *The Sages*, 1.411; 2.866, n. 66. Harry Orlinsky, "Studies in the Septuagint of the Book of Job," *HUCA* 28 (1957) 53-74; 29 (1958) 229-271; 30 (1959) 153-167; and 32 (1961) 239-268, rejects the view that the Septuagint translator was motivated by any given trend, and attempts to prove that the many divergences in the translation are due either to a Hebrew original differing from our present text, or to the character of the translator's particular style. Urbach, however, concludes after lengthy discussion, *The Sages*, 2.867, n. 66, that it is not possible to accept Orlinsky's general thesis concerning the character and method of the translator.

[86]Gordis, *Book of Man*, 222.

[87]Urbach, *The Sages*, 1.411.

[88]Septuagint version of Job 2:9, quoted in Pope, *Job*, 22.

[89]Pope, 22.

[90]Pope, xliv.

[91]Septuagint version of Job 42:17, quoted in Pope, *Job*, 354.

[92]The identification of Job with Jobab is also found in a late *Targum* of I Chron 1:43. See Ginzberg, *Legends*, 5.384, n. 14.

[93]Robert Doran, "Aristeas the Exegete," in J. H. Charles-worth, *The Old Testament Pseudepigrapha* (forthcoming, Doubleday, 1984), writes that the work of this Aristeas is known to us only third-hand through Eusebius (d. 339) (*Praep. Evang.* 9.25, 430d-431). His identification with the author of the *Letter of Aristeas* is problematic and the issue remains open. Aristeas portrays Job as a silent sufferer, tested by God. His friends arrive not to berate, but to comfort him, and "While he was being comforted, he said that even without comfort he would be steadfast in piety, even in such trying circumstances. God amazed at his high courage, freed him from his illness and made him master of many possessions" (trans. from Eusebius by Robert Doran). Doran suggests that the language Aristeas uses is typical of that found in Jewish accounts of persecution and martyrdom. "Aristeas," he writes, "has transformed the tragedy and problem of suffering in the canonical book of Job into an edifying story of endurance for the sake of religion." As for the relationship between Aristeas and the Septuagint addition, Doran suggests that both may share a common tradition: "A source for this common tradition may be the 'Syriac book' which the Septuagint addition claims that it is quoting."

[94]Jerome, *Letter* 73 (*PL* 22, col. 677), and see below, 38-39.

[95]Simon, *Verus Israel*, 223-224. *EJ*, "Edom," notes that "at the end of the tannaitic period, and still more in the amoraic, the identification [of Edom and Rome] became very widespread, and the overwhelming majority of homilies about Edom speak explicitly of Rome. Thus it was stated that Rome was founded by the children of Esau, and Rome was identified as one of the cities of the chiefs of Esau enumerated at the end of Genesis 36." See also G. D. Cohen, "Esau as Symbol in Early Medieval Thought," *Jewish Medieval and Renaissance Studies* (ed. A. Altmann; Cambridge, Ma., 1967) 19-48.

[96]On the *Test. Job*, see Kaufmann Kohler, "Testament of Job," *Semitic Studies in Memory of Alexander Kohut* (Berlin, 1897), 264-338, which includes an English translation of the book; his article, "Job, Testament of," in *JE*; and Robert A. Kraft, *The Testament of Job. TextsT 5. Pseudepigrapha Series 4.* SBL (Missoula, Montana, 1974), which contains Greek text and English translation, and an annotated, chronological bibliography; see also Nahum Glatzer, *The Dimensions of Job, A Study and Selected Readings* (New York, 1969), 13-14; "The Testament of Job," *EJ*.

[97]Marc Philolenko, "Le Testament de Job et les Thérapeutes," *Sem* 8 (1958) 41-53, believes the *Test. Job* is probably pre-Christian and was written in an Essene setting. Robert Kraft, on the other hand, has suggested that in its present form the book may reflect a Christian setting. For an indication of other views, see annotated bibliography in Kraft, *The Testament of Job*.

[98]Job is said to have married Dinah in *B. B. Bat.* 15b and in *Gen. Rab.* 57:4; see above, 13. The pseudepigraphical *Biblical*

Antiquities of Philo (trans. M.R. James, prolegomenon by Louis
Feldman; New York, 1971), also records this tradition at 8.8
(p. 97): "And thereafter Job took her [Dinah] to wife and begat
of her fourteen sons and six daughters, even seven sons and three
daughters before he was smitten with affliction, and thereafter
when he was made whole seven sons and three daughters." The *Biblical Antiquities* agrees with midrashic tradition in making Dinah
Job's sole wife, before, during and after his afflictions, while
in the *Test. Job*, Job's first wife, Sitis, dies of her sufferings,
and he marries Dinah after he is restored to prosperity.

[99]*Num. Rab.* 14:2 recounts that Job and Abraham were among
those who discovered the existence of the one God on their own.

[100]Job's great generosity is described in *B. Meg.* 28a, *B.
Pesaḥ.* 112a, and *'Abot R. Nat.* 2 and 7.

[101]*Test. Job* 1: 3b-5a (Kraft, 23).

[102]*Test. Job* 43: 1-13b (Kraft, 75-77).

[103]Kohler, "Job, Testament of," *JE*.

[104]*Test. Job* 53: 1b-4 (Kraft, 85).

[105]Glatzer, *Dimensions*, 12-16.

[106]Glatzer, 14, discusses an addendum to the midrash *'Abot
R. Nat.*: "This Addendum, compiled somewhere between the seventh
and ninth centuries, like the *Testament*, presents Job as a man of
perfect, unquestioning faith. Throughout all his troubles Job
acknowledges and praises God for all his attributes until 'all the
world believed there was none like him in the land.' Satan, who
had not succeeded in destroying Job's trust in God, is finally
condemned and cast down from Heaven." The Hebrew text has been
published as Addendum II to Version I of the work, (ed. S.
Schechter; Vienna, 1887), 150-166. The passage on Job is on p.
164. See also Ginzberg, *Legends*, 2.57 and n. 15. Urbach, *The
Sages.* 2.868, n. 73, believes this addition was influenced either
directly or indirectly by *Test. Job*.

[107]The Church Father, Theodore of Mopsuestia (d. 428), for
example, usually a strict follower of the letter of the biblical
text, accepted the popular story of Job found in the *Testament* as
the true account. He dismissed the bulk of the biblical book as a
mere literary product, written by a man anxious to parade his
learning and to gain repute. Theodore, quoted in G.D. Mansi,
Sacrorum Conciliorum nova et amplissima collectio (Venice, 1759-
98) IX, 233 ff. (reference in Glatzer, *Dimensions*, 15), thought
the speeches attributed to Job by the biblical author unbefitting
a man "who mastered his life with great wisdom and virtue and
piety."
    Job is mentioned by neither Philo nor Josephus. This is
not surprising, however, for both refer almost exclusively to the
Pentateuch in their exegetical writings.

[108]Jaroslav Pelikan, *The Emergence of the Catholic Tradition 100-600* (Chicago and London, 1971) 66, recounts that when
Pope Gregory I instructed the missionary Augustine to adapt both
pagan temples and pagan holy days to Christian usages, he was "but
following the practice widely current in the days when the Roman
Empire was being converted."

[109]Pelikan, 66.

[110]*Ibid.*

[111]Jean Daniélou, *Holy Pagans of the Old Testament* (London, New York, Toronto, 1957) 17-20. See Rom 1:19-21; 2:14-15; also Acts 14:14-17; 17:17, 25-26.

[112]Greenberg, "Mankind, Israel and the Nations," 36-38; and see above, 8, n. 8.

[113]Irenaeus, *Against the Heretics* III, 16:1 (Harvey 2, 81).

[114]Augustine, *De Catechizandis Rudibus* § 3 and § 9 (*PL* 40).

[115]Justin, *Apology* I, 46:2-5 (Goodspeed, 58-59).

[116]*Constitutions of the Holy Apostles* VIII.5 (*ANF* 7, 482). The principal criterion for being considered a priest of God was the offering of sacrifices. This is the reason why Abel, Seth, Noah, Melchizedek and Job were considered pagan priests: each is described in the Bible as sacrificing to the Lord. See Marcel Simon, "Melchisédech dans la polémique," and "Les Saints d'Israel dans la dévotion de l'Eglise ancienne," *RHPR* 34 (1954) 80-151, and above, n. 56

[117]Gregory the Great, *Moralia on Job*: Preface § 5 (*F of Ch* 18, 18).

[118]Daniélou, *Holy Pagans*, 97. Two recent books which contain discussions of Job in patristic literature are Lawrence Besserman, *The Legend of Job in the Middle Ages* (Cambridge, Mass., 1979), and Günther Datz, *Die Gestalt Hiobs in der Kirchlichen Exegese und der Arme Heinrich Hartmanns von Aue* (Goppingen, 1973).

[119]I Clement XVII.

[120]Tertullian, *Treatise on Patience* XIV (*ANF* 3, 716).

[121]*Apostolic Constitutions* VII:8,7. This work is tentatively dated in the fourth century.

[122]*Apoc. Paul*, Edgar Hennecke, *New Testament Apocrypha*, (ed. W. Schneemelcher, trans. R. McL. Wilson; 2 vols., Philadelphia, 1965) 2. 755-798.

[123]*Apoc. Paul* v. 49 (Hennecke, 2.793).

[124]Gregory, *Moralia*: Preface § 13 (*F of Ch* 18, 25). On Job as a model for human sufferers see J. R. Baskin, "Job as a Moral Exemplar in Ambrose," *VC* 35 (1981), 9-19.

[125]Zeno, *Tractate* 11.15.

[126]Gregory, *Moralia*: Preface § 14 (*F of Ch* 18, 26).

[127]Daniélou, *Holy Pagans*, 99.

[128]On Jerome's consulting Jewish teachers, see below, 38, and Simon, *Verus Israel*, 211-212.

[129]Jerome, *Preface to Job* (*NPNF*, ser. ii 6, 491).

[130]Ibid. By Arabic, one assumes Jerome means whatever Aramaic translations were available to him.

[131]Ibid.

[132]Ibid.

[133]Ibid.

[134]This tradition is found in *Gen. Rab.* 57:4, see above, 13. Ginzberg, *Legends*, 5.384, n. 14, notes that echoes of rabbinic teachings about Job are found in the works of two other Church Fathers. Origen, in *Homilies on Ezek* 4 (*PG* 13, col. 724), writes that Job is said to have lived in the time of the patriarchs and of Moses. The Syrian Father Aphraates writes that Job lived two hundred and ten years (see above, n. 18).

[135]Jerome, *Liber Hebraicorum Quaestionum in Genesim* (*PL* 23, col. 971).

[136]Ibid. This tradition is found in *J. Soṭa* 20d. The Rabbis were unsure whether the part Elihu played in the Book of Job was deplorable or praiseworthy. This confusion is evident here, where R. Akiba understands "Then was kindled the wrath of Elihu, the son of Barachel the Buzite, of the family of Ram" (Job 32:3) to refer to Balaam. According to Akiba, he was called "the Buzite," because his prophecy was misapprehended, or in Hebrew, בזויה , "made contemptible," a pun on Buzite. Balaam too was from the family of Ram, as it says, "Balak the King of Moab brought me from Aram" (Num 23:7).

[137]Jerome, *Letter* 73 (*PL* 22, col. 677).

[138]Jerome, *Commentaria in Epistolam ad Ephesios* III.5 (*PL* 26, col. 527).

[139]According to Pope, *Job*, 147, Job 19:26 is a notoriously difficult verse. He renders it, "Even after my skin is flayed, without my flesh I shall see God." He notes that many Christian interpreters since Origen have tried to read into this verse an affirmation of immortality or resurrection, but without success.

[140]Jerome, *Liber Contra Joannem Hierosolymitana* 30 (*PL* 23, cols. 381-382).

[141]For Augustine's remarks on the significance of Job's patience in suffering, see *Enarrationes on Psalms* 56.18 (*NPNF* ser.i 8, 224); *On the Creed* 10 (*NPNF* ser.i 3, 373); *On Patience* 9 (*NPNF* ser.i 3, 530); and *On the Gospel of St John* XLI.9 (*NPNF* ser. i 7, 233).

[142]Augustine, *City of God* 18.47 (*CC* 48, 645-646).

[143]Ibid.

[144]Ibid.

[145]Augustine, *Quaestionum in Heptateuchum* LXIX (*CC* 33, 100-101).

[146]Augustine, *On Christian Doctrine*, Prologue § 7 (Robertson, 6).

[147]Augustine, *Sermon* XXXI.2 (*NPNF* ser.i 6, 353).

[148]Gregory, *Moralia*: Introductory epistle to Leander § 3 (*F of Ch* 18, 5).

[149]*Moralia*: Preface §§ 1,2 (*F of Ch* 18, 14-15).

[150]Beryl Smalley, *The Study of the Bible in the Middle Ages* (Notre Dame, Indiana, 1970) 34.

[151]Jean Leclercq, "From Gregory the Great to Bernard," *CHB* 2. 183-196; 185.

[152]Gregory, *Moralia*: Preface § 4 (*F of Ch* 18, 17).

[153]Ibid.

[154]Ibid., § 5 (18).

[155]Ibid., § 12 (24).

[156]Ibid., § 13 (26).

[157]Ibid., § 14 (26).

[1]Urbach, *The Sages*, 1.542; and see E.J. Hamlin, "Nations," *IDB*.

[2]Although Num 10:29 is unclear as to whether Hobab is Moses' father-in-law, or his brother-in-law, the son of Reuel, Moses' father-in-law, an attempt to remove the ambiguity is made in Judg 4:11, where Hobab is identified as the father-in-law of Moses. On the difficulty of identifying Moses' father-in-law, see W.F. Albright, "Jethro, Hobab and Reuel in Early Hebrew Tradition," *CBQ* 25 (1963) 1-11; R. deVaux, "Sur l'origine Kénite ou Madianite du Yahvisme," *Eretz-Israel* 9, *W.F. Albright Volume* (ed. A. Malamat; Jerusalem, 1969) 28-32; and B. Mazar, "The Sanctuary of Arad and the Family of Hobab the Kenite," *JNES* 24 (1965) 297-303.

[3]Martin Noth, *Numbers. A Commentary* (Philadelphia, 1968), 75, believes that Hobab acquiesced: "It is true that this is not now stated, but it must have been the original outcome of this story which otherwise would have no *raison d'être*."

[4]References to Jethro as one of Pharaoh's counsellors are found in *B. Soṭa* 11a, *B. Sanh.* 106a, and *Exod. Rab.* 1:9.

[5]On Jewish proselytism in the rabbinic period, see Bernard Bamberger, *Proselytism in the Talmudic Period* (Cincinnati, 1939); William Braude, *Jewish Proselyting in the First Five Centuries of the Common Era* (Providence, 1940); Marvin Pope, "Proselyte," *IDB*; "Proselytes," *EJ*; Simon, "Le proselytisme juif," *Verus Israel*, 315-355; and Urbach, *The Sages*, 1.541-554.

[6]*M. 'Abot* 1:12.

[7]*B. 'Abod. Zar.* 3b, 24a.

[8]Urbach, *The Sages*, 1.542.

[9]*B. Pesaḥ.* 87b. Urbach, *The Sages*, 1.546-547, shows that this justification for Israel's dispersal was used in disputations with Christians such as Origen (*Contra Celsum* 1,55), and notes that "It is inconceivable that a Jew would have advanced this argument, if it could have been easily refuted by an actual situation at variance with it."

[10]*Lev. Rab.* 6:5.

[11]*Eccl. Rab.* 5:11.

[12]*B. Yebam.* 47a. The reception of proselytes, following instruction in the commandments, consisted of three parts: circumcision, for male converts; ritual immersion; and the offering of a sacrifice in the Temple. These requirements are justified in *B. Ker.* 81a: "As the Israelites in the wilderness had to fulfill three conditions before the conclusion of the covenant, namely circumcision (Exod 12:48), sprinkling with water (Exod 19:10) and an offering (Exod 24:5), so proselytes must fulfill the same three conditions on entering the covenant."

[13]*Sipra*, Kedoshim 8:3 (Weiss, 91a).

[14]In the Pentateuch the term for an alien living within
the bounds of Israel is גר . By rabbinic times the word had come
to refer specifically to proselytes, and the Rabbis read certain
biblical verses, originally intended to apply to foreign so-
journers, as referring to converts to Judaism. To obviate confusion the term for a proselyte became   גר צדק   , while a resident
sojourner was dubbed גר תושב .

[15]*Tanḥ.*: Vayakhel 8.

[16]R. Ḥelbo (fl. 290-320 *CE*), for example, is quoted in *B.
Yebam.* 109b, to the effect that "Proselytes are as bad as the
scab for the Jews." See Bamberger, *Proselytism*, and Braude, *Jewish Proselyting*, for other negative comments.

[17]Greenberg, "Israel and the Nations," 29.

[18]Urbach, *The Sages*, 1.543, comments: "The type of Gentile
that they encountered and their experiences with the pagans who
were drawn towards Judaism and read the Bible also determined the
reactions of the Sages." Of R. Ḥelbo's remark, Urbach notes, 550,
that even it is not clear and unambiguous evidence against proselytism, "for other things are described as difficult; nevertheless a man is not obliged, nor is he even able, to refrain from
them."

[19]Urbach, 1.552.

[20]*B. Giṭ.* 56a; *B. Sanh.* 96b. Of these legends which tell
of descendants of Israel's cruelest enemies who later became converts to Israel, G.F. Moore, *Judaism* 1.347, writes: "It gratified
Jewish pride in the demonstrated superiority of the true God, and
the true religion to play with the imagination that bitter enemies
of Israel had been constrained to acknowledge this superiority and
become converts to Judaism . . . Present too was the feeling that
the sins of the heathen fathers did not exclude their posterity
from the Jewish people or from the highest honor the Rabbis could
conceive, that of being Doctors of the Law." Along these lines,
Braude, *Jewish Proselyting*, 28, recounts that only once did Abraham's zeal as "father of the proselytes" slip and the consequences
were tragic: "R. Eleazar b. Pedat (fl. 250-290 *CE*) asked: 'Why
were the children of Israel enslaved in Egypt 210 years?' 'Because,' answered R. Johanan, 'in returning the rescued captives to
the king of Sodom, Abraham allowed some of them to slip from under
the wings of the Shekinah.'" This legend is found in *B. 'Abod.
Zar.* 9a, and *B. Sanh.* 97a.

[21]Bamberger. *Proselytism*, 11.

[22]See below, 54, n. 41.

[23]Of the Rechabites, Ginzberg, *Legends* 3.76, writes: "One
of the descendants of Jethro was Jonadab, son of Rechab, who, when
he heard from a prophet that God would destroy the Temple, bade
all his children, as a token of mourning, to drink no wine, use no
oil for anointing themselves, nor cut their hair, nor dwell in
houses. The Rechabites obeyed this command of their sire, and as
a reward for this, God made a covenant with them that their
descendants should always be members of the Sanhedrin, and
teachers of Israel." Both the *Mek* Yitro 2 (Horovitz-Rabin, 200)
and *Sipre Num.* 78 (Horovitz, 73) discuss the Rechabites in great
detail as Jethro's descendants.

[24]Tradition records that Jethro's descendants were given the privilege of sitting in the Sanhedrin for which usually only pure-blooded Israelites were qualified. *T. Bik.* 1:2 maintains that with respect to the first fruit offerings Jethro's progeny were to enjoy the legal status of pure-blooded Israelites, and not of proselytes. Two reasons are given in *B. Sanh.* for this special treatment. According to *B. Sanh.* 106a, Balaam, Job and Jethro served as Pharoah's counsellors at the time of the Israelite captivity. When Pharoah wished to kill all Israelite male children, Jethro was outraged and fled. As a reward for refusing to obey Pharoah, Jethro's descendants were privileged to sit in the San-hedrin. *B. Sanh.* 103b-104a recounts that Jethro's descendants merited such honor because of his hospitality to Moses in Midian. See Ginzberg, *Legends* 2.254; 5.393, n. 21.

[25]On the problem of identifying Moses' father-in-law, see above, n. 2.

[26]*Mek.* Yitro 1 (Horovitz-Rabin, 189). In Exod 4:18, Moses' father-in-law is designated by the variant reading Jether instead of Jethro.

[27]*Mek.* Yitro 1 (Horovitz-Rabin, 189). The name Putiel, which is identified with Jethro in this source, derived from "And Eleazar, Aaron's son took him one of the daughters of Putiel to wife and she bore him Phineas" (Exod 6:25). Although the relation to Jethro, beyond his also having daughters, seems to be nil, the identification also occurs in such rabbinic texts as *B. B. Bat.* 109b-110a, *B. Soṭa* 43a and *B. Sanh.* 82b.

[28]*Sipre Num.* 78 (Horovitz, 72-73).

[29]On Rahab the harlot in rabbinic literature, see my "The Rabbinic Transformations of Rahab the Harlot," *Notre Dame English Journal* 11 (1979) 141-157.

[30]*Mish. R. El.*, p. 304.

[31]See above, n. 24.

[32]Bamberger, *Proselytism*, 190.

[33]Jethro appeared at Moses' camp with his daughter Zippo-rah, Moses' wife, and their two sons. Zipporah and her sons had last appeared in Exod 4:4, when they were accompanying Moses back to Egypt. There is no biblical hint, prior to Exod 18:2, that Zipporah had been sent away and returned to her father. According to *Mek.* Yitro 1 (Horovitz-Rabin, 190-191) Moses had divorced Zippo-rah at the instigation of Aaron because of the dangers involved in Moses' mission to Egypt.

[34]*Mek.* Yitro 1 (192).

[35]Ibid., 193.

[36]Ibid. With traditional pointing, this verse reads, "Am I a God near at hand saith the Lord, and not a God afar off?" R. Eleazar, however, reads it in a way suitable to his homiletical point, that God welcomes converts. The same verb, "to bring near," (להקריב) in this prooftext from Jer is used in the *Sipre Num.* 78 (Horovitz, 73-74) with the meaning "to convert." Thus, "And as these [Jethro, Rahab] drew themselves near to God [that is, converted] so God will draw near to him all those of Israel who observe the Torah."

[37]*Mek.* Yitro 1 (Horovitz-Rabin 193).

[38]*Tg. Ps.-J.* on Exod 18:7.

[39]*B. Sanh.* 94a. The Septuagint reading for ויחד is
'εξέστη "he shuddered." Brevard S. Childs, *The Book of Exodus.
A Critical Theological Commentary* (Philadelphia, 1974) 320, suggests that this reading is based on either the Hebrew root חרד
("tremble, be terrified"), or on the root חתת ("be dismayed,
frightened"). According to Umberto Cassuto, *A Commentary on the
Book of Exodus* (trans. I. Abrahams; Jerusalem, 1967) 218, however,
the Greek should be translated "he shuddered," and derives not
from a different Hebrew reading like ויחרד, but from midrashic
interpretations such as those found in *B. Sanh.* 94a.

[40]*Mek.* Yitro 1 (Horovitz-Rabin 194).

[41]Thus the *Mek* Yitro 1 (194-195), contrasts Jethro's statement of faith with those of Naaman and Rahab: "Jethro, still believing that there was some substance in other gods, said, 'I know
that the Lord is greater than all the gods' (Exod 18:11). Naaman
came nearer the truth [although he still confined God to one point
of the universe], for he said, 'Now I know that there is no other
God in all the earth but in Israel' (2 Kgs 5:15). Rahab [made
even further progress] and placed God both in heaven and earth,
saying, 'For the Lord your God, He is God in Heaven above and in
earth beneath' (Josh 2:11). But Moses made Him fill all the space
of the world, as it is said, 'The Lord, He is God in the heaven
above, and upon the earth beneath: there is none else' (Deut
4:39)." *Tg. Onq.* removes any ambiguity, and strengthens Jethro's
position by rendering the verse, "Now I know that there is no God
but He."

[42]*Mek.* Be-Shallaḥ 1 (Horovitz-Rabin, 177); claims of past
excesses are typical of rabbinic remarks about converts.

[43]*Exod. Rab.* 7:6.

[44]On traditions of Zipporah's conversion to Judaism prior
to meeting Moses, see Ginzberg, *Legends* 6.136, n. 791.

[45]*Mek.* Yitro 1 (Horovitz-Rabin 190).

[46]Ibid. This comment, changing the word "priest," to the
neutral "chief" is reflected in *Tg. Onq.* on Exod 18:1.

[47]Jethro's meal with Aaron and the elders of Israel gave
rise to various homiletical remarks. In *B. Ber.* 63b, this comment
is found: "R. Abin the Levite [fl. ca. 350 *CE*] also said: If one
partakes of a meal at which a scholar is present, it is as if he
feasted on the effulgence of the divine presence, as it is said,
'And Jethro, Moses' father-in-law, took a burnt offering and sacrifices for God: And Aaron came and all the elders of Israel to
eat bread with Moses' father-in-law before God' (Exod 18:12). Was
it before God that they ate? Did they not eat before Moses? This
tells you that if one partakes of a meal at which a scholar is
present, it is as if he feasted on the effulgence of the divine
presence." A kindred remark in the *Mek.* Yitro 1 (Horovitz-Rabin,
195), also inquires where Moses was during the meal (since there
is no scriptural indication that he participated in it): "Here we
learn that Moses was serving the entire company. And there is no
reason why great men should not serve lesser men, for the Holy
One, blessed be He, gives everyone his wants, and to everybody

according to his needs. And not to good people alone, but also to wicked people, and even to people who are worshipping idols."

[48]*Mish. R. El.*, p. 304. Also, *Sipre Num.* 78 (Horovitz, 72) and 80 (77): "It had been part of God's plan to reward Jethro for the love he bore the Torah; and for this reason He allowed it to come to pass that Moses had to have his attention called to the plan of installing elders through his father-in-law, that the Holy Scriptures might devote a whole chapter to the plan of Jethro." Jethro's name, in fact, is given to a weekly portion of the Torah that extends from Exod 18:1 to 20:23.

[49]*Mek.* Yitro 2 (Horovitz-Rabin, 199).

[50]The Rabbis wondered why Jethro/Hobab should be so insistent in Num 10 to return to his own land. For a synthesis of rabbinic speculation, see Ginzberg, *Legends* 3.73-74.

[51]*Mek.* Yitro 2 (Horovitz-Rabin, 199-200). As is noted above, Judg 1:16 was regarded as proof by the Rabbis that Jethro's descendants dwelt as proselytes in Israel.

[52]*Sipre Num.* 78 (Horovitz, 76).

[53]Ibid. 80 (77).

[54]Ginzberg, *Legends* 3.74, based on *Sipre Num.* 78.

[55]*Sipre Num.* 80 (Horovitz, 77).

[56]Ibid., see above, n. 14, for a discussion of the rabbinic understanding of the biblical גר .

[57]*Pesiq. Rab Kah.* 12:16; and *Tanḥ.* B: Exod. 73-74.

[58]*Pesiq. Rab Kah.* 12:11.

[59]Greenberg, "Israel and the Nations," 29-30.

[60]*Sipre Num.* 78 (Horovitz, 73).

[61]Philo Judaeus, *On the Giants, Works of Philo Judaeus.* (*LCL*, 12 vols; ed. and trans. by F.H. Colson and G.H. Whitaker; London, New York, 1930), § 50 (2.471). Here Philo calls Jethro ὁ περίσσος τῦφος ; in *On Drunkenness* (see below, 151-153), Jethro is again ὁ τῦφος, while Moses is ὁ σοφος.

[62]*On the Change of Names* §§ 103-104 (*LCL* 5.193).

[63]Hans Lewy, editor and introduction, *Philo: Selections,* published in *Three Jewish Philosophers* (New York, 1969), 13. Lewy believes that Philo's etymologies of Hebrew names were passed on to him by his Alexandrine teachers.

[64]*On the Change of Names* §§ 103-104 (*LCL* 5. 193). A comparison makes clear that Philo's etymologies do not derive from the rabbinic etymologies preserved in our sources. Philo's word-lists derived "Jethro" or "Jethor" from the Hebrew root יחר in its primary meaning of "remainder," or "excess." The Rabbis also derived "Jethro" from this root, but in its pi'el (intensive) form where it means "to add," or "to do much." The pi'el form of this root is a post-biblical form. Similarly, Philo's source took "Reuel" to mean "shepherding of God," from ריעה, "shepherd," and

אל "God."   The Rabbis understood "Reuel" as "God's friend," from
the word רׇיע, "friend" or "companion."   While Philo does identify
Hobab of Num 10 with Jethro, he does not use the name Hobab, and
therefore provides no etymology for it.

[65]*On the Change of Names* §§103-104 (*LCL* 5.193).

[66]Ibid.

[67]Ibid. §§ 107-110 (5.197).   Philo here supports his
account of Jethro's double nature with a second allegory based on
the meaning of the word "Midian," which he takes to mean "judgement" or "sifting."   "Midian" has a two-fold significance to
Philo.   It can mean those who have been judged to be unfit such as
the Midianites who initiated the unholy rites of Baal Peor in Num
25:3, it can also mean those who are worthy to dispense justice.
According to this second meaning, Jethro, when he is called Reuel,
is the priest of judgement, allegorically, the mind.

[68]*On the Change of Names* § 105 (5.195).

[69]Ibid. § 114 (5.210).

[70]Ibid.

[71]E.R. Goodenough, *By Light, Light* (New Haven, 1935) 200.
Goodenough contends, p. 200, that in the allegory of Jethro and
his daughters, Philo identifies Moses as the agent if not the
exact equivalent of the Logos, the intermediary force connecting
the remote diety with his creation.   In a sense it is through the
transforming power of the Logos/Moses that the vain and interfer-
ing Jethro becomes Reuel, a member of the divine flock subject to
the shepherding of God.   This theme is also expressed in Philo's
treatise *On Agriculture* § 43 (*LCL* 3.131), where the flocks which
represent the thoughts and commands of the bad shepherd, Jethro,
have to be put into order by Moses and led into justice.

[72]*On Drunkenness* § 37 (*LCL* 3.337).   In Greek mythology
Proteus was a wise sea god who had the ability to foresee the
future.   However, since he never spoke oracularly unless forced to
do so, his questioner had first to catch hold of him.   This was no
easy matter, for Proteus could change shape at will.   He figures
in the *Odyssey of Homer*, lines 416-419.   Proteus was called
"Egyptian," probably because of confusion with a fabled king of
Egypt, also named Proteus.   In *On Drunkenness* § 37 (*LCL* 3.337),
Philo writes that like Proteus, Jethro is the type "which bows
down to the opinions of the multitude and undergoes all manners of
transformations in conformity with the ever-varying aspirations of
human life."

[73]*On Drunkenness* § 37 (*LCL* 3.337).

[74]Ibid. § 40 (3.339).

[75]Ibid. §§ 44-45 (3.341).

[76]See above, 49-50, notes 23-24.

[77]Lewy, *Selections*, 13.

[78]Josephus, *Jewish Antiquities of Flavius Josephus* (*LCL*, 9
vols; trans. H. St J. Thackery; London, New York, 1930) III. 64
(*LCL* 4.349-350).

[79]Ibid. III. 65 (4.350).

[80]Ibid. III. 73 (4.351).

[81]Ibid. III. 73 (4.353).

[82]Ibid. III. 74 (4.353). Rabbinic tradition pays a similar tribute to Moses in *Sipre Deut.* for recording, without appropriating, the oracles of Balaam, see below, 80-83.

[83] For a discussion of patristic interest in the literal import of Scriptures, see B. Smalley, *Study of the Bible in the Middle Ages*, 1-26.

[84]See below, 69-72 for the comments of Augustine and Bede.

[85]See below, 72-73, for Cyril of Alexandria's adaptation of Philo's Jethro.

[86]In the Septuagint the word used for "father-in-law," in Exod 18 and Num 10 is γαμβρός, which can mean any kinsman by marriage. Its secondary meanings are "son-in-law," "brother-in-law," and thirdly, 'father-in-law"; the more specific word for "father-in-law," is πενθερός. This confusion over Hobab's relationship to Moses is reflected in the Vulgate as well. In Exod 18, Jethro is described as *socer*, "father-in-law," a literal translation of חתן , but in Num 10:29 that same Hebrew word is translated by *cognatus*, "kinsman."

[87]See, for example, B. Childs, *The Book of Exodus*, 322.

[88]In *B. Zebaḥ.* 116a, this discussion is recorded as a controversy of the Tannaim."

[89]Origen, *In Exodum Homiliae* (*SC* 16; trans. P. Fortier; Paris, 1940) 237. An interesting explanation of this same problem is presented anonymously by the *Glossa Ordinaria: Liber Exodus* 18:1 (*PL* 113, col. 244): "When Moses was about to free the children of Israel, he sent his wife and sons away, whom he afterwards met in the desert. This signifies that preachers, when they are sent to a work of preaching, must seclude themselves from temporal worries; if they should afterwards assume a bishopric, or other position of dignity, then they ought to carry all the concerns of their parishioners, both temporal and spiritual."

[90]See above, 60, n. 58.

[91]Origen, *In Exodum Homiliae* XI. 6 (*SC*, 241).

[92]J. Pelikan, *The Emergence of the Catholic Tradition*, writes, 31-32: "As the apologists came to grips with the defenders of paganism, they were compelled to acknowledge that Christianity and its ancestor Judaism, did not have a monopoly on either the moral or doctrinal teachings whose superiority Christian apologetics were seeking to demonstrate."

[93]Origen, *Homiliae* XI. 6 (*SC*, 242).

[94]Augustine, *Quaestionum in Heptateucham* (*CC* 33; Series latina; Turnholt, Belgium, 1953) LXIX, 100-101.

[95]*On Christian Doctrine* (trans. D.W. Robertson; Indianapolis, 1958), Prologue § 7, 11.

[96]The actual text upon which Augustine exercised his exegetical talents varied during the course of his life. Although
there was at that time no official Latin version, Augustine recom-
mended the *Itala* as being superior to all other versions. However, as G. Bonner, "Augustine as Biblical Scholar," *CHB* 1.541-
562, writes, 547, Augustine was prepared to appeal to several
different readings of the same passage without making any attempt
to discriminate among them: "So far as he was concerned, one form
[was] as good as another for the purpose of preaching."

[97]Augustine, *Locutionum in Heptateuchum* LXXXII (*CC* 33,
415). In the Hebrew, the verb is "took," ויקח . *Tg. Onq.*, the
Syriac, and the Vulgate on this verse have "sacrificed," the apparent intent of the Hebrew "took."

[98]Augustine, *Quaest.* LXIX (*CC* 33, 100-101).

[99]Bede,*Exegetica Genuina* XVIII (*PL* 91, col. 316).

[100]Cyril of Alexandria, *Glaphyrorum in Exodum* I.8 (*PG* 69,
cols. 406-410).

[101]For Philo's Jethro, see above, 62-63.

[102]Cyril, *Glaphyr.* I.8 (*PG* 69, col. 406).

[103]Ibid. (col. 407).

[104]Ibid. (col. 408).

[105]Jacob Neusner, *Aphrahat and Judaism. The Christian-
Jewish Argument in Fourth-Century Iran* (Leiden, 1971) 4.

[106]Aphraates, *Demonstration* 16: Summary (Neusner, *Aphrahat*,
60).

[107]Ibid., *Demonstration* 16:6 (Neusner, 65).

[108]Neusner, *Aphrahat*, 5.

[109]Ibid.

[110]Scholars such as Louis Ginzberg, "Aphraates, the Persian
Sage," *JE*; and Frank Gavin, *Aphraates and the Jews* (Toronto,
1923), have pointed out apparent parallels in Aphraates and
aggadic literature, and have written of "Aphraates' dependence
upon, or affiliation with, Jewish thought" (Gavin, 37). Neusner,
Aphrahat, 151-195, discusses the whole question of "Aphrahat and
the Rabbis," and concludes, 195, that prevailing impressions of
Aphraates' closeness to rabbinic sources are at best imprecise and
exaggerated.

[111]Neusner suggests, 172, that a few apparently derogatory
remarks in rabbinic texts concerning Jethro (he cites Jethro's
part in the conspiracy in Egypt, quoting *B. Sanh.* 106a) may be an
effort to denigrate Jethro in response to Aphraates' claim that he
was a righteous gentile and superior to Israel. This seems unlikely given the rabbinic exoneration of Jethro from any evil-
doings in Egypt, the glorification of Jethro as a proselyte in
rabbinic sources, and the uniqueness of Aphraates among Church
Fathers in his wholehearted praise of Jethro.

[1]Geza Vermes, *Scripture and Tradition in Judaism* (Leiden, 1961), 175; and Alexander Rofe, *"The Book of Balaam" (Numbers 22:2-24:25). A Study in Methods of Criticism and the History of Biblical Literature and Religion* (Jerusalem, 1979) [Hebrew]; 45-49.

[2]Rofe, *"Book of Balaam,"* 47-49.

[3]Vermes, *Scripture and Tradition* 175-176, points out that the Priestly circles who completed the redaction of the Torah are generally responsible for the negative picture of Balaam which later commentators projected back on to the main narrative of Num 22-24. "Thus," he writes, "the pejorative interpretation of the Balaam story is consequently not a product of rabbinic exegesis, but a contribution of the priestly redactors of the Torah." Rofe, *"Book of Balaam,"* 45-49, holds that the turning point has its root in the Deuteronomic concept of prophecy which would deny the existence of heathen prophecy, and therefore sought to discredit Balaam. He suggests, pp. 49-52, that the ass episode is a burlesque of Balaam's prophetic abilities. Its composition reflects the shift in attitude toward Balaam, and is intended to deny the possibility of gentile prophecy.

An interesting context for these biblical transformations of Balaam is provided by the Aramaic Deir 'Alla plaster inscriptions discovered in the Jordan Valley in 1967. One of the major texts contains a prophecy delivered by the gods at night to "the divine seer" Balaam. Jacob Hoftijzer, one of the scholars involved in the discovery, reconstruction and publication of the texts (*Aramaic Texts from Deir 'Alla* [ed. J. Hoftijzer and G. van der Kooij; Leiden, 1976]); writes in "The Prophet Balaam in a 6th Century Aramic Inscription," *BA* 39 (1976) 11-17;13, that "If one combines the biblical data [about Balaam] with those of Deir 'Alla, one must conclude that for a considerable period of time the figure of Balaam took up a prominent position in a specific religious tradition in Transjordan." Baruch Levine, in a review article, "The Deir 'Alla Plaster Inscriptions," *JAOS* 101 (1981) 195-205; 204, writes that "The biblical traditions are, of course, the work of Israelite writers, who convey their negative view of divination. At Deir 'Alla we perceive the arts of the diviner through the eyes of those who take omens seriously." He goes on to note that while Balaam's powers are seen as efficacious at Deir 'Alla, ". . . the biblical tradition epitomized Yahweh's supremacy, and Balaam's use of divination is ineffectual (Num 24:1)." Rofe, *Book of Balaam*, 69-70, speculates that the inscription served as a *hieros logos* for a house of sacral prostitution. This would explain why the Priestly writer transformed Balaam into a Midianite sorcerer who lured Israelites into prostitution with the daughters of Midian.

[4]Moshe Greenberg, "Mankind, Israel and the Nations," 30.

[5]*Sifre Deut.* 54 (Finkelstein, 122).

[6]Urbach, *The Sages*, 1.26. Urbach, 26, n. 30, relates that at the end of the first century CE, R. Tarfon (fl. 80-110 CE) declared that if the books of the Minim--which Urbach understands to refer to the writings of the early Christians--fell into his hands, he would burn them, including the Divine Names that they contain, "for even if a pursuer were pursuing me, I would enter an

idolatrous shrine, but not one of their temples, because idolaters
disavow Him out of ignorance, whereas these know Him and yet deny
Him" (*T. Sabb.* 13:5).

[7]Urbach, *The Sages*, 1.116.

[8]Ibid., 1.116, n. 56.

[9]Ibid., 1.116.

[10]*B. Sanh.* 105a.

[11]Ibid.

[12]*M. Sanh.* 10:2; this statement is also found in *B. Ḥag.*
15b.

[13]The gemara on this mishnah in *B. Sanh.* 105a states that
Balaam's plea, "Let me die the death of the righteous / And let my
end be like his" (Num 23:10), is clear testimony that Balaam knew
his future fate. His meaning was, "If I die the death of the
righteous, that is, a natural death, my last end will be like his,
that is, I will enter the world to come; but if not, if I die a
violent death, then 'Behold, I will go unto my people' (Num
24:14), that is, down into Gehenna." Since Balaam did die a violent death, he was accordingly barred from the world to come.
Similarly, another etymology of Balaam, "without a people"
(בלא עם), is cited here as proof that Balaam was indeed among
those who have no portion in the future life.

[14]*B. Sanh.* 106b.

[15]Thus, Ginzberg, *Legends*, 5.313, writes: "The man whom
the Midianites and Moabites believed to be Moses's peer [Balaam]
was none other than Laban, Israel's arch-enemy, who in olden days
had wanted to root out entirely Jacob and all his family, and who
had later on incited Pharaoh and Amalek against the people of
Israel to bring about their destruction." In *B. Sanh.* 105a, Laban
is said to be identical with Beor, Balaam's father.

[16]*J. Soṭa* 20d.

[17]See below, 91-93.

[18]This passage is typical of many in rabbinic literature
which compare the qualities of a gentile unfavorably against those
of an Israelite. Thus, Job is also contrasted with Abraham to
Abraham's advantage (see chapter 1, 18-20). Similarly, in *Gen.
Rab.* 55:8 (as well as *B. Sanh.* 105a and *Num. Rab.* 20:12), the commentators seize on the similarity of diction in Num 22:21,
Balaam's departure for Moab, and Gen 22:3, Abraham's preparations
for his journey to Mount Moriah. They explain that Balaam was so
overjoyed at the opportunity to curse Israel that in his haste to
set out he himself saddled his ass, although he did not lack servants; similarly, Abraham was so eager to obey God's command that
he made his own preparations, although he too had many servants.
In the case of Abraham love upset the natural order, but for
Balaam the natural order was upset by hate. See below, however,
81, where Balaam is favorably compared with Moses.

[19]*Sipre Deut.* 357 (Finkelstein, 430).

[20]*Mek.* Yitro 1 (Horovitz-Rabin, 188).

[21] *Gen. Rab.* 65:20 attempts to deal with the problem of Balaam by transforming him from a prophet to a philosopher: "R. Abba b. Kahana [fl. 290-320 *CE*] said: Never arose such great philosophers in the world as Balaam the son of Beor and Abnomos of Gadara." Abnomos was a friend of Rabbi Meir, and is probably identical with the cynic Oenomaus. Of Oenomaus, *EJ* writes that he was a pagan philosopher of the school of younger cynics, who lived during the reign of Hadrian (117-139 CE). Due to his gibes at the gods and oracles, coupled with his sympathy and closeness to rabbinic circles, the Rabbis regarded him as the greatest heathen philosopher of all time. It is interesting to find Balaam linked with him. Perhaps this was an effort to demystify Balaam, and transform him from one who appeared to have actual contact with the divine to the kind of gentile wise man the Rabbis were familiar with from their own times. See Ephraim Urbach, "Homilies of the Rabbis on the Prophets of the Nations and the Balaam Stories," *Tar* 25 (1955-56) 272-289 [Hebrew]; English summary, III-VII; and below, 91-93.

[22] Urbach, "Homilies," VII.

[23] *Tanḥ.* Balak 11, quoted in Urbach, "Homilies," VI.

[24] *Lev. Rab.* 1:13.

[25] *Num. Rab.* 20:10. Also *Lev. Rab.* 1:13, and *Tanḥ.* Balak 8. The complete passages cite numerous scriptural verses corroborating the claim that God speaks to prophets of the nations only at night. So too, it maintains that all the miracles wrought for Israel, as well as the punishments of the wicked on Israel's behalf, take place at night.

[26] See above, 82.

[27] This passage originates in a midrash on "O My people, remember now what Balak king of Moab devised, / And what Balaam the son of Beor answered him; / From Shittim unto Gilgal / That ye may know the righteous acts of the Lord" (Mic 6:5). The question of God's anger is raised in *B. Ber.* 7a, which concludes that wrath is a mood of the Holy One, blessed be He, on the evidence of "A God that hath indignation every day" (Ps 7:12). The topic is also discussed in *B. 'Abod. Zar.* 4a, where God's indignation is said to last but one moment, and that moment lasts but one fifty-eight thousandth eight hundred and eighty-eighth part of an hour. It was this exact moment that Balaam knew.

[28] See ch. 1, 11-14 for discussions of when Job lived.

[29] *S. 'Olam Rab.* 69. Also *B. B. Bat.* 15b.

[30] *Lev. Rab.* 1:12; see also *Deut. Rab.* 1:4.

[31] *B. Sanh.* 105b.

[32] *Tanḥ.* B.: Num. 13; *Num. Rab.* 20:19.

[33] This remark appears to be polemical in intent and probably echoes popular anti-Christian sayings of the day. That the remark is juxtaposed with a comment on Balaam, however, does not mean that he is to be identified directly with Jesus. See below, 91-93.

[34] For Balaam as one of Pharaoh's counsellors, see *B. Soṭa* 11a, *B. Sanh.* 106a, and *Exod. Rab.* 27:3.

[35]See *Mek.* Yitro 1 (Horovitz-Rabin, 188); and *B. Zebaḥ.*
116a for this midrash, based on Ps 29:9-11, in full.

[36]*Tanḥ.* B.: Lev. 16. Similar is *Num. Rab.* 20:18, quoted
above, 83.

[37]An etymology of Balaam's name in *B. Sanh.* 105a is given
to support this claim: "Son of Beor denotes that he committed
bestiality." This is based on the similarity of בעור (Beor) and
בעיר ("cattle"). In the same location a similar accusation is
lodged against Beor himself. This theme reappears in *B. Sanh.*
105b, in the exegesis of Balaam's dialogue with the ass. The
ass's statement, "Ever since I was thine unto this day" (Num
22:30) is explained, "Moreover, I serve thee as a companion by
night."

[38]*B. Sanh.* 105a.

[39]Jonathan Slater, "The Character of Balaam as a Villain in
Midrash Numbers Rabbah," unpublished bachelor's thesis in Folklore
and Mythology, Harvard University, 1974, 32. That God hates lewd-
ness is declared in *B. Sanh.* 106a.

[40]Slater, 32.

[41]See Ginzberg, *Legends*, 1.298, 2.159, and 3.334, as well
as relevant notes, for a number of traditions about Balaam's magical abilities.

[42]*B. Sanh.* 106a.

[43]In *Num. Rab.* 20:20, where a similar account is recorded,
the evidence that the tribes of Israel had with them the holy
plate mentioned in Exod 28:36 is found in the following verse,
"And Moses sent them, a thousand of every tribe to the war, them
and Phinhas the son of Eleazar the priest, to the war, with the
holy vessels and the trumpets for the alarm in his hand" (Num
31:6). This verse almost directly precedes the account of the
death of Balaam in Num 31:8.

[44]Ginzberg, *Legends* 6.144, n. 853, notes that in Jewish and
Christian legends flying through the air is one of the accomplish-
ments of the sorcerer. Similar stories are told by Christian
sources about Simon Magus. On Simon Magus, see below, n. 121.

[45]*B. Sanh.* 106a preserves the tradition that Phinehas
killed Balaam. The plate Phinehas held up is identified in
Yelammedenu on Yalkut I, 785.

[46]*Tg. Yer.* on Num 31:8.

[47]R. Travers Herford, *Christianity in Talmud and Midrash*
(London, 1903), for example, painted a vivid picture of the violent hatred the Rabbis bore towards Jesus as manifested in their
comments on Balaam. He attempted to find in the names associated
with Balaam secret references to others in the drama of Jesus who
were also to be shut out from the world to come. Thus, he concluded that Peter, Judas Iscariot and Paul are meant by the references to Ahitophel, Doeg and Gehazi in such texts as *M. Sanh.* 10:2
and *B. Ḥag.* 15b. Herford writes, p. 69, that ". . . in the Talmud, Balaam and Jesus are classed together, and that therefore
Balaam serves frequently as a type of Jesus. I do not mean that
wherever Balaam is mentioned Jesus is intended, or that everything
said about the former is really meant for the latter. I mean that

wherever Balaam is mentioned, there is a sort of undercurrent of reference to Jesus, and that much more is told of Balaam than would have been told if he and not Jesus had really been the person thought of."

[48]Louis Ginzberg, "Some Observations on the Attitude of the Synagogue towards the Apocalyptic-Eschatological Writings," *JBL* 41 (1922) 115-136, 122, n. 18. Also see the *Legends*, 6.124.

[49]Morris Goldstein, *Jesus in the Jewish Tradition* (New York, 1950) 63-66, reviews past scholarship on the question. The identification of Balaam with Jesus was apparently initiated in a letter written by S.J.L. Rapaport in 1833. Abraham Geiger gave impetus to the suggestion in 1868 with the publication of *Bileam und Jesus*. S. Krauss wrote on "Balaam," *JE*: "As Balaam the magician and, according to the derivation of his name, 'destroyer of the people,' was from both of these points of view a good prototype of Jesus, the latter was also called Balaam."

[50]Goldstein, 66. Traditions exist to the effect that Balaam was both lame and blind in one eye. He is supposed to have been lame because in, "And he went to a bare height" (Num 23:3), the word for "bare height" שׁפי could also mean lame, rendering the verse, "And he went lame." This tradition is recorded in *B. Sanh.* 105a, and *B. Soṭa* 10a. The belief that Balaam was blind in one eye is based on "The man whose *eye* is open" (Num 24:3), and is found in *B. Sanh.* 105a, and *B. Nid.* 31a.

[51]Urbach, "Homilies," V.

[52]Ibid.

[53]See above, ch. 1.

[54]This verse was also understood as a messianic prophecy by Jewish readers. Vermes, *Scripture and Tradition*, 165-166, records that the Septuagint, Peshitta and the Targums interpret "sceptre" symbolically, as referring to the Messiah. He writes that in the Palestinian Targums "star" is also used as a metaphor for "king." Thus, *Tg. Yer.* on this verse reads, "When the mighty king from the house of Jacob shall reign, and the Messiah, the mighty sceptre of Israel shall be anointed." The verse was considered an allusion to the Messiah by some of the Rabbis as well. R. Akiba (fl. 110-135 CE) believed the verse had been fulfilled by the rebel leader Bar Kokhba. The real name of the leader of the Second Jewish Revolt against Rome (132-136 CE) was Simeon ben Kosiba. Akiba played on the words Kosiba and Kokhba "star." See *J. Ta'an.* 68d. Num 24:17 also had messianic connotations for the Qumran sect. J.M. Allegro, "Further Messianic References in Qumran Literature," *JBL* 75 (1956) 174-187, reports, p. 182, that Num 24:15-17 appears with several other biblical testaments with messianic overtones in Qumran document, *4 QTestim*, a collection of scriptural sources referring to a coming prophet. The verse also appears in the Qumran *Damascus Document* VII:12-21, which reads in part: "The star is he who searches the Law, who came to the region of Damascus, as it is written, 'A star shall rise out of Jacob, and a sceptre shall spring up from Israel.' The sceptre is the leader of the whole gathering: when he arises he will destroy all the children of Seth." For the use of this verse by Jewish Christians, Jewish ascetic groups and early Christians, see Jean Daniélou, "The Star of Jacob," *Primitive Christian Symbols* (Baltimore, 1964) 102-123, and below, section iv.

[55]Urbach, "Homilies," writes, p. V: "Balaam is transformed
into the chief representative of the prophets of the nations, and
is described in the image of those who claimed to be the prophets
either of heathen or of Christian (especially Gnostic) groups with
whom the Rabbis came into contact."

[56]J. Ta'an. 65b. The conclusion of this verse from Num
23:19 is more usually rendered, "Or when he hath spoken, will he
not make it good?" (JPS).

[57]B. Sanh. 107a.

[58]Urbach, "Homilies," VI.

[59]Philo, Life of Moses (LCL 6).

[60]G.F. Moore, Judaism 1.239: "The rabbinic schools had no
theory of the mode of prophetic inspiration such as Philo approp-
riates from Plato, a state of ecstasy or enthusiasm; but it was
with them an uncontested axiom that every syllable of Scripture
had the veracity and authority of God."

[61]Hans Lewy, "Philo," in Three Jewish Philosophers, 18.

[62]Philo, On the Special Laws, iv § 49 (LCL 8. 37 ff.).

[63]Plato, Timaeus and Critias, trans. H.D.P. Lee (Middlesex,
England, 1971) § 72, p. 97.

[64]Ibid., 98.

[65]Philo, On the Migration of Abraham §§ 32-35 (LCL 4. 151).

[66]Philo, The Life of Moses 263 (LCL 6. 413).

[67]Ibid., 268 (6.415).

[68]Ibid., 273 (6.417).

[69]Ibid., 274 (6.417).

[70]Ibid., 277 (6.419).

[71]Ibid., 294 (6.429).

[72]See above, 87-88, Num. Rab.20:19; and below, 100,
Pseudo-Philo's Bib. Ant. 18:4; where similar views are expressed.

[73]Philo, On the Cherubim (LCL 2. 27).

[74]The origin of Philo's etymology is unclear. Professor
Judah Goldin has suggested to me that it may come from בלא עם ,
understanding "non-people," as a "foolish people."

[75]Philo, On the Cherubim (LCL 2.27).

[76]Jewish Antiquities of Flavius Josephus (LCL 4).

[77]Josephus, J. Ant. IV.102 (LCL 4. 527).

[78]Ibid. Of Balaam's origin, Num 22:5 recounts, "And he
sent messengers to Balaam the son of Beor, to Pethor, which is by
the river, to the land of the children of his people." Geza

Vermes *Scripture and Tradition*, 129, explains that "Pethor" has
been understood in various ways: "In the biblical text 'Pethor'
is a place name, and the Septuagint, Peshitta and *Tg. Onq.* interpret it as such. Other traditions, because of Balaam's converse
with God during the night, discern in 'Pethor' an allusion to
Balaam's profession, the root *ptr* signifying 'to interpret
dreams'." This explains Josephus' comment, as well as Philo's "a
man far famed as a soothsayer" (*Life of Moses* § 264); also *Bib.
Ant.* 18:2, and the Vulgate, *hariolus*, "a soothsayer or prophet."
Num. Rab. 20:7 and *Tanḥ. B.: Num.* 134, offer both interpretations:
"Pethor was his native city. . . . Others say that he was interpreter (פותר) of dreams."

[79]Josephus, *J. Ant.* IV.107 (*LCL* 4.531).

[80]*Num. Rab.* 20:9, for example, comments: "And as he had
led others astray, so he was himself led astray. By the counsel
that he gave he was himself tripped up. And the Holy One, blessed
be He, led him astray." Also similar is *Num. Rab.* 20:11 : "The
Holy One, blessed be He, concealed from him that his going would
destroy him from the world and lead him to the nethermost pit."

[81]Josephus, *J. Ant.* IV.111 (*LCL* 4.531). Of Balaam's sincerity, *Num. Rab.* 20.15 recounts: "'Balaam said to the angel of
the Lord: "I have sinned,"' (Num 23:24. [He] said so because he
was a subtle villain and knew that nothing can prevent punishment
except repentance, and that if any sinner says 'I have sinned,'
the angel is not permitted to touch him." Philo's attitude is
similar, see above, 95.

[82]*J. Ant.* IV.118 (*LCL* 4.533).

[83]Ibid., IV.119-122 (*LCL* 4.533-535).

[84]Ibid., IV. 129-130 (*LCL* 4.537-539).

[85]Ibid., IV. 118-119 (*LCL* 4.531).

[86]Ibid., IV. 127 (*LCL* 4.537), Josephus does not mention
Balaam's ignominious end. In his version of Num 31:8, in *J. Ant.*
IV.161 (*LCL* 4.553), he recounts only the names of the five Midian-
ite kings said to have been killed in battle.

[87]*The Biblical Antiquities of Philo*, (trans. M.R. James;
prolegomenon, Louis H. Feldman; New York, 1971). In his detailed
introduction, Feldman discusses the history of the text, its
influence on other biblical commentators, and summarizes scholarly
speculation on its date and purpose. He also provides a thorough
line by line commentary on the text in which he notes many parallel passages in rabbinic, hellenistic and patristic literature.

[88]Feldman, "Prolegomenon," *Bib. Ant.*, ix.

[89]*Bib. Ant.* 18:3, 123.

[90]Ibid.

[91]Ibid. 18:8, 125. 18:9 records Balaam's encounter with
the angel, and here again Balaam receives divine reassurance:
"And his she-ass came by way of the desert and saw the angel, and
He opened the eyes of Balaam and he saw the angel and worshipped
him on the earth. And the angel said to him: 'Hasten and go on,
for what thou sayest shall come to pass with him.'" Here, as in

Josephus, Balaam's consternation on perceiving the angel is not questioned.

[92]Ibid., 18:10.

[93]Ibid.

[94]Ibid. 18:4. Compare with *Num. Rab.* 20:19, above, 87-88.

[95]Ibid., 18:13.

[96]Vermes, *Scripture and Tradition*, 175.

[97]See above, 87-88.

[98]See above, 87-88.

[99]For other mild views of Balaam, see below, the comments of Origen, 104-109, and Jerome, 112-113.

[100]The notion of those who follow after, or are disciples of Balaam is found in rabbinic literature as well. *M. 'Abot* 5:19, for example, contrasts such men to the disciples of Abraham: "Every man who has three things is a disciple of Abraham our father. Has he three other things, he is a disciple of Balaam the villain. A generous eye, a humble spirit, and a lowly soul belong to the disciple of Abraham. An evil eye, a haughty spirit, and enormous greed to the disciple of Balaam."

[101]Bo Reicke, *The Epistles of James, Peter and Jude.* AB (New York, 1964) 191, points out that Jude was written with great regard for a Jewish Christian audience, and this is evident in its references to Old Testament figures. Norman Perrin, *The New Testament. An Introduction* (New York, 1974) 270, notes 2 Peter's use of material from Jude, and also his awareness of and respect for Jewish convictions of what constituted biblical canon.

[102]R.P.C. Hanson, *Allegory and Event* (Richmond, Va., 1959) 73.

[103]Ibid. Other common proofs were Gen 49:10ff., Jacob's prophecy about Judah; Ps 110; Isa 7:14, the virgin who is to conceive; Isa 8:14; Isa 28:16; Mal 3:1, the forerunner; and Deut 28:66, "Thy life shall hang before thee."

[104]Justin, *Apology* I 32.12-13 (ed. E.J. Goodspeed, *Die ältesten Apologeten*; Göttingen, 1915, 14). For a survey of patristic comments on Balaam's role as prophet of Christ and ancestor of the Magi, see E. Kirschbaum, "Der Prophet Balaam und die Anbetung der Weisen," *RQ* 49 (1954) 129-171, 130.

[105]Justin, *Dialogue with Trypho* 126.1 (Goodspeed, 246).

[106]Athanasius, *Oratio de Incarnatione Verbi* 33, (PG 25, col. 153).

[107]Augustine, *City of God* 18.47 (CC 48, 645-646).

[108]Augustine is particularly hostile to Balaam, and must find a way to reconcile his prophetic gift with his evil character; by holding that one could be taught by bad angels Augustine shows that an evil man could prophesy Christ. See below, 110-112.

[109]Thus, Augustine in *De Diversis Quaestionibus ad Simplicianum* 2 (*PL* 40, cols. 129-130). Also, see below, 110-112.

[110]Athenagoras, *Legatio pro Christianis* 9.1 (Goodspeed, 323).

[111]Hanson, *Allegory*, 194, writes: "The parallels to this type of inspiration are clearly pagan, the Delphic Oracle and the oracle at Cumae described in the sixth book of the Aeneid spring to mind."

[112]Justin, *Apology* I 36.1 (Goodspeed, 50).

[113]Clement of Alexandria, *Stromata* 6.18.168.3.

[114]Irenaeus, *Ex Catena in Numeros. Fragment 23* (*PG* 7, col. 1241.

[115]Jerome, *In Ezekiel* 6.18.3 (*PL* 25, col. 170c).

[116]Augustine, *Sermo 33. De Balaam et Balac* (*PL* 39, col. 1810).

[117]Origen, *Homily* 19.3 (*PG* 12, col. 724).

[118]Ambrose, *Epistle* 50:14 (*PL* 16, col. 1157).

[119]Ibid., 50:8.

[120]Origen, *Homily on Numbers* 13.7 (*PG* 12, col. 675): "Ex illo Balaam denique fertur Magorum genus et institutio in partibus Orientis vigere, qui descripta habentes apud se omnia quae prophetaverat Balaam, etiam hoc habuerunt scriptum quod 'Orietur stella ex Iacob et exsurget homa ex Israhel.' Haec scripta habebant Magi apud semetipsos et ideo, quando natus est Iesus, agnoverunt stellam et intellexerunt adimpleri prophetiam."

[121]Joseph Bidez, Franz Cumont, *Les Mages Hellénisés. Zoroastre, Ostanès et Hystaspe d'après la Tradition Grecque* (2 vols.; Paris, 1938) 1.48. The authors write, p. 47, that if there is a biblical character whose identification with Zoroaster is easy to explain, it is Balaam: "The resemblance of the character of Balaam with that of Zoroaster, magician of Babylon, to whom were attributed predictions of the coming of the Messiah destined to establish justice and happiness on earth, made easy the confusion of one with another." On the possible connections of Jewish groups such as the Essenes with Iranian magic, and the resultant formation of dualist sects, such as that of Simon Magus, see Daniélou, *Primitive Christian Symbols*, 115-118. Daniélou writes, p. 118: "So we see Simon, as a disciple of the Zadokite Dositheus, converted to dualism by Magi. All this tends to show that the center for the development of the theme of the star, Balaam's prophecy, was the Essenian group that remained at Damascus. It kept in touch with Qumran and Samaria, but came into contact with magism, which affected its theology. Perhaps it even tried to make converts among the Magi, in particular by making use of Balaam's prophecy about the star. On the other hand, the Magi made converts among them, as the case of Simon shows." According to H.J. Schoeps, *Theologie und Geschichte des Judenchristums* (Tubingen, 1949) 249-254, Simon Magus was denoted in Jewish legend under the figure of Balaam. For more information on Simon Magus, see Jean Daniélou, "Judeo-Christianisme et Gnose," *Aspects du Judeo-Christianisme. Travaux du centre d'études supérieures*

spécialisé d'histoire des religions de Strasbourg, 139-164 and G.
van Groningen, *First Century Gnosticism: Its Origins and Motifs*
(Leiden, 1967) 128-164.

[122]For Balaam's place in Epiphany and Christmas sermons, see
below, 112. Bidez and Cumont, *Les Mages*, recount a Syrian legend
that the prophetic words of Balaam were preserved by the kings of
Assyria and passed on from reign to reign by their dynasty to that
of Iran until the time of Augustus when the star appeared in heav-
en; the Persians, struck with fear, were able to recognize in it
the star which was announced by Balaam, and their king prepared
splendid gifts which he sent by the hands of the Magi, under the
guidance of the Star, to Bethlehem. (This is recounted in a
Syriac tract, *On the Star of the Magi*, falsely attributed to
Eusebius, and preserved in a sixth century ms.; it has been published by Wright, *Journal of Sacred Literature* [1866]). Other
Syriac texts recounting similar legends testify to the popularity
of Balaam as the first of the Magi in the Syriac Church.

[123]Hanson, *Allegory*, 195.

[124]Origen, *Homilies on Ezekiel* 6.1 (*PG* 13, col. 709).

[125]Ibid.

[126]Hanson, *Allegory*, 196.

[127]Origen, *Commentary on John* 13.26 (*PG* 14, col. 443).

[128]Smalley, *Study of the Bible*, 13.

[129]Origen appears to show an awareness here of rabbinic traditions. A similar comment on this verse appears in both editions
of the midrash collection *Tanḥ.*; and in *Num. Rab.* 20:4, which
reads: "'And Moab said unto the elders of Midian: Now will this
multitude lick up all that is round about us, as the ox licketh up
the grass of the field' [Num 22:4]. As the ox, they implied, has
his strength in his mouth, so have these their strength in their
mouths; as in the case of the ox, all that he licks up loses every
sign of fertility, so in the case of these people, any nation that
harms them loses all signs of prosperity; as the ox gores with his
horns so do these do battle with their prayers, as it says, 'His
horns are the horns of the wild-ox' [Deut 33:7]." The sources of
Origen's knowledge about rabbinic traditions have been much discussed. N.R.M. de Lange, *Origen and the Jews. Studies in
Jewish-Christian Relations in Third-Century Palestine* (Cambridge,
1976) 25, notes that Origen himself says that he consulted many
Jews, and that he sometimes quotes more than one of them in the
same passage. He goes on to say that "At least one of Origen's
Jewish informants was a convert to Christianity, and it may be
that he made use of several converted Jews." It seems probable
that such a convert was Origen's informant on rabbinic material
relating to Balaam since he refers to such a man in his *Homily on
Numbers* 13.5 (*PG* 12, 672B): "Ut autem scias tale aliquid cogitasse
regem, ex Scripturae verbis intellige, quae ego a magistro quodam,
qui ex Hebraeis crediderat, exposita didici."

[130]Origen, *Selecta in Numeros*, Latin text (*PG* 12, col. 578);
the same comment is also found in his *Homily* 15.4 (*PG* 12, col.
672).

[131]*Homily* 13.6 (*PG* 12, col. 674).

[132]*Homily* 15.4 (*PG* 12, col. 671).

[133] *Selecta* (*PG* 12, col. 579).

[134] *Selecta* (*PG* 12, col. 579).

[135] Ibid.

[136] *Homily* 14.4 (*PG* 12, cols. 682-683).

[137] *Homily* 14.4 (*PG* 12, col. 683). For a comparison of Balaam to Caiaphas, see this text at col. 683B, and also Origen's *Commentary on John* 28.12 and 13 (*PG* 14, cols. 705 and 713).

[138] *Homily* 13.8 (*PG* 12, col. 676); Also see *Selecta* (*PG* 12, col. 579).

[139] See below, p. 107 and n. 144.

[140] *Homily* 15.1 (*PG* 12, col. 684).

[141] *Homily* 15.1 (*PG* 12, col. 683).

[142] Ibid.

[143] Ibid.

[144] Ibid., cols. 683-684.

[145] Ibid., col. 684.

[146] *Commentary on John* 28.12 (*PG* 14, col. 707), Latin text: " . . . perspicuum est quod propheta non erat; augurem enim fuisse scriptam est. Ac profecto si quis propheta est, is quidem prophetat; sin vero quis prophetat, non continuo etiam est propheta." Origen writes in a similar vein of Caiaphas (Ibid, col. 706), Latin text: "Non, si quis prophetat, ideo propheta est."

[147] *Homily* 14.4 (*PG* 12, col. 683).

[148] *Homily* 14.3 (*PG* 12, col. 681).

[149] Ibid., cols. 681-682.

[150] Origen takes the Septuagint reading which translates the Hebrew "end," as "seed;" in Latin: "Ut fiat semen meum sicut semen justorum."

[151] *Homily* 15.4 (*PG* 12, cols. 689-690).

[152] See below, 112-113.

[153] Ambrose, *Epistle* 50 (*PL* 16, cols. 1152-1153). For Philo, see above, 93-96.

[154] *Epistle* 50.6.

[155] *Epistle* 50.7.

[156] *Epistle* 50.8. Compare with Philo, 95-96, who says that from the moment Balaam was invaded by the Spirit of God he lost all of his own augurer's abilities.

[157]*Epistle* 50.15. Philo, too, stresses Balaam's avaricious-
ness, as do the New Testament traditions.

[158]Augustine, *De Diversis Quaestionibus ad Simplicianum* 2
(*PL* 40, cols. 129-130).

[159]Ibid. cols. 129-130.

[160]See above, 102.

[161]Augustine, *Quaestionibus* (*PL* 40, col. 130).

[162]Augustine, *Quaestionum in Heptateucham* (*PL* 34, cols.
739-740).

[163]Ibid. col. 740. This is very reminiscent of the rabbinic
remark that God speaks to prophets of the nations only at night,
see above, 84, notes 24,25.

[164]Augustine, *Quaestionibus* (*PL* 40, col. 136).

[165]Gregory of Nyssa, *In Diem Natalem Christi* (*PG* 46, col.
1133).

[166]Augustine, *Sermo CC in Epiphania Domini* (*PL* 38, col.
1028).

[167]Augustine, *Sermo CCIII in Epiphania Domini* (*PL* 38, col.
1035). In both these sermons Augustine maintains that the Magi
were the "first fruits" of the nations, as if explicitly denying
their descent from an earlier gentile witness to Christ.

[168]Jerome, *Epistle* 77 (*PL* 22, col. 695).

[169]Jerome, *Quaestiones in Genesim* (*PL* 23, cols. 971-972).
Jerome apparently takes this verse to apply to Balaam's anger when
he found he could not curse Israel. The identification of Elihu
with Balaam is found in *J. Soṭa* 20d. Here R. Akiba understands
Job 32:2, "Then was the kindled the wrath of Elihu, the son of
Barachel the Buzite, of the family of Ram" to refer to Balaam.
See above, 79. Clearly, Jerome was acquainted with this tradi-
tion.

[170]This etymology probably derives from Origen: "Balaam was
a symbol to the gentile nations who previously followed omens, but
seeing God did not fulfil these, ceased. His name is interpreted
'vain people'" (*Selecta* [*PG* 12, col. 579]). Origen and Jerome's
etymology may derive in turn from Philo's "foolish people" see
above, 96, and n. 74.

[171]Jerome, *Commentarium in Ezechielem* 6 (*PL* 25, col. 170).

[172]Jerome, *Commentariorum in Evangelium Matthaei* 1.2 (*PL* 26,
col. 26).

[173]Ephraem, *Hymni de Nativate Christi in Carne* 20 (Lamy II,
482).

[174]See above, 105, n. 129.

[175]Origen, *Homily 11 on Exodus* (*PG* 12, col. 577d).

[176]See above, n. 169. Jerome makes the same identification
in *Commentarii in Librum Job* 37 (*PL* 26, col. 721).

[177]*Num. Rab.* 20:11 recounts that God concealed Balaam's doom from him until he had destroyed his own soul: "When he had taken leave of his glory and realized the position he was in, he began to pray for his soul, 'Let my soul die the death of the righteous' (Num 23:10)."

[178]Jay Braverman, "Balaam in Rabbinic and Early Christian Tradition," *Joshua Finkel Festschrift*, (ed. Sidney B. Hoenig and Leon D. Stitskin; New York, 1974) 41-50; 50.

[179]Balaam appears frequently in medieval sculpture and manuscript illustration as a prophet of Christ. Perhaps his dual qualities were best merged in medieval liturgical drama. Emile Mâle, *L'art religieux du XIIIe siècle en France* (Paris, 1902) 216, describes Balaam's role in a typical play of the prophets: "Then came Balaam riding upon his ass and prophesied that a star would rise over Jacob. The ass played a part too in showing by its presence that the Spirit of God may sometimes speak through the mouth of the simplest creature, for the animal saw the angel, even though he remained invisible to the eye of man." E.N. Stone, "Adam, A Religious Play of the Twelfth Century," *University of Washington Publications in Language and Literature* 4 (1926-28) 159-193, 188, n. 50, suggests that Balaam seated on the ass was included for comic relief: "It is not improbable that the introduction of Balaam and his ass was a concession made to the popular craze for boisterous amusements, or an attempt on the part of the Church to turn the ribaldry of the long-established medieval Saturnalia to purposes of edification." Such ridicule of Balaam, while it preserved his role as a prophet, also echoed his pejorative characterization by the Church Fathers, and its continuation in medieval sermons and commentary. It seems fitting that in a popular solution to his contradictory character the wicked prophet should end as a clown.

[1]See Ch. I, 8-9.

[2]*B. Sanh* 105a.

[3]Ch. II, 47-49; 61.

[4]Ch. II, 49; 60-61.

[5]Ch. III, 79.

[6]Ch. III, 91-93.

[7]Ch. III, 87-88.

[8]Ch. I, 16-20.

[9]Ch. I, 19.

[10]Ch. I, 17-18.

[11]Ch. I, 14-16.

[12]Ch. I, 21.

[13]Augustine, *City of God* 18.47 (*CC* 48, 645-646).

[14]Ibid.

[15]Ch. I, 32-37.

[16]Ch. I, 36, and see n. 124.

[17]Ch. I, 34-35.

[18]Ch. II, 71.

[19]Ch. II, 69-72.

[20]Ch. III, 102.

[21]Ch. III, 107-108.

[22]Ch. III, 112.

[23]Ch. III, 103-104.

[24]Ch. III, 108-109; and also see Jerome's similar comments on 111.

[25]See, for example, Ch. I, 24, 38-39, and notes 70, 134, 135 and 136; Ch. III, 105 and n. 129, and 113.

[26]Ch. I, 38; and Ch. III, 113 and n. 129.

[27]Ch. I, 22-24, notes 56-73.

[28]Ch. I, 38-39.

[29]Ch. III, 91-93.
[30]Ch. III, 102.

BIBLIOGRAPHY

Abelard, Peter. *Dialogue of a Philosopher with a Jew and a Christian.* Tr. Pierre J. Payer. *Medieval Sources in Translation* 20. Pontifical Institute of Medieval Studies. Toronto, 1979.

'Abot de-Rabbi Nathan. Ed. Solomon Schechter. Vienna, 1887.

Albright, W. F. "Jethro, Hobab and Reuel in Early Hebrew Tradition," *CBQ* 25 (1963) 1-11.

Allegro, J. M. "Further Messianic References in Qumran Literature," *JBL* 75 (1956) 174-187.

Altmann, Alexander. "*Homo Imago Dei* in Jewish and Christian Theology," *JR* 48 (1968) 235-259.

Ambrose. *Epistle* 50. *PL* 14.

The Ante-Nicene Fathers. The Writings of the Fathers down to AD 325. Ed. A. Roberts, J. Donaldson and A. C. Coxe. 10 vols. N.Y., 1890-1899.

Aptowitzer, Viktor. *Kain und Abel in der Agadah, den Apokryphen, der hellenistischen, christlichen und muhammedanischen Literatur.* Vienna and Leipzig, 1922.

Athanasius. *Oratio de Incarnatione Verbi.* *PG* 25.

Athenagoras. *Legatio pro Christianis. Die ältesten Apologeten.* Ed. E. J. Goodspeed. Göttingen, 1915.

Augustine. *City of God.* CC 48.

_____. *De Catechizandis Rudibus.* *PL* 40.

_____. *De Diversis Quaestionibus ad Simplicianum.* *PL* 40.

_____. *Enarrationes on Psalms.* Tr. Philip Schaff. *NPNF* 8.

_____. *Enchiridion.* *CC* 46.

_____. *Locutionum in Heptateuchum.* *CC* 33.

_____. *On Christian Doctrine.* Tr. D. W. Robertson. Indianapolis, 1958.

_____. *On the Creed.* Tr. Philip Schaff. *NPNF* 3.

_____. *On the Gospel of St. John.* Tr. Philip Schaff. *NPNF* 7.

_____. *On Patience.* Tr. Philip Schaff. *NPNF* 3.

_____. *De Praedestinatione Sanctorum Liber* PL 44.

_____. *Quaestionum in Heptateucham.* *CC* 33.

_____. *Sermo CC in Epiphania Domini.* *PL* 38.

_____. *Sermo CCIII in Epiphania Domini.* *PL* 38.

_____. *Sermo* 33. *PL* 39.

_____. *Sermon* 31. Tr. Philip Schaff. *NPNF* 6.

Baer, Yitzhak. "Israel, the Christian Church, and the Roman Empire from the time of Septimus Severus to the Edict of Toleration," *SH* 7 (1961) 79-149.

Bamberger, Bernard. *Proselytism in the Talmudic Period.* Cincinnati, 1939.

Bardy, Gustave. "Les traditions juives dans l'oeuvre d'Origène," *RB* 34 (1925) 217-252.

Baskin, J. R. "Job as Moral Exemplar in Ambrose," *VC* 35 (1981) 9-19.

_____. "Origen on Balaam: The Dilemma of the Unworthy Prophet," *VC* 37 (1983) 22-35.

_____. "The Rabbinic Transformations of Rahab the Harlot," *Notre Dame English Journal* 11 (1979) 141-157.

Bede. *Exegetica Genuina. PL* 91.

Benamozegh, Elie. *Israël et Humanité: Etude sur le Problème de la Religion Universelle et sa Solution.* Paris, 1914.

Bergman, Samuel Hugo. "Israel and the Oikumene," *Studies in Rationalism, Judaism and Universalism. In Memory of Leon Roth.* Ed. R. Loewe. London, New York, 1966, 47-65.

Bertholet, Alfred. *Die Stellung der Israeliten und Juden zu den Fremden.* Freiburg and Leipzig, 1896.

Besserman, Lawrence. *The Legend of Job in the Middle Ages.* Cambridge, Mass., 1979.

The Biblical Antiquities of Philo. Ed. Montague R. James. New edition, ed. Louis H. Feldman. New York, 1971.

Bidez, Joseph and Franz Cumont. *Les Mages Hellénisés. Zoroastre, Ostanès et Hystaspe d'après la Tradition Grecque.* 2 vols. Paris, 1938.

Bloch, Joseph. *Israel and the Nations.* Berlin and Vienna, 1927.

Bonner, G. "Augustine as Biblical Scholar," *CHB* I, 541-562.

Bowker, John. *The Targums and Rabbinic Literature. An Introduction to Jewish Interpretation of Scriptures.* Cambridge, 1969.

Braude, William. *Jewish Proselyting in the First Five Centuries of the Common Era* (Providence, R. I., 1940).

Braverman, Jay. "Balaam in Rabbinic and Early Christian Tradition," *Joshua Finkel Festschrift.* Ed. Sidney B. Hoenig and Leon D. Stitskin. New York, 1974, 41-50.

_____. *Jerome's "Commentary on Daniel": A Study of Comparative Jewish and Christian Interpretations of the Hebrew Bible. CBQMS* 7. Washington, D. C., 1978.

Cambridge History of the Bible.   Ed. P. R. Ackroyd and C. F.
   Evans. 3 vols. Cambridge, 1970.

Caquot, A.   "Un écrit sectaire de Qoumran: Le 'Targum de Job,'"
   RHR 185 (1974) 9-27.

Cassuto, Umberto.   *A Commentary on the Book of Exodus*.   Tr. I.
   Abrahams. Jerusalem, 1967.

Childs, Brevard S.   *The Book of Exodus*. *A Critical Theological
   Commentary*. Philadelphia, 1974.

Cohen, Gerson D.   "Esau as Symbol in Early Medieval Thought," *Jewish Medieval and Renaissance Studies*. Ed. A. Altmann. Cambridge, Mass., 1967, 19-48.

Constitutions of the Holy Apostles.   Tr. A. Roberts and J. Donaldson. *ANF* 7. New York, 1896.

Corpus Christianorum.   Series latina. 176 - volumes. Turnholt,
   Belgium, 1953 - .

Cyril of Alexandria.   *Glaphyrorum in Exodum*.   *PG* 69.

Daniélou, Jean.   *From Shadows to Reality*.   Westminster, Maryland,
   1960.

_____.   *Holy Pagans of the Old Testament*.   London, New York,
   Toronto, 1957.

_____.   *Primitive Christian Symbols*.   Baltimore, 1964.

Datz, Günther.   *Die Gestalt Hiobs in der Kirchlichen Exegese und
   der Arme Heinrich Hartmanns von Aue*. Goppingen, 1973.

de Lange, N. R. M.   *Origen and the Jews*. *Studies in Jewish-
   Christian Relations in Third-Century Palestine*.   Cambridge,
   1976.

de Vaux, R.   "Sur l'origine Kénite ou Madianite du Yahvisme,"
   Eretz-Israel 9. *W. F. Albright Volume*.   Ed. A. Malamat.
   Jerusalem, 1969.

Doran, Robert.   "Aristeas the Exegete," *The Old Testament Pseudepigrapha*. Ed. J. H. Charlesworth, New York, forthcoming 1984.

Encyclopedia Judaica.   16 vols. Jerusalem and New York, 1971.

Ephraem.   *Hymni de Nativate Christi*.   Ed. Thomas Joseph Lamy.
   Sancti Ephraem Syri hymni et sermones . . . Malines, Belgium,
   1882 - 1902.

Fitzmeyer, J. A.   "Some Observations on the Targum of Job from
   Qumran Cave 11," *CBQ* 36 (1974) 503-524.

Fraade, Steven D.   *Enosh and his Generation: Pre-Israelite Hero
   and History in Post-biblical Interpretation*. *SBLMS*.   Chico,
   Ca., forthcoming.

Gard, Donald H.   "The Concept of Job's Character according to the
   Greek Translator of the Hebrew Text," *JBL* 72 (1953) 182-186.

Gerleman, G.   *Book of Job*. *Studies in the Septuagint* I.   Lund,
   1946.

Ginzberg, Louis. "Aphraates, the Persian Sage," *JE*.

_____. *Die Haggada bei den Kirchenvätern. Erster Theil: Die Haggada in den pseudo-hieronymianischen Quaestiones*. Amsterdam, 1899.

_____. *Die Haggada bei den Kirchenvätern und in der apokryphischen Literatur* [2: Genesis]. Berlin, 1900.

_____. "Die Haggada bei den Kirchenvätern [3] Exodus," *Livre d'hommage à la mémoire du Dr. Samuel Poznanski*. Warsaw, 1927, 199-216.

_____. "Die Haggada bei den Kirchenvätern. Numeri- Deuteronomium [4]," *Studies in Jewish Bibliography . . . in Memory of Abraham S. Freidus*. New York, 1929, 503-518.

_____. "Die Haggada bei den Kirchenvätern. V. Der Kommentar des Hieronymus zu Koheleth," *Abhandlungen zur Erinnerung an Hirsch Perez Chajes*. Vienna, 1933, 22-50.

_____. "Die Haggada bei den Kirchenvätern: VI. Der Kommentar des Hieronymus zu Jesaja," *Jewish Studies in Memory of George A. Kohut*. New York, 1935, 279-314.

_____. *The Legends of the Jews*. 7 vols. Philadelphia, 1909-1938.

_____. "Some Observations on the Attitude of the Synagogue towards the Apocalyptic-Eschatological Writings," *JBL* 41 (1922) 115-136.

Glatzer, Nahum. "The Book of Job and its Interpreters," *Biblical Motifs. Origins and Transformations*. Ed. Alexander Altmann. Cambridge, Mass., 1966, 197-220.

_____. *The Dimensions of Job. A Study and Selected Readings*. New York, 1969.

Glossa Ordinaria: Liber Exodus. PL 113.

Goldin, Judah. *The Fathers According to Rabbi Nathan. Yale Judaica Series* 10. New Haven, 1955.

_____. *The Song at the Sea*. New Haven, 1971.

Goldstein, Morris. *Jesus in the Jewish Tradition*. New York, 1950.

Goodenough, E. R. *By Light, Light*. New Haven, 1935.

Goodspeed, E. J. *Die ältesten Apologeten*. Göttingen, 1915.

Gordis, Robert. *The Book of Man and God*. Chicago and London, 1965.

Grant, Robert. *The Letter and the Spirit*. London, 1957.

_____. *A Short History of the Interpretation of the Bible*. New York, 1963.

Greenberg, Moshe. "Mankind, Israel and the Nations in the Hebraic Heritage," *No Man is Alien. Essays on the Unity of Mankind*. Ed. J. Robert Nelson. Leiden, 1971, 15-40.

_____. *Understanding Exodus*. New York, 1969.

Gregory of Nyssa. *In Diem Natalem Christi*. *PG* 46.

Gregory the Great. *Moralia on Job*. *F of Ch* 18, 21, 23, 31.
     Oxford, 1844-50.

Hamlin, E. J. "Nations," *IDB*.

Hanson, R. P. C. *Allegory and Event*. Richmond, Va., 1959.

_____. "Biblical Exegesis in the Early Church," *CHB* I, 412-
     454.

Hennecke, Paul. *New Testament Apocrypha*. 2 vols. Ed. W. Schnee-
     melcher; tr. R. McL. Wilson. Philadelphia, 1965.

Herford, R. Travers. *Christianity in Talmud and Midrash*. London,
     1903.

Hoftijzer, J. and G. van der Kooij. Edd. *Aramaic Texts from Deir
     'Alla* (Leiden, 1976).

Hoftijzer, J. "The Prophet Balaam in a 6th Century Aramaic
     Inscription," *BA* 39 (1976) 11-17.

Interpreter's Dictionary of the Bible. Ed. G. A. Buttrick et al.
     5 vols. Nashville and New York, 1962, 1976.

Irenaeus. *Against the Heretics*. Ed. W. W. Harvey. *Sancti
     Irenaei . . . Adversus Haereses*. Cambridge, 1857.

_____. *Fragment* 23. *Ex Catena in Numeros*. *PG* 7.

Jerome. *Oeuvres Complètes de Saint Jérome*. Tr. Abbé Bareille.
     Paris, 1879.

_____. *Liber Contra Joannem Hierosolymitanum*. *PL* 23.

_____. *Commentarium in Ezechielem*. *PL* 25.

_____. *Commentariorum in Evangelium Matthaei*. *PL* 26.

_____. *Commentarii in Librum Job*. *PL* 26.

_____. *Commentaria in Epistolam ad Ephesios*. *PL* 26.

_____. *Epistolae*. *PL* 22.

_____. *Liber Hebraicorum Quaestionum in Genesim*. *PL* 23.

_____. *Preface to the Book of Job*. Tr. W. H. Fremantle.
     NPNF. Series 2, vol. 6. Oxford and New York, 1896.

Jewish Encyclopedia. 12 vols. New York, 1903.

Josephus. *Jewish Antiquities of Flavius Josephus*. Tr. H. St. J.
     Thackeray. 9 vols. *LCL*. New York and London, 1930.

Justin. *Apology*. Ed. E. J. Goodspeed. *Die ältesten Apologeten*.
     Göttingen, 1915.

_____. *Dialogue with Trypho*. Ed. E. J. Goodspeed. *Die
     ältesten Apologeten*. Göttingen, 1915.

Kaufmann, Herman Ezekiel. *Die Anwendung das Buches Hiob in der Rabbinischen Agadah.* Frankfurt am Main, 1893.

Kimelman, Reuven. "Rabbi Yohanan and Origen on the Song of Songs: A Third Century Jewish-Christian Disputation," *HTR* 73 (1980) 567-595.

_____. *Rabbi Yohanan of Tiberias. Aspects of the Social and Religious History of Third Century Palestine.* Yale University Dissertation, 1977.

Kirschbaum, E. "Der Prophet Balaam und die Anbetung der Weisen," *RQ* 49 (1954) 129-171.

Klauser, Theodor. "Bileam," *Reallexikon für Antike und Christentum.* Stuttgart, 1950 - .

Klijn, A. F. J. *Seth in Jewish, Christian and Gnostic Literature.* *NovTSup* 46. Leiden, 1977.

Kohler, Kaufmann. "Job, Testament of," *JE.*

_____. "Testament of Job," *Semitic Studies in Memory of Alexander Kohut.* Berlin, 1897, 264-338.

Kraft, Robert A. *The Testament of Job. TextsT* 5. *SBL Pseudepigrapha Series* 4. Missoula, Montana, 1974.

Krauss, Samuel. "Balaam," *JE.*

_____. "Church Fathers," *JE.*

_____. "The Jews in the Works of the Church Fathers," *JQR* o.s. 5 (1893), 122-157; 6 (1894), 89-99, 225-261.

Lamirande, Emilien. "Etude bibliographique sur les pères de l'Eglise et l'aggadah," *VC* 21 (1967) 1-11.

Lampe, G. W. H. "The Exposition and Exegesis of Scripture: To Gregory the Great," *CHB* 2, 155-183.

Lauterbach, Jacob Z. "The Attitude of the Jew toward the Non-Jew," *CCAR Yearbook* 31 (1921) 186-233.

Leclercq, Jean. "From Gregory the Great to Bernard," *CHB* 2, 183-196.

Levine, Baruch. "The Deir 'Alla Plaster Inscriptions," *JAOS* 101 (1981) 195-205.

Lewis, Jack P. *A Study of the Interpretation of Noah and the Flood in Jewish and Christian Literature.* Leiden, 1968.

Lewy, Hans. Ed. *Philo: Selections,* in *Three Jewish Philosophers.* New York, 1969.

Loewe, Raphael. "The Jewish Midrashim and Patristic and Scholastic Exegesis of the Bible," *SP* 1 (1957) 492-512.

Majan-Gannim. Commentary on Job of Rabbi Samuel ben Nissim Masnuth. Ed. Solomon Buber. Berlin, 1889.

Mâle, Emile. *L'art religieux du XIIIe siècle en France.* Paris, 1902.

Margalioth, Mordechai. Ed. *Encyclopedia of Talmudic and Geonic Literature. A Biographical Dictionary of the Tannaim, Amoraim, and Geonim*. [Hebrew] 2 vols. Jerusalem, 1942.

Marmorstein, A. "Judaism and Christianity in the middle of the Third Century," *HUCA* 10 (1935) 223-263.

Mazar, B. "The Sanctuary of Arad and the Family of Hobab the Kenite," *JNES* 24 (1965) 297-303.

Mekilta d'Rabbi Ishmael. Ed. H. S. Horovitz and I. A. Rabin. Frankfurt am Main, 1930.

Mekilta de-Rabbi Ishmael. Ed. and tr. Jacob Z. Lauterbach. 3 vols. Philadelphia, 1933-35.

Mekilta de-Rabbi Simeon. Ed. J. N. Epstein and E. Z. Melamed. Jerusalem, 1955.

Midrash Rabbah. Ed. Elimelech Epstein. 5 vols. Tel Aviv, 1956-63.

Midrash Rabbah: Genesis. Ed. Hanoch Albeck. Jerusalem, 1965.

Midrash Rabbah: Numbers. Ed. Isaac Zev Adler. B'nai B'rak, Israel, 1962.

Midrash Rabbah. Tr. H. Freedman and Maurice Simon. London, 1939, 1961.

Midrash Tanhuma. Ed. Solomon Buber. Vilna, 1885.

Midrash Tanhuma. Berlin, New York, 1924.

Mishnah. *Shisha Sidre Mishnah*. 6. vols. Ed. H. Albeck and H. Yalon. Jerusalem, 1952-56.

The Mishnah. Tr. H. Danby, Oxford, 1933.

Mishnat R. Eliezer. Ed. H. G. Enelow. New York, 1933.

Moore, G. F. *Judaism in the First Centuries of the Christian Era*. 2 vols. Cambridge, Mass., 1927, 1931.

Neusner, Jacob. *Aphrahat and Judaism. The Christian-Jewish Argument in Fourth Century Iran*. Leiden, 1971.

Noth, Martin, *Numbers. A Commentary*. Philadelphia, 1968.

Origen. *Commentary on John*. *PG* 14.

_____. *Homiliae in Numeros*. *PG* 12.

_____. *Homiliae in Ezechielem*. *PG* 13.

_____. *In Exodum Homiliae*. Tr. P. Fortier. *SC* 16.

_____. *Libellus De Oratione*. *PG* 11.

_____. *On Prayer*. Tr. Eric George Jay. London, 1954.

_____. *Selecta in Numeros*. *PG* 12.

Orlinsky, Harry. "Studies in the Septuagint of the Book of Job,"
    HUCA 28 (1957) 53-74; 29 (1958) 229-271; 30 (1959) 153-167; 32
    (1961) 239-268.

Patrologiae Cursus Completus: Series Graeca. Ed. J. P. Migne.
    162 vols. Paris, 1857-1866.

Patrologia Cursus Completus: Series Latina. Ed. J. P. Migne.
    221 vols. Paris, 1844-1864.

Pelikan, Jaroslav. *The Emergence of the Catholic Tradition 100-
    600*. Chicago and London, 1971.

Perrin, Norman. *The New Testament. An Introduction*. New York,
    1974.

Pesiqta de-Rab Kahana. Ed. Solomon Buber. Vilna, 1925.

Pesiqta de-Rab Kahana. Tr. William G. Braude and Israel J. Kap-
    stein. Philadelphia, 1975.

Pesiqta Rabbati. Ed. M. Friedmann. Vienna, 1880.

Philo. *Works of Philo Judaeus*. Ed. and tr. F. H. Colson and G.
    H. Whitaker. 12 vols. *LCL*. London and New York, 1930.

Philolenko, Marc. "Le Testament de Job et les Thérapeutes," *Sem* 8
    (1958) 41-53.

Pirqe Rabbi Eliezer. Ed. David ben Edel Luria. New York, 1946.

Plato. *Timaeus and Critias*. Tr. H. D. P. Lee. Middlesex, Eng-
    land, 1971.

Pope, Marvin. *Job. A New Translation and Commentary*. *AB*. New
    York, 1973.

_____. "Proselyte," *IDB*.

Reicke, Bo. *The Epistles of James, Peter and Jude*. *AB*. New
    York, 1964.

Rofe, Alexander. *"The Book of Balaam" (Numbers 22:2-24:25). A
    Study in Methods of Criticism and the History of Biblical Lit-
    erature and Religion*. [Hebrew] Jerusalem, 1979.

Sandmel, Samuel. *Philo's Place in Judaism: A Study of Concep-
    tions of Abraham in Jewish Literature*. New York, 1956, 1971.

Schechter, Solomon. *Aspects of Rabbinic Theology*. New York,
    1909, 1969.

Schoeps, Hans Joachim. *The Jewish-Christian Argument. A History
    of Theologies in Conflict*. London, 1963.

_____. *Theologie und Geschichte des Judenchristums* (Tubingen,
    1949).

Schützinger, Heinrich. "Die arabische Bileam-Erzählung. Ihre
    Quellen und ihre Entwicklung," *Der Islam* 59 (1982) 195-221.

Seder 'Olam Rabbah. Ed. M. D. Yerushalmi. Jerusalem, 1954, 1971.

A Select Library of the Nicene and Post Nicene Fathers of the Christian Church. Ed. Philip Schaff. 14 vols. New York, 1886-1890.

A Select Library of the Nicene - Post Nicene Fathers of the Christian Church. Second Series. Ed. H. Wace and P. Schaff. 14 vols. Oxford and New York, 1890-1900.

Semahot. Ed. and tr. Dov Zlotnick. New Haven, 1966.

Simon, Marcel. "Melchisédech dans la polémique entre juifs et chrétiens et dans la legende," *RHPR* 17 (1937) 58-93.

_____. "Les Saints d'Israel dans la devotion de l'Eglise ancienne," *RHPR* 34 (1954) 80-151.

_____. *Verus Israel. Etude sur les relations entre Chrétiens et Juifs dans l'Empire Romain 135-425*. Paris, 1948.

Sipra deve Rav. Ed. I. H. Weiss. Vienna, 1862; reprinted New York, 1966.

Sipre ad Deuteronomium. Ed. L. Finkelstein. Berlin, 1939.

Sipre d'be Rab, Sipre ad Numeros. Ed. H. S. Horovitz. Jerusalem, 1966.

Slater, Jonathan. "The Character of Balaam as a Villain in 'Midrash Numbers Rabbah,'" Bachelors Thesis in Folklore and Mythology. Harvard University, 1974.

Smalley, Beryl. *The Study of the Bible in the Middle Ages*. Notre Dame, Indiana, 1970.

Sokoloff, M. *The Targum to Job from Qumran Cave XI*. Ramat-Gan, Israel, 1974.

Sources chrétiennes. 267 - vols. Paris, 1941 - .

Spiegel, Shalom. "Noah, Danel and Job, touching on Canaanite Relics in the Legends of the Jews," *Louis Ginzberg Jubilee Volume*. English Section. New York, 1945, 305-357.

Stone, E. N. "Adam, A Religious Play of the Twelfth Century," *University of Washington Publications in Language and Literature* 4 (1926-28) 159-193.

Talmud. *Talmud Babli*. 20 vols. New York, 1937.

_____. *The Babylonian Talmud* Ed. and tr. I. Epstein. London, 1935-1952.

_____. *Talmud Yerushalmi*. Venice Edition. Berlin, 1925.

Tcherikover, Victor. "Social Conditions," *The Hellenistic Age. World History of the Jewish People* 6. Ed. A. Schalit. New Brunswick, N. J., 1972, 87-114.

Tertullian. *Treatise on Patience*. Tr. A. Roberts and J. Donaldson. *ANF* 3. New York, 1899.

Tuinstra, E. M. *Hermeneutische Aspecten van de Targum van Job uit Grot XI van Qumran*. Groningen Dissertation, 1971.

Urbach, Ephraim. "The Homiletical Interpretations of the Sages and the Expositions of Origen on Canticles and the Jewish-Christian Disputation," *SH* 22 (1971) 247-275.

_____. "Homilies of the Rabbis on the Prophets of the Nations and the Balaam Stories," *Tar* 25 (1955-56) 272-289 [Hebrew], English summary iii-vii.

_____. *The Sages. Their Concepts and Beliefs*. 2 vols. Jerusalem, 1975.

Van der Ploeg, J. and A. van der Woude. *Le Targum de Job de la Grotte de Qumran*. Leiden, 1971.

Van Groningen, G. *First Century Gnosticism: Its Origins and Motifs*. Leiden, 1967.

Vaserstein, A. "A Rabbinic Midrash as a Source of Origen's Homily on Ezekiel," *Tar* 46 (1977) 317-318 [Hebrew], English summary vi.

Vermes, Geza. *Scripture and Tradition in Judaism*. Leiden, 1961.

Wiles, M. F. "Origen as Biblical Scholar," *CHB* I, 454-488.

Wilken, R. L. *Judaism and the Early Christian Mind. A Study of Cyril of Alexandria's Exegesis and Theology*. New Haven, 1971.

Williams, A. Lukyn. *Adversus Judaeos; A Bird's Eye View of Christian Apologetics until the Renaissance*. Cambridge, 1935.

Zuckerman, Bruce. *The Process of Translation in 11QTGJOB; A Preliminary Study*. Yale University Dissertation, 1980.

INDEX OF PRIMARY SOURCES

An entry in the form 123/34 indicates "page 123, note 34."

1. *Hebrew Bible*

4. *Testament of Job*

    1:3   31
    1:3b-5a   140/101
    1:4   31
    27:3-9   31
    38:2   31
    43:1-13b   140/102
    45:1-4   31
    53:1b-4   140/104

5. *Biblical Antiquities*

    8:8   139-140/98
    18:2   159/78
    18:3   159/89,/90
    18:4   158/72, 160/94
    18:8   159/91
    18:9   159/91
    18:10   160/92,/93
    18:13   160/95

6. *Apocalypse of Paul*

    v. 49   36, 141/122,/123

7. *Dead Sea Scrolls*

    Damascus Document 157/54
    4QTestimonia   157/54
    11QTGJOB   138/80

8. Philo

Life of Moses (by section)
    263   158/66
    264   159/78
    268   158/67
    273   158/68
    274   158/69
    277   158/70
    294   158/71

On Agriculture (by section)
    43   150/71

On Drunkenness (by section)
    37   150/72,/73
    40   150/74
    44-45   150/75

On the Change of Names
    (by section)
    103-104   149/62,/64,
                 150/65,/66
    105   150/68
    107-110   150/67
    114   150/69,/70

On the Cherubim (by page)
    27   158/73,/75

On the Giants   (by section)
    50   149/61

On the Migration of Abraham
    (by section)
    22-25   158/65

On the Special Laws
    (by book and section)
    iv. 49   158/62

9. Josephus

Jewish Antiquities
    (by book and section)
    iii. 61-66   65
    iii.64   150/78
    iii.65   151/79
    iii.73   151/80,/81
    iii.74   151/82
    iv.102   158/77
    iv.107   159/79
    iv.111   159/81
    iv.117-118   159/85
    iv.118   159/82
    iv.119-122   159/83
    iv.127   159/86
    iv.129-130   159/84
    iv.161   159/86

10. *Mishnah*

Megilla
    4:9   27

Nedarim
    3:11   133/29

Sota
    5:5   10, 19

Baba Meṣi'a
    4:10   48

Sanhedrin
    10:2   154/12, 156/47

'Eduyyot
    2:10   135/48

'Abot

    1:1   133/29
    1:12   145/6
    3:14   8
    4:15   133/32
    5:19   80, 160/100

11.   *Tosepta*

Bikkurim
    1:2   147/24

Šabbat
    13:2   137/78
    13:5   154/6

Sanhedrin
    13:2   9

SUBJECT INDEX

An entry in the form 123/34 indicates "page 123, note 34."